World Music Pedagogy, Volume VII

World Music Pedagogy, Volume VII: Teaching World Music in Higher Education addresses a pedagogical pathway of varied strategies for teaching world music in higher education, offering concrete means for diversifying undergraduate studies through world music culture courses. While the first six volumes in this series have detailed theoretical and applied principles of World Music Pedagogy within K-12 public schools and broader communities, this seventh volume is chiefly concerned with infusing culture-rich musical experiences through world music courses at the tertiary level, presenting a compelling argument for the growing need for such perspectives and approaches.

These chapters include discussions of the logical trajectories of the framework into world music courses, through which the authors seek to challenge the status quo of lecture-only academic courses in some college and university music programs. Unique to this series, each of these chapters illustrates practical procedures for incorporating the WMP framework into sample classes. However, this volume (like the rest of the series) is not a prescriptive "recipe book" of lesson plans. Rather, it seeks to enrich the conversation surrounding cultural diversity in music through philosophically rooted, social justice-conscious, and practice-oriented perspectives.

Listening Episode music examples can be accessed on the eResource site from the Routledge catalog page.

William J. Coppola is Assistant Professor of Music Education at the University of North Texas. He is the coauthor of *World Music Pedagogy, Volume IV: Instrumental World Music* and is a Smithsonian Folkways World Music Pedagogy certified music educator.

David G. Hebert is Professor at Western Norway University of Applied Sciences, Professor-II at Lund University, and Manager of Nordic Network for Music Education.

Patricia Shehan Campbell is Donald E. Peterson Professor at the University of Washington. She is Editor of the Routledge World Music Pedagogy Series and a board member for Smithsonian Folkways Recordings and the Association for Cultural Equity.

Routledge World Music Pedagogy Series
Series Editor: Patricia Shehan Campbell, University of Washington

The **Routledge World Music Pedagogy Series** encompasses principal cross-disciplinary issues in music, education, and culture in seven volumes, detailing theoretical and practical aspects of World Music Pedagogy in ways that contribute to the diversification of repertoire and instructional approaches. With the growth of cultural diversity in schools and communities and the rise of an enveloping global network, there is both confusion and a clamoring by teachers for music that speaks to the multiple heritages of their students, as well as to the spectrum of expressive practices in the world that constitute the human need to sing, play, dance, and engage in the rhythms and inflections of poetry, drama, and ritual.

Volume I: Early Childhood Education
Sarah H. Watts

Volume II: Elementary Music Education
J. Christopher Roberts and Amy C. Beegle

Volume III: Secondary School Innovations
Karen Howard and Jamey Kelley

Volume IV: Instrumental Music Education
Mark Montemayor, William J. Coppola, and Christopher Mena

Volume V: Choral Music Education
Sarah J. Bartolome

Volume VI: School-Community Intersections
Patricia Shehan Campbell and Chee-Hoo Lum

Volume VII: Teaching World Music in Higher Education
William J. Coppola, David G. Hebert, and Patricia Shehan Campbell

World Music Pedagogy

Teaching World Music in Higher Education

Volume VII

William J. Coppola

University of North Texas

David G. Hebert

Western Norway University of Applied Sciences

Patricia Shehan Campbell

University of Washington

Routledge
Taylor & Francis Group

NEW YORK AND LONDON

First published 2021
by Routledge
605 Third Avenue, New York, NY 10158

and by Routledge
2 Park Square, Milton Park, Abingdon, Oxon, OX14 4RN

Routledge is an imprint of the Taylor & Francis Group, an informa business

Library of Congress Cataloging-in-Publication Data
Names: Roberts, J. Christopher, author. | Beegle, Amy C., author.
Title: World music pedagogy.
Description: New York ; London : Routledge, 2018– | Includes bibliographical
    references and index.
Identifiers: LCCN 2017050640 (print) | LCCN 2017054487 (ebook) |
    ISBN 9781315167589 () | ISBN 9781138052727 | ISBN 9781138052727q
    (v.2 : hardback) | ISBN 9781138052796q(v.2 : pbk.)
Subjects: LCSH: Music—Instruction and study.
Classification: LCC MT1 (ebook) | LCC MT1 .W92 2018 (print) | DDC
    780.71—dc23
LC record available at https://lccn.loc.gov/2017050640

ISBN: 978-0-367-23172-9 (hbk)
ISBN: 978-0-367-23173-6 (pbk)
ISBN: 978-0-429-27861-7 (ebk)

Typeset in Times New Roman
by Apex CoVantage, LLC

Visit the eResource: www.routledge.com/9780367231736

Dedication

We were in the final frenzied weeks of preparing this volume for press when the distinguished ethnomusicologist, musicologist, and educator, Professor Bruno Nettl, passed from this world. He inspired us, and we continue to be guided by his wisdom, his devotion to scholarship and teaching, and his enthusiasm for articulating the beauty and logic of the world's musical cultures to his students. We humbly dedicate this book to Bruno, as we resonate deeply with his belief that musical study in higher education should include three components—Western classical music, local music traditions, and "something of the rest of the world."

Contents

Chapter 4   **Performing World Music**   **76**

Series Foreword

Turning and turning in the widening gyre
The falcon cannot hear the falconer;
Things fall apart; the centre cannot hold;
Mere anarchy is loosed upon the world . . .

from "The Second Coming", W. B. Yeats

There is a foreboding tone to the above stanza, which at first may seem out of sync with a book on the pedagogy of world music. After all, music education is an intact phenomenon, arguably innocent and pure, that envelops teachers and their students in the acts of singing, playing, and dancing, and this field is decidedly not about falcons. Instead, music education conjures up long-standing images of spirited high school bands, choirs, and orchestras, of young adolescents at work in guitar and keyboard classes, of fourth grade xylophone and recorder players, of first grade rhythm bands, and of toddlers accompanied by parents playing small drums and shakers. At a time of demographic diversity, with a wide spectrum of students of various shapes, sizes, and hues laid wide open, music education can press further, as the field has the potential to hold court in a child's holistic development as a core avenue for the discovery of human cultural heritage and the celebration of multiple identities based upon race, ethnicity, gender, religion, and socioeconomic circumstance.

Yet there is a correspondence of the stanza, and the disquiet that Yeats communicates, with this book and with the book series, *World Music Pedagogy in School and Community Practice*. I refer the reader to the start of the third line, and also to the title of a novel by Nigerian author Chinua Achebe. A landmark in the world's great literature, *Things Fall Apart* has been very much in mind through the conception of this project, its design and development by a team of authors and its thematic weave in these tempestuous times. Achebe's writing of cultural misunderstanding, of the arrogance and insensitivity of Western colonizers in village Africa, of competing cultural systems, is relevant.

We raise questions relative to music teaching and learning: Do things fall apart, or prove ineffective, when they do not reflect demographic change, do not respond to cultural variation, and do not reasonably reform to meet the needs of a new era? Can music education remain relevant and useful through the full-scale continuation of conventional practices, or is there something prophetic in the statement that things fall apart, particularly in music education, if there are insufficient efforts to revise and adapt to societal evolution? There is hard-core documentation of sparkling success stories in generations of efforts to musically educate children. Yet there is also evidence of frayed, flailing, and failing programs that are the result of restrictive music selections and exclusive pedagogical decisions that leave out students, remain unlinked to local communities, and ignore a panorama of global expressions. There is the sinking feeling that music education programs exclusively rooted in Western art styles are insensitive and unethical for 21st-century schools and students, and that choices of featured music are statements on people we choose to include and exclude from our world.

Consider many school programs for their long-standing means of musically educating students within a Western framework, featuring Western school-based music, following Western literate traditions of notation, Western teacher-directed modes of learning, and Western fixed rather than flexible and spontaneously inventive musicking potentials. All good for particular times and places, and yet arguably unethical in the exclusion of music and music-makers in the world. Certainly, all practices deserve regular review, upgrades, even overhauls. Today's broad population mix of students from everywhere in the world press on diversifying the curriculum, and the discoveries of "new" music culture potentials are noteworthy and necessary in making for a more inclusive music education.

So, the Nigerian author selected the Irish poet's phrase as meaningful to his seminal work, much as we might reflect upon its meaning so to muster a response to the societal disruption and contestation across the land, and in the world. The practice of musically educating children, youth, and adults may not at first appear to be the full solution to the challenges of local schools and societies, nor is it essential to meeting mandates in cultural and multicultural understanding. But music is as powerful as it is pan-human, musicking is musical involvement in what is humanly necessary, and the musical education of children and youth benefit their thoughts, feelings, and behaviors. When things fall apart, or seem to be on the brink of breaking up, of serving fewer students and to a lesser degree than they might be served, we look to ways in which the music of many cultures and communities can serve to grow the musicianship of our students as well as their understanding of heritage and humanity, of people and places. Thus, from cynicism springs hope, and from darkness comes light, as this book and book series rises up as a reasoned response to making music relevant and multiply useful in the lives of learners in schools and communities.

THE SERIES

Each of the six volumes in the World Music Pedagogy Series provides a sweep of teaching/learning encounters that lead to the development of skills, understandings, and values that are inherent within a diversity of the world's musical cultures. Written for professionally active teachers as well as students in undergraduate and certification programs on their way to becoming teachers, these volumes encompass the application of the World Music Pedagogy (WMP) process from infancy and toddlerhood through late adolescence and into the community.

The books are unified by conceptualizations and format, and of course by the series' aim of providing theoretical frameworks for and practical pedagogical experiences in teaching the world's musical cultures. Individual WMP volumes are organized by music education context (or class type) and age/grade level.

For every volume in the World Music Pedagogy Series, there are common elements that are intended to communicate with coherence the means by which learners can become more broadly musical and culturally sensitive to people close by and across the world. All volumes include seven chapters that proceed from an introduction of the particular music education context (and type), to the play-out of the five dimensions, to the reflective closing of how World Music Pedagogy contributes to meeting various musical and cultural goals, including those of social justice through music as well as issues of diversity, equity, and inclusion.

Scatterings of music notations appear across each volume, mostly meant to assist the teacher who is preparing the orally based lessons rather than to suggest their use with students. Many of the chapters launch from vignettes, real-life scenarios of teachers and students at work in the WMP process, while chapters frequently close on interviews with practicing music educators and teaching musicians who are devoting their efforts to effecting meaningful experiences for students in the world's musical cultures. Authors of several of the volumes provide commentaries on published works for school music ensembles, noting what is available of notated scores of selected world music works, whether transcribed or arranged, and how they can be useful alongside the adventures in learning by listening.

LISTENING LINKS FOR THE SERIES

Of central significance are the listening links for recordings that are featured in teaching-learning episodes. These episodes are lesson-like sequences that run from 3 minutes to 30 minutes, depending upon the interest and inclination of the teacher, which pay tribute to occasions for brief or extended listening experiences that may be repeated over a number of class sessions. The listening links are noted in the episode descriptions as well as at each chapter's end, and users can connect directly to the recordings (audio as well as video) through the Routledge eResource site for each of the series' volumes, linked to the catalog page of each volume through www.routledge. com/Routledge-World-Music-Pedagogy-Series/book-series/WMP.

All volumes recommend approximately 20 listening links, and Chapters 2–6 in each volume provide illustrations of the ways in which these listening selections can develop into experiences in the five WMP dimensions. From the larger set of recommended listening tracks, three selections continue to appear across the chapters as keystone selections, which are intended to show the complete pathways of how these three recordings can be featured through the five dimensions. These learning pathways are noted in full in Appendix 1, so that the user can see in one fell swoop the flow of the teaching-learning process, from Attentive Listening to Engaged Listening, Enactive Listening, Creating World Music, and Integrating World Music. A second Appendix (2) provides recommended resources for further reading, listening, viewing, and development of the ways of World Music Pedagogy.

As a collective of authors, and joined by many of our colleagues in the professional work of music teachers and teaching musicians, we reject the hateful ideologies that blatantly surface in society. We are vigilant of the destructive choices that can be made in the business of schooling young people and that may result from racism, bigotry, and prejudice. Hate has no place in society or its schools, and we assert that music is a route to peace, love, and understanding. We reject social exclusion, anti-Semitism, White supremacy, and homophobia (and other insensitive, unfeeling, or unbalanced perspectives). We oppose the ignorance or intentional avoidance of the potentials for diversity, equity, and inclusion in curricular practice. We support civility and "the culture of kindness" and hold a deep and abiding respect of people across the broad spectrum of our society. We are seeking to develop curricular threads that allow school music to be a place where all are welcome, celebrated, and safe, where every student is heard, and where cultural sensitivity can lead to love.

ACKNOWLEDGMENTS

This collective of authors is grateful to those who have paved the way to teaching music with diversity, equity, and inclusion in mind. I am personally indebted to the work of my graduate school mentors, William M. Anderson, Terry Lee Kuhn, and Terry M. Miller, and to Halim El-Dabh and Virginia H. Mead, all who committed themselves to the study of music as a worldwide phenomenon, and who paved the way for me and many others to perform, study, and teach music with multicultural, intercultural, and global aims very much in mind. I am eternally grateful to Barbara Reeder Lundquist for her *joie de vivre* in the act of teaching music and in life itself. This work bears the mark of treasured University of Washington colleagues, then and now, who have helped to lessen the distance between the fields of ethnomusicology and music education, especially Steven J. Morrison, Shannon Dudley, and Christina Sunardi. Many thanks to the fine authors of the books in this series: Sarah J. Bartolome, Amy Beegle, William J. Coppola, Karen Howard, Jamey Kelley, Chee Hoo Lum, Chris Mena, Mark Montemayor, J. Christopher Roberts, and Sarah J. Watts. They are "the collective" who shaped the course of the series and who toiled to fit the principles of World Music Pedagogy into their various specialized realms of music education. We are grateful to Constance Ditzel, music editor at Routledge, who caught the idea of the series and enthusiastically encouraged us to write these volumes, and to her colleague, Peter Sheehy, who carried it through to its conclusion.

As in any of these exciting though arduous writing projects, I reserve my unending gratitude for my husband, Charlie, who leaves me "speechless in Seattle" in his support of my efforts. Once again, he gave me the time it takes to imagine a project, to write, read, edit, and write some more. It could not have been done without the time and space that he spared me, busying himself with theories behind "the adsorption of deuterated molecular benzene" while I helped to shape, with the author-team, these ideas on World Music Pedagogy.

Patricia Shehan Campbell
December 2017

Acknowledgments

The pages of this final volume of the Routledge World Music Pedagogy Series are filled with ideas about music, culture, and the bi-directional flow of the ideas that comprise the teaching-learning process in higher education. Our collective experience at the tertiary level spans many decades, with experiences in teaching world music courses on faculties in colleges and universities in the U.S. and abroad. We've held teaching posts in public and private institutions, in community colleges, four-year colleges, comprehensive universities, and universities with "R-1" research ratings. We have worked in liberal arts and conservatory-like settings, and have taught world music in large-enrollment classes open to all university students, smaller classes of music-only majors, and small seminars for students of ethnomusicology. While we do not have all the answers, we do sense that the time is ripe to share insights on teaching world music in higher education in ways that are musical, culturally sensitive, and of course, globally expansive.

We are indebted to many: Our students, our teachers, our colleagues in the fields of ethnomusicology and education, and our collaborating musicians and educators who have offered us "slices of musical life" in the world's cultures.

Many thanks to those who allowed themselves to be interviewed for this book, including Steven Friedson, Lois Hicks-Wozniak, Jonathan McCollum, Amanda C. Soto, and Deborah Wong. Their insights underscore the key pedagogical considerations they have honed through their own experiences as ethnomusicologists and educators. We are grateful to all who have provided images for the book, especially Rahim AlHaj.

We wish to express our gratitude "in particulars," too. Will would like to thank Kari Adams, Julie M. Song, Juliana Cantarelli Vita, and Jared Critchfield for providing suggestions for musical selections throughout this book, as well as the students of UNT's Spring 2019, Autumn 2019, and Autumn 2020 MUED 3200 classes for their willingness to workshop several of the activities presented in the following pages. Patricia is grateful for the years of support, in this and other professional projects, to

Michiko Sakai and Hidaat Ephrem of the University of Washington School of Music. David offers his thanks to participants of the 2019 Sharq Taronalari conference in Uzbekistan and the 2019 Nordic Network for Music Education intensive course in Sweden, where helpful comments were provided on material developed for this book.

Finally, thanks to you, our dear reader, for taking to heart the ways in which music can be known by students as a world phenomenon and as a "sonic reflection" of cultural behaviors, meanings, and values.

William J. Coppola, Denton, Texas, U.S.A.
David G. Hebert, Bergen, Norway
Patricia Shehan Campbell, Seattle, Washington, U.S.A.
February 14, 2020

Episodes and Activities

Listening Episode and Performance Activity music examples can be accessed on the eResource site from the Routledge catalog page.

1

Teaching and Learning in Context

> *"Music may be universal to humankind, but, contrary to the poet Longfellow, music is not the universal language of mankind but, rather, a group of discrete languages or, perhaps better stated, systems of communication, each integrated and unified, and each of them must be learned."*
>
> —Bruno Nettl, 2010, p. 3

Brad Peterson, Assistant Professor of Percussion at a medium-sized northeastern university, is unexpectedly asked by his dean to teach a survey course called "Music in Culture." The faculty is currently short-staffed but the dean thinks that Brad will be an effective instructor, assuming a generalist—if slightly uninformed—stance in holding that all percussionists should be proficient in plenty of world music styles. Believing strongly in the importance of teaching music as a universal human activity, Brad is enthusiastic for the opportunity but hesitates to tell the dean that he is only experienced in Afro Caribbean and jazz styles. Nor is he an ethnomusicologist, although he has already been gently advocating for one or two such scholars to be hired to the faculty. Brad realizes he will have to do some personal research to prepare for the task of teaching the several other musical traditions beyond his specialty. Identifying as an active drummer first and foremost, he seeks to make the semester-long "Music in Culture" course as engaging and interactive as possible—especially since the class will be made up of mostly science and engineering majors who have few other opportunities to make music in their daily lives.

***

As part of her graduate fellowship, Felicia Kwan, a third-year PhD student of music history, is asked to be the instructor-of-record for a freshman-level music course called "Music of the World's Cultures." As a budding scholar of the French Baroque period,

Felicia realizes that her specialization has left her ill-equipped to teach a course featuring musical practices from outside the Western European idiom. All summer she has been studying a borrowed world music textbook, hoping to prepare herself for the new course. But as she studies the book and the previous year's syllabus for the course, she is disappointed by the inevitable dry lecture format that the materials presume. From personal experience, Felicia understands that students develop a deeper appreciation for music through active participation, whether by singing, dancing, or playing instruments. She begins to jot down a list of deeply meaningful musical experiences she recalls from her own life and travels: attending a performance of a Cantonese opera troupe, learning tango in the city's Latin ballroom, participating in taiko *drumming with an on-campus Japanese cultural group, and observing a powwow at the local state fair. "This will be a good starting point," she says to herself, ripping up the syllabus from last year.*

***

Mark Rosenstein, Regents Professor of Ethnomusicology, brushes a thin layer of dust from his office filing cabinet. Having recently returned from a two-week trip to Morocco, he feels rejuvenated and eager to begin his 29th year of teaching in higher education. From his filing cabinet he pulls out an envelope labeled "MUSC151: Introduction to World Music," which has become discolored with age over the decades. Recalling his visceral reaction to the Moroccan malhun *music he had heard in the streets and squares of Marrakech last month, he feels a twinge of yearning as he disinterestedly reads over the syllabus of his course that he's taught for the past 17 years now. The repetitiveness of his syllabus once gave him comfort, but now it suddenly feels stale and uninteresting, styled as a series of top-down presentational lectures with few music-making opportunities. While his passion for teaching this world music course had never waned, lately it seemed to him that students were losing interest. A pang of guilt rises in his chest.* How is it, *he thinks to himself,* that with so much in constant flux—the identities of our students, the consistent changes in our society, and the very nature of the music we study and explore—I have continually insisted on teaching the same exact material, in the very same way, over all these years? *Taking his seat at his desk, Prof. Rosenstein makes a personal vow to himself:* This year will be different. *He finds himself sketching out a participatory plan for the first day's class session, replete with listening that will invite student participation, creative expression, and thoughts about the cultural meaning of* malhun *music of Morocco.*

This book seeks to address relevant and applicable strategies for teaching world music in higher education. It is the seventh and final volume in the Routledge World Music Pedagogy Series and is geared as a guide to all who may teach a course on world music cultures. Its purpose is to reach beyond and counterbalance the study of Western European art music. It is launched from the premise that the study of world music need not get short shrift in higher education music departments and schools, nor should such courses consist of dry and impersonal lectures. While it may be the first book of its kind to guide the teaching-learning process in university-level world music courses, it is also long overdue and vital as a means of knowing how best to shape the experiences of world music study. World Music Pedagogy fixes on a dynamic peda-gogical approach that requires students' ongoing involvement through listening, think-ing analytically, and "doing"—thus conceiving of music as an essential act of human expression conveyed through performative and creative acts. It considers music as both sonic and social and underscores the importance of knowing the cultural contexts of music that give it meaning.

Setting the Scene for Courses in World Music Studies

On most any college campus, when approaching the façade of the music building, one is greeted warmly by a gradual crescendo of melody and harmony. Eclectic music from a range of European art music composers, styles, and historical eras mix together, reverberating from within the walls and bursting from the windows like the impetuous whistling of a tea kettle. Music of the great European masters is typically the steady diet for students in studios, ensembles, and academic courses, while at the periphery there may lie an opportunity to sample jazz, popular, and folk music beyond the core studies. Within this campus environment of a school or department of music, art is living, creative expression is encouraged, and *doing* is expected. Among both music majors and students from other fields and disciplines, those enrolled in music courses usually find themselves working closely with a music professional—a seasoned per-former, a gifted intellectual, or a thoughtful educator. *Music is social*, after all, and cannot be taught impersonally.

While the description of the campus music building may appear inviting, it also reflects a myopic view of musical study that has changed little since the birth of the Conservatoire de Paris in 1795. This Western European model of music, so pervasive among colleges, conservatories, and universities, should give us pause today, knowing what we do about the wider world of which we are a part, with its numerous cultural, artistic, and musical practices. One of the world's great practices, consisting of multiple sub-practices, is Western European Art Music (WEAM). It is referred to as "art music" or "classical music," sometimes even "serious music"—as opposed to the music that is called "folk," "vernacular," or even "light." Not only are WEAM repertoires and techniques emphasized in studio-applied study, ensembles, and academic courses in music history and theory, but in many four-year programs, music majors typically give full focus to WEAM with little to no study of music beyond the West. For students of majors other than music, the focus of their elec-tive studies tends to be music appreciation courses centered on WEAM practices, as well as upper-level seminars on "The Orchestra," "The Opera," and "Chamber Music." These courses are surely valuable, and yet they do not open their reach to the musical realities of a global and intercultural era.

There is rich potential for tertiary-level music programs to serve as welcoming environments for students to learn music in a wide-span way, to learn to listen ana-lytically to the music of people across the globe, to join in with music (live or with recordings) in a participatory and performative manner. Students deserve to know why music is necessary for people everywhere in the world and to understand music for its culture-specific and cross-cultural functions. Spanning courses such as "World Music Cultures," "Music in Africa," "Music and Migration," "Latin American Music," "Music and Protest," "Music of Multicultural America," "Music and Ritual," "Music in Asia," and "American Popular Music," the territory for teaching music of the world's cultures is ripe for meaningful and active musical participation, regardless of students' prior experience, ability, or so-called talent. In these times, tertiary music classrooms are wide open for learning more of the world's musical cultures through recordings, videos, and online sites. Facilitated by their professors, students can come to make sense of the wide array of musical possibilities, to explore themes, to experience ways of delving deeply into listening until it beckons their participation, performance, and even creativity in the shaping of new music. Whether they major in piano performance or music education, or history or bioengineering, students can study in earnest music and its cultural meaning through explorations of its roles, functions, and sonic styles in the world's cultures.

The three opening vignettes illustrate real-life attitudes and challenges among teaching faculty, from first-time lecturers who are assigned a world music course without prior study or experience, to veteran professors who seek imaginative ways to recapture student interest. On campuses where faculty are seeking to fulfill diversity initiatives and globalize their reach of topical studies, music faculty charged with teaching world music courses are finding that they require time to educate themselves about developing relevant lectures, discussions, and experiences to meet these needs. They study topical areas of interest and review available textbooks, recordings, videos, online sites, and various ancillary materials in order to renew and redo their teaching approaches, be it for their students' in-person or remote learning. For novices and experts alike, there is a learning curve among tertiary-level teaching faculty in coming into the preparation and delivery of courses that spark the musical thinking—and musical *doing*—of their students.

The philosophical position of providing students with a broad view of music as a pan-human phenomenon should surely be one that is shared by faculty of music, and yet there is discernable variance across institutions. Some universities, colleges, and conservatories have courses in place, or action plans in development, for the design and delivery of courses in world music cultures for music majors and students of various fields of study. Yet in some university programs, world music courses are scheduled as elective offerings for students of every major *except* music, thus asserting the importance for music majors to continue the practice of four solid years toward the concentrated and uninterrupted study of Western European art music. In yet other programs, world music is stuffed into a mix of music history courses, with two or three courses dedicated to WEAM history and merely one relegated to "all the rest of the music"—including world, jazz, folk, and popular styles.

On many faculties, courses in world music are appropriately—and logically—taught by ethnomusicologists. However, in many programs it falls to faculty without ethnomusicological training to provide world music courses. In fact, it is not uncommon that in tertiary-level institutions, it is the specialists in subfields such as music theory, music education, composition, and instrumental and vocal performance who are assigned the responsibility of teaching world music courses. Depending upon the faculty member, such an assignment may feel energizing, or daunting, or both.

For ethnomusicologists who may prefer not to claim expertise in all the world's musical cultures, it is sometimes their challenge to broaden course content beyond specialized fieldwork study in order to address styles, traditions, and/or geographic locations of the musical world. After all, just as it would seem reasonable for a musicologist to specialize in music of the Italian Renaissance or the Viennese school of the early 20th century, ethnomusicologists typically specialize in a specific genre and region, thus identifying as an "Asianist" or "Africanist" with lesser experience in music elsewhere in the world. Just as a Bach scholar might need to stretch to teach 19th-century music, so would a scholar of Near Eastern music need to stretch to teach music of the Caribbean. Thus, ethnomusicologists may join with other music faculty in probing pedagogical ways to extend music course content to areas beyond their research expertise and to search for ways of teaching all the world's musical cultures. Ethnomusicologists may seek to creatively feature avenues that infuse interdisciplinary perspectives and mix musicological and anthropological ideals together. Moreover, professors within and beyond ethnomusicology, and with past experience in teaching world music courses, may struggle to find new inspiration when their course content becomes outdated and loses resonance with students.

This volume is designed to support tertiary-level music faculty in their integration of innovative and globally conscious pedagogies in order to effectively teach world music in higher education. We seek to illustrate how, through stronger interdisciplinary and international connections, music's roles and functions across cultures can be more widely understood—all while musical skills and understandings are strengthened through a more robust pedagogical approach. We recommend ways that world music courses, with pedagogical interventions that draw students into the thick of the musical and cultural content, are vital to the development of students' musical understandings, skills, and values. The strategies we describe emanate from pedagogical research and experiences in which teaching faculty can communicate to students that music is a basic human behavior—and one that is as universal as it is culture-specific in its sonic constructions and social functions. Because music is an activity that bolsters community health and well-being, enables social cohesion, and contributes to intercultural understanding and conflict resolution, we recommend avenues of experience that balance the cerebral with the embodied and feature both analytical and holistic ways of knowing music in culture and as a global phenomenon. *Teaching World Music in Higher Education* espouses the instructional approach of World Music Pedagogy, offering a way forward for the design and delivery of experiences that lead to musical and cultural discoveries and understandings. This volume appears as a compendium of strategies for invigorating course content with participatory activities and a deeper involvement with the vast expanse of the world's musical cultures.

Music in Higher Education: Tradition and Change

Musical study knows a long life in higher education, and because North American universities were historically influenced by European institutions, musical study in North America is understandably quite Western European in nature. Universities such as those at Cambridge, Oxford, Paris, and Salamanca established music as one of a quadrivium of studies that consisted also of arithmetic, geometry, and astronomy. Music courses emphasized the logic of the ancient Greeks, and then drew upon the ideals of the Roman theorist Boethius in shaping academic studies. Performing musicians of the Middle Ages learned their trade well outside the university, in conservatories and professional music schools that were first associated with orphanages and church choirs. As European universities eventually opened their theoretically based programs to performance studies, the works of Western European composers were central to the curriculum. North American universities imported European-styled learning in the way of both content and method such that by 1900, music programs in U.S.-based public universities typically offered a standard body of courses in vocal and instrumental performance and music history and theory—again, all Western European in nature. To these courses were added programs of study in music education, and by the mid-20th century, undergraduate music major studies had settled into a standard menu of studio lessons, ensembles, and academic courses focused on Western European art music. Now well into the 21st century, relatively small changes to that arrangement have been made, even when universities are serving students whose heritages are increasingly traced to Africa, Asia, the Americas, and places beyond Europe.

In response to these deep-rooted historical circumstances, a Task Force on the Undergraduate Music Major was established by The College Music Society in 2013–14. Teaching faculty on the task force engaged in a systematic analysis of four-year degree programs in universities, colleges, and conservatories. A group of eight seasoned tertiary-level faculty with specializations in music history, music theory, performance (solo, chamber, and large ensembles), ethnomusicology, composition, jazz studies, and music education convened to consider the challenges of preparing students over their four-year programs for professional work as thoughtful musicians in the world beyond the academy. In task force discussions, three concepts arose as critical to the reform of music in higher education and were dissected every which way to achieve a meaningful overhaul of 19th-century institutional prerogatives: *creativity, diversity, and integration*. Questions of a more musically diverse array of courses surged forward, as did practical avenues for students to engage creative musical processes while allowing for the merging of performance and academic studies in order to achieve deep and meaningful understandings. The collective ideas, with an accent on the three pillar themes, were put to print in a documentary report called the Manifesto (2014), which was both applauded and disputed and which triggered a flood of activity that included departmental examinations, full-faculty retreats, pilot courses, and wholesale change from the ground level up. A post-Manifesto book, *Redefining Music Studies in an Age of Change: Creativity, Diversity, and Integration* (Sarath, Myers, & Campbell, 2017), contains the complete Manifesto while also working through the backdrop of its development, expanding upon issues of creativity, diversity, and integration, examining models of change, and offering some practical steps toward realizing the Manifesto's vision.

The dialogue on diversity has continued in recent years as teaching faculty seek to shape music studies on points of relevance, tradition, transition, and full-on transformation. Faculty in schools and departments of music in institutions of various sizes and contexts are working to hone more relevant undergraduate studies. Where there were once no courses in "non-Western" music, some faculty are making their way forward in figuring ways to introduce students to world music cultures through a single academic course. Where there was once only Western European art music (and Euro-American art music) programmed for ensembles, some faculty are pioneering experiences and exercises in performing transcriptions, arrangements, and newly commissioned works from various world regions. Where there were once only symphonies, choirs, and wind ensembles, there are now greater opportunities on some campuses to enroll in an "African drumming ensemble," a salsa band, an Indonesian *gamelan*, an Irish "trad" group, a Mexican *mariachi*, a Balkan dance troupe, or a bluegrass group. Where there was once no ethnomusicologist on faculty, some institutions are finding faculty lines for hiring specialists who are at the frontline for diversifying musical study. Where only students with training on Western orchestral instruments and voice were admitted to major in music, openings are now apparent for some whose experience is primarily centered on nontraditional instruments such as electric bass, accordion, gospel-style piano, or Persian *tar*. Where a Western European base for musical study is yet continuing, there are indications that multiple musical expressions are finding their way into institutions of higher education.

Teaching World Music in Higher Education

For decades various accreditation agencies, such as the National Association for Schools of Music (NASM), have encouraged the inclusion of studies of musical diversity in undergraduate music major programs. Recommendations are not mandates, however, and institutions vary in their interpretations of how calls for musical diversity shall be served. Some universities have advanced world music as a course for students in programs other than music, while others have prescribed a course for students in degree programs other than music. Occasionally, world music is inserted as a short unit within an overfull music education methods course in order to meet multicultural education requirements. Still other programs may meet their diversity mandate by offering an evening's African drumming workshop for all music majors, a required half-day experience with a visiting artist from Japan or Turkey, or even an online assignment. Musical diversity may be variously defined, too, so that students may be credited and approved for their enrollment in a jazz band, a guitar class, or a "new music" course.

When a musical diversity requirement best translates to the successful study of music as a world phenomenon, and that position is embraced as vital to the evolution of students as world-conscious citizens, then the faculty of an institution's music department or school should be ready to commit to reflecting this stance. They can consider it their social responsibility to enlighten students of the notion that Western European art music is just one of many musical expressions in the world, and that art, folk, traditional, and popular forms of music exist in societies everywhere. When faculty share the position that the study of the music's diverse expressions is a necessary component of educating a music major, then they are also prepared to commit to channels of knowledge and skills that are substantive and even integrative in manner.

Music faculty can choose to require students to enroll in four semester-long history-culture courses, which could reasonably consist of two courses each in "Western European Art Music" and "World Music." Or they may provide a more generalized, broad-based introductory course in which music of many cultures is sampled in understanding sonic features. Topics in such a course might feature broader musical concepts such as pentatonic melodies (e.g., Javanese *gamelan*, Northumberland folk fiddle tunes), harmonic cluster-chords (e.g., the works of Charles Ives, Bela Bartok, Cecil Taylor, and Japanese *gagaku*), or additive meter (e.g., Bulgarian folk song, works by Philip Glass, Dave Brubeck, and Igor Stravinsky). Such an introductory course could be followed by a blend of Western history-theory courses over the first several years of study, and then an upper-level set of courses that include world music cultures of largely art and traditional forms, American music (including art, folk, and traditional styles), and popular music in global perspective. Clearly, the precise configuration of courses will vary widely from one institution to another, and performance-based programs at conservatories will be comprised of selections that differ from those in liberal arts colleges or comprehensive universities. Still, world music studies may be important at both the introductory and concluding stages of degree studies. In the first year, they are valuable for stimulating students to consider the broad range of music genres and traditions from the very start. In a student's senior year, such courses enable students to rethink and reflect on what they already know and how it fits into the vast forms of music-making found in the world.

While a single course in world music is an important step to take in diversifying a program that has been previously centered on Western European art music, there are then the challenges that arise in determining ways to adequately cover all of the world's music in courses that run just 10–15 weeks. World music courses, whether for music majors or university students at large, tend to sample in survey fashion a variety of musical cultures and their expressive forms. World music textbooks have commonly featured forms of art music and folk music from East Asia, Southeast Asia (e.g., Indonesia), South Asia (e.g., India), the Near East, sub-Saharan Africa (e.g., West Africa), the Americas (including long-standing cultural groups in North America as well as one or more cultures in the Caribbean, and in Central and South America), and occasionally the Pacific Islands. If European folk cultures are featured at all, they are likely from the European periphery—such as Bulgaria, Ireland, or Spain. For courses with just 30 sessions per term, the result is a sweeping survey of sometimes too much information, while 50-session courses afford a little more time to "sink in" to the musical practices.

Naturally, seminars provide opportunities for greater exploration of places, people, genres, and issues in greater depth. For example, senior seminars or capstone courses in world music offer opportunities for students to have guided excursions across cultures into such topical areas as music and race, gender/sexuality, class, transnationalism, rituals/ceremonies, healing, and children/youth. Or they may focus attention on the music of a single region, nation, or ethnic cultural group, such as "Music of the Pacific Islands," "Music in Brazil," or "Music of the African Diaspora." Seminar courses are well suited to ethnomusicologists who have deep knowledge of particular musical cultures, forms, and issues and may be successfully taught by faculty teams from music and anthropology, sociology, history, and area studies.

Pluralism, Innovation, and Interdisciplinary Study

Further concepts associated with the changing landscape of higher education today include *pluralism, innovation,* and *interdisciplinary study,* all of them resonant with efforts to diversify musical study through courses in world music. Pluralism refers to the growing recognition that diversity of all kinds may contribute to a strengthening of music programs: Diversity of musical practices and genres, diversity of student cultural backgrounds and identities, and diversity of approaches to teaching and learning (Campbell, 2018). Innovation is the systematic application of newer and increasingly effective teaching-learning strategies. Such strategies are bolstered by the latest technological developments, including the provision of music and all the performing arts through mediated channels. Websites, streaming services, YouTube videos, and various means of online and hybrid learning are vital to bringing diverse learners in touch with diverse musical expressions from local and global communities. Finally, interdisciplinary study goes to the heart of the ethnomusicological concept of knowing music for its sonic *and* social meanings, and for understanding music and musicians in the context of the cultures that value particular timbres, tonalities, and texts, but also express themselves for their religious, ritualistic, social, political, and environmental contexts. By studying music through interdisciplinary filters, what then emerges are perspectives of music as part-and-parcel of the valued beliefs and customary practices of people—both in local communities and across the globe.

Decades of discussion regarding matters of pluralism, innovation, and interdisciplinary studies have spurred active and ongoing change in many institutional settings where music is taught and learned. Even a moderate redesign of undergraduate programs in music for 21st-century students requires attention to diversity as it is conceptualized by thoughtful responses to the realities of these concepts. Experienced faculty as well as newcomers to teaching positions at the tertiary level are in positions to shape learning in ways that resonate well with the interests and needs of their students, and these concepts can lead the way in transforming music practices in higher education.

Core Matters of Culturally Inclusive Music Programs

For music faculty in universities, colleges, and conservatories, the desire to teach with a focused attention to the cultural identities of their students may come quite naturally. Both music majors and nonmajors arrive to campus with experience in (or familiarity with) Western European art music, popular music genres such as hip-hop, country, and indie rock, and the distinctive music of their families and local communities. Because the music is "in the air" and surrounding them in their particular cultural communities, they may know well African American–based gospel and blues, Mexican *mariachi* and *son jarocho*, Korean K-Pop, *p'ung mul*, and *pansori*, Puerto Rican *jibaro* and *bomba*, Filipino *kulintang* and *rondalla*, and music for Chinese *dizi* (flute), *erhu* (two-string fiddle), and *guqin* (plucked zither). These musical expressions have cultural significance for many students, and they contribute to the cultural mosaic of North America's contemporary soundscape.

Despite a recognition by faculty of the musical realities of their students, they may not necessarily possess the practical skills to feature these instruments, ensembles, and styles in ways that properly celebrate the diversity of their student populations. Trained as they are on the various instruments and styles of Western European art music, faculty are justified in their desire to maintain their knowledge and skills on the musical practices of their own education and training, even as they may be intrigued with instruments and styles that are less familiar to them. Particularly when their students are more than just aware of "Other" musical practices and are sometimes even steeped in it, faculty are finding themselves uncertain and yet also in earnest to understand these traditions better, as their time allows. In the process they shift toward prospects for a more culturally inclusive education in music for their students.

As important as it may be to develop a culturally responsive and student-centered environment, it is equally necessary to recognize and respond to the diversity of the world's musical cultures "writ large." Faculty know that as globalization continues to bring people together from cultures across the world, there is wisdom in preparing students for a more globally conscious future. Knowing more of the world's musical cultures is necessary in order to become more musically fluent—or even musically aware—of music as a subject, field, and discipline. Thus, exposure, experience, and formal education in diverse musical cultures can—and *should*—happen regardless of the presence or absence of students whose heritage traces to Mumbai or Madras, India; to Recife or Rio de Janeiro, Brazil; to Shanghai or Xian, China; or to San Juan, Puerto Rico; Havana, Cuba; or Kingston, Jamaica.

This commitment by faculty to knowing more of the musical world joins well with efforts to know the musical identities of students, and together these efforts can provide a more powerful complement to fashioning a culturally responsive program of musical study (Lind & McKoy, 2016). Such a broadening of musical study provides restorative representation to those who have been socially marginalized within society. Through meaningful musical engagements that move beyond historically rigid definitions of musical practices, such efforts may help marginalized groups reclaim their identities, even while more privileged European-heritage students develop cultural sensitivity, empathy, and humility through an attitude of open-mindedness and activism. A truly globalized curriculum holds that music should also be recognized as a pan-human phenomenon which has enriched the lives of every known civilization on earth. From this standpoint, providing students with an understanding of how music is performed, consumed, and shared among some of the world's countless societies becomes a matter of social and ethical responsibility. That is, experiences with diverse musical practices are intrinsically worthwhile and indispensable simply because they celebrate life-as-art—a behavior in which humans are naturally compelled to engage.

Surely, cultural diversity is inherently complicated, and the responsibility of developing more appropriate responses to diversity in higher education raises questions of practicality. Music faculty question matters of depth versus breadth in undergraduate programs, leading them to contemplate whether world-comprehensive musical approaches could ultimately jeopardize students' pursuits of specialized musical abilities within singular traditions. They argue that it may be counter-educative to develop musicians who are "jacks of all trades" but "masters of none." Collegiate instructors further lament their own lack of expertise with culturally unfamiliar music when they have studied WEAM music all their lives. Finally, as faculty are awakening to the importance of shaping a greater cultural sensitivity with regard to the identities of their students and of the musicians whose music they teach, a climate of uncertainty and even some fear has arisen among well-intentioned music faculty. Positive developments have indisputably developed, however, and will continue to evolve as a result of the profession's reinvigorated attention toward such delicate matters.

Acknowledging Positionality and Personal Limitations

Many ethnomusicologists contend that teaching cultural diversity through music is an inherently political act. This matter is particularly relevant within a global climate in which isolationism, nationalism, and xenophobia are on the rise. At the same time, it is no secret that academia at large continues to consist of mostly White-dominated disciplines. Accordingly, faculty must consider the implications of their own identities and experiences within the grander scheme of the cultural narratives that they present through their teaching. They must work to deconstruct narratives that reinscribe hegemonic ways of thinking, and instead must centralize the experiences of communities beyond themselves in order to come to terms with culturally situated musical logic and beauty. After all, the music of a Javanese *gamelan* or a Mexican *mariachi* is as brilliant as a Mozart string quartet, although structures, functions, and cultural meanings require study so that their logic and beauty can be known. In the process of making curricular spaces for previously unfamiliar music and musicians, faculty are effectively working to *decolonize* the field.

Such a process of decolonization requires that instructors first acknowledge their own *positionality*, or how their social and political identities are constructed by their race, gender, class, gender/sexuality, and so on with respect to their ensuing perspectives and biases. Moreover, instructors must continually own their personal limitations and gaps in knowledge through the practice of *intellectual humility* (Church & Samuelson, 2016), as well as their gaps in cultural understanding through the practice of *cultural humility* (Hook, Davis, Owen, Worthington, & Utsey, 2013). Accordingly, we the authors wish to model the importance of recognizing our specific positionalities as world music educators. In particular, we three acknowledge our identities as White music scholars and own the limitations that our identities afford us.

William J. Coppola is a third-generation American of Irish-Italian descent, raised by mostly nonmusical working-class parents in a relatively nondiverse suburb of New York City. His deeper exposure to cultural diversity was late in coming—not

Photo 1.1   William J. Coppola (photo credit: Juliana Cantarelli Vita)

until graduate school—but after living and teaching in New York City for nearly a decade, his understanding of cultural diversity expanded as he sought to connect more deeply with friends, colleagues, and community members from backgrounds unique from his own. Within New York City, he lived among diverse mixtures of African American, Afro Caribbean, and Hasidic Jewish communities (Crown Heights, Brooklyn), as well as lived and taught in Asian American and Latinx neighborhoods (Bayside, Queens). Finally, his pursuit of doctoral study in Seattle resulted in exploring ethnomusicological principles at the very center of his education. Beyond learning from culture bearers and colleagues from around the world while attending the University of Washington, his learning-and-doing of world music cultures was supplemented by enriching musical experiences in Tanzania, Nepal, China, Morocco, Scotland, and Israel.

David G. Hebert was born in Seattle in the 1970s. Most of his immediate family is regarded as White, but through marriage and adoption, African Americans, Asian Americans, and Hispanic Americans all make his extended family rather ethnically diverse. His grandfather was missing in action in the Korean War, and his parents lived long-term in China as U.S. expats, so East Asia naturally became a region of long-term interest and eventually one of his research specializations. He has taught world music at universities and colleges in academic posts within the U.S., Russia, Japan, China, Sweden, Norway, Finland, Brazil, and New Zealand. These

Photo 1.2 David G. Hebert (right) and Dr. Arnold Chiwalala (left)

experiences also provided opportunities to mentor postgraduate students from Tanzania, Guyana, and Iraq and to have music projects in Vietnam and Ethiopia. As a multi-instrumentalist, he has played in professional bands that perform music from Zimbabwe, South Africa, Cuba, and Brazil. In addition to subjects in ethnomusicology and music education, he teaches courses in cultural policy and non-Western educational philosophy for international students, with whom he continues to learn.

Patricia Shehan Campbell grew up in an American-hyphenated (Irish-Austrian) working-class family in the nitty-gritty industrial Midwest. She attended schools during a period of racially discriminatory housing practices and felt the impact of "White flight" as her family remained in Cleveland while friends and neighbors of various European ancestries were suddenly gone and replaced by new friends of racially mixed heritage. She learned of redlining and restrictive covenants and felt the racial tensions of busing that led to civil unrest in the streets. Her commitment to social justice through music education grew as 1970s-style multicultural education was shaping into a set of strategies encompassing principles of equity and inclusion. She credits her work in urban schools, her studies in ethnomusicology, and her associations with activist musicians as critical influences of her efforts in intercultural understanding and global competence in and through music. Through decades of work in the U.S. and in global contexts (via Fulbright grants and international projects), she sees music as key to increasing social cohesion, understanding, and empathy. Her work continues with the Lomax archives through the Association for Cultural Equity and with Smithsonian Folkways Recordings.

Photo 1.3   Patricia Shehan Campbell (photo credit: Skúli Gestsson)

Ethnomusicology and World Music: Overlaps and Distinctions

"World music" and "ethnomusicology" are related yet distinctive terms, but at times they have been erroneously joined together as a one-and-the-same entity. Particularly in conversations concerning musical diversity, faculty who teach world music courses have been colloquially referred to as ethnomusicologists, even when their primary training has been in another subfield such as percussion performance, composition, or music education. While ideally, all institutions of higher education would have fully trained PhDs in ethnomusicology on faculty, such an ideal has not (yet) been attainable in a widespread way. In fact, many music major programs are served by a handful of professors whose charge is coverage of many realms of performance and academic study. Thus, the reality is that in many departments and schools of music, world music courses are taught quite skillfully by non-ethnomusicologists.

As discussed thoroughly, courses in music history, music theory, and music appreciation have historically featured the works and lives of composers from the European tradition. In response to the changing context of the late 20th century, "world music" merely became a marketing category preferred by the recording industry to replace such earlier categories as folk, traditional, ethnic, and international music. The term then seeped into common academic parlance and was taken to mean all forms of traditional art music, folk music, and even popular music genres from continents other than Europe and North America. The term was initially assigned to studies of music of African villages and of the high-art Asian music in such places as Jogjakarta (Indonesia) and Jaipur, Kolkata, and Madras (India). Eventually, European and American folk music traditions were incorporated under the same umbrella term of world music, so to include musical cultures of the Balkan countries, Scandinavia, Iberia, and the northwest European islands of the United Kingdom and Ireland, as well as music of African American, European American, Latin American, Asian American, and Native American cultures.

Over millennia and continuing even today, cultural borrowings and influences have resulted in musical hybridity and the formation of new genres. Just as surely as the Silk Road was a conduit of cultural exchange, such that the plucked lutes and dulcimers in China, Japan, and Korea bear a resemblance to those found as far west as Iran and the Mediterranean region, so too are fusion genres, including the results of efforts by Paul Simon and Ry Cooder in South Africa, Brazil, and Cuba considered bona fide within conceptualizations of world music. These genres make their appearance in world music courses, too, including Tex-Mex *conjunto* (Mexican-German fusion), *reggaeton* (Jamaican dancehall, derived from reggae, mixed with Latin merengue, *plena*, and *bomba*), and *bhangra* (Punjabi folk, Bollywood, and Western popular music featuring Indian and Pakistani instruments along with electric guitars, bass, and drum kits). Surely, all music—but particularly music beyond the realm of Western European art music—qualifies as "world music," and they are awaiting opportunities for experience and study by students under the guidance of thoughtful music faculty of various specializations.

As a distinctive area of research, *ethnomusicology* is the study of music in culture, and music as culture. It is its own scholarly field and is interdisciplinary in its reach of music as it relates to language, geography, politics, economics, gender, and other disciplines. It embraces the social and cultural dimensions of musical behaviors and values, and also includes study of the material features of musical instruments and the cognitive processes of singers, players, dancers, and creative composers-improvisers. Ethnomusicologists may be equally likely to find themselves conducting research in an American conservatory, at a street parade, in a church, or in a club as in an African village. While ethnomusicology was once rooted in a kind of 19th-century comparative musicology in which all music was examined through a Western analytical lens, the shift toward anthropological and sociological theory and method in the mid-20th century brought a greater emphasis on understanding music's local uses, functions, and meanings. It is common for ethnomusicologists to pursue ethnographic fieldwork research by spending extended periods of a year or more working directly in the field with musicians in villages, neighborhoods, musical studios, dancehalls, and even virtually online. They learn the musical practices as they enter, invited, into the community of musicians who know the music from the inside out and are willing to share it with visiting scholars. For several generations, ethnomusicologists have produced an array of publications and field recordings, resulting in an ever-growing corpus of knowledge about music as a global phenomenon. It follows that ethnomusicology serves as the research base for the specialized knowledge vital to teaching world music.

World Music Pedagogy

At the nexus of ethnomusicology and education, World Music Pedagogy (WMP) arises from a belief in the principles of democracy, both cultural and musical, as a driving force for the steady presence of musical diversity in classrooms, seminar rooms, and rehearsal halls. The disciplinary blend of ethnomusicological principles and multicultural-intercultural tenets in WMP make for an approach to teaching and learning that is intended to result in both the development of musical knowledge and skills and the honing of multicultural-intercultural understandings. Foundational to World Music Pedagogy is the assumption that all music teaching-learning ventures need to be firmly anchored to matters of diversity, equity, and inclusion, so much so that the exclusion of musical styles for study is viewed as inherently an act of exclusion of those *people*. Democratically speaking, music from every culture is deemed worthy of study by proponents of World Music Pedagogy, and thus the approach is meant to serve as a guide to the design of course content and method, the selection of repertoire for study and experience, and the full play-out of encounters with the world's musical expressions in courses and across programs.

World Music Pedagogy emerged from the blended efforts of (a) culturally conscious ethnomusicologists, who teach world music courses from their vast knowledge of musical ethnographies, and (b) music educators, who know through research and practice the multiple layers of musical experience that are required for music to be humanly learned and retained. WMP is anchored in a half-century's work by both (a) ethnomusicologists, who communicate their fieldwork understandings beyond the niche of specialist scholars and out to the public at-large, and (b) music educators to meet global mandates in schools and university programs by encompassing cultures beyond the Western European art forms. The term "World Music Pedagogy" and its framework were first introduced by Patricia Shehan Campbell (2004), although the components have been alive and well for much longer. Where there are institution-wide mission statements on diversity, equity, and inclusion, these aims have driven content and modes of mindful involvement in the musical experience and its cultural sources. Because WMP advocates that learning be musically alive and active, rather than continuing a tradition of static lecture-and-listening classes, it opens avenues for challenging Eurocentric perspectives of not only the content of tertiary-level courses but also the process by which music outside the spectrum of Western European art music is transmitted and learned.

The WMP approach underscores the logic of making sense of music as an aural art, a channel of creative practice, and a means of personal and communal human experience. As a systematic and semi-sequential route to musical understanding, WMP assumes learning by listening, and it entails all manner of musical participation, performance, creative activities, and the critical need to contextualize the music, to tell the stories behind the music, and to honor the people whose music it is. WMP is applicable in teaching dance tunes, rhythmic percussion pieces, children's songs, choral works, and music of instrumental ensembles from around the world. It is practical and transferable to any music, anywhere, anytime.

While there are many avenues to teaching world music and to developing cultural understandings through music, some are unsystematic, incomplete, and even superficial. Some approaches are geared to a steady stream of lectures by faculty who talk to their students rather than facilitate musical understanding in more active ways. World Music Pedagogy aims at equipping faculty members who go it alone, often without an array of "exotic" instruments of the world or the financial means to regularly support featured world music artists in their courses. The approach is intended to realize the aims of opening ears and minds to more of the world in and through music. It pays tribute to performing musicians, on audio recordings, video recordings, and "live" (when possible). It provides the strategies by which faculty can facilitate repeated listenings and opportunities to join in, to ultimately embody the music via performance of the recorded piece—even to the point of extending or creating new music in the style of the learned musical work. Along the way, the approach requires integration so that the music is backed with stories that bring on cultural understanding. Teaching world music via World Music Pedagogy provides a comprehensive perspective that all music, musicians, and music students deserve.

As a teaching-learning process, World Music Pedagogy espouses five dimensions, or phases, each of which holds powerful potential for drawing students into musical-cultural involvement, insights, and understandings of a recorded or video-recorded musical selection (see Figure 1.1). Three listen-to-learn dimensions form the core of the WMP process:

1. *Attentive Listening*, directed and focused listening to music's elements and structures, guided by specific points of attention raised by the instructor's questions;

2. *Engaged Listening*, participatory listening to the recorded selection through active participation by listeners in some extent of music-making (by singing a melody, patting a rhythm, playing a percussion part, moving to a dance pattern); and

3. *Enactive Listening*, the performance of the recorded work in which, through intensive listening to every musical nuance, the music is re-created by learners in as stylistically accurate a way as possible.

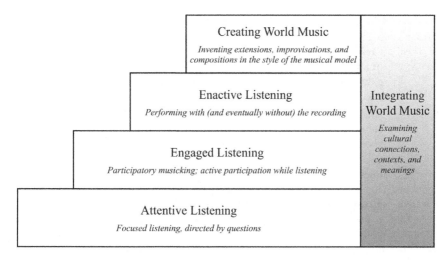

Figure 1.1   World Music Pedagogy in five dimensions

These first three dimensions are quite obviously sequential in that one must have initial listening encounters (Attentive Listening) before one can participate, and this is followed by an invitation to participate in sounding musical components while listening to the recording (Engaged Listening). Continued listening and "participatory musicking" lead to performance-level acquisition of the musical work through the knowledge that is gained in multiple in-depth listening experiences, in which learners are singing or playing all or most parts of the recorded selection (Enactive Listening). This third dimension suggests that learners are capable of "realizing the recording" by performing along with it, and eventually without it, as they work toward a more confident and nuanced level of performance.

The first three dimensions may be utilized as separate entities within one session of a world music cultures course, or they may be linked in a sequence that runs 20 or 30 minutes. The recorded segments the instructor chooses for these three listening phases are typically brief—for example, just 30–45 seconds, so that concentrated attention can be given to learning the musical excerpt well and thoroughly through multiple repetitions. It is likely that multiple opportunities are necessary for learners to listen with attention to the discovery of elemental features of a selection and style (Attentive Listening), which allow them to contribute one or more vocal or instrumental parts to the music (Engaged Listening), and then to perform the music close to the manner in which it sounds on the source recording (Enactive Listening). These three core dimensions may double back on each other, too, so that students may be directed by their instructors to return to the first phase so that they can "check themselves" even as they are striving to match the musical style and substance of a recording in a performance of the music.

Beyond these three initial listening dimensions are two more essential dimensions:

4. *Creating World Music*, the invention by students of new music in the style of a musical model through composition, improvisation, songwriting, and extending a piece beyond what is represented on the recorded model; and

5. *Integrating World Music*, the examination of music as it connects to culture and illuminates a prism-like grasp of integrated topics and interdisciplinary subjects as varied as history, geography, language and literature, the sciences, the visual arts, dance, and drama.

These dimensions may naturally seep in between and around the listening dimensions and need not be reserved chronologically for end-points in the process. Although creative-expressive moments may occur in playful ways throughout the process, creativity in the style of the musical model requires considerable familiarity with the music's structures, with listening leading to familiarity. Of course, it is understood that the musical model needs to be acknowledged, and a return to the musical model is necessary in order to understand differences between "them" (the musical originators) and "us" (the musical learners). When learners have progressed to the point of performing the musical work, they are then in the thick of understanding its constituent parts so that they can ornament, embellish, extend the music, or shape something new that adheres to stylistic features of the learned selection.

The dimension of Integrating World Music may well be inserted at any point along the way, from start to finish. A curiosity of music's functions, uses, and meanings often comes from students at any point, as these are teaching moments that allow for the integration of ideas about music and culture that need not be left to the end of the process. Questions that naturally arise from students often include why the music sounds the way it does, who the singers and instrumentalists may be, what the lyrics mean, and why a particular culture might find this music important to them as a component of their cultural heritage, values, and identities.

While listening inherently develops and proceeds across the first three phases, the World Music Pedagogy dimensions are not lock step, but rather can be used with a balance of logic, flexibility, and relevance to the given teaching-learning situation. Altogether, these five WMP ways of knowing can be used to facilitate student understanding of music as sound, behavior, and values. The dimensions can be used while co-teaching with culture bearers, heritage musicians, or teachers of other disciplinary specializations (e.g., historians, language specialists, experts in African or Asia studies). World Music Pedagogy offers a practical plan for honoring those whose music we study by listening to it and learning it well enough to participate in it, to enact it through performance, to fashion music in creative new ways based on studied musical selections, and to understand its meaning in culture.

Overview of the Book

Chapter 2 launches into the first stage of the WMP process: *Attentive Listening*. This stage stresses the value of listening as central to the WMP framework—beginning with brief, repeated listening to a recording, and asking deliberate questions to tune listeners' ears to specific musical features.

Chapter 3 describes the next two stages of the WMP framework, *Engaged Listening* and *Enactive Listening*—a two-stage continuum of events in which students, through careful interaction with a recording, dive into salient musical features and develop deeper understandings and basic performance techniques through careful interaction with a recording.

Chapter 4 details how these deep listening exercises and participatory activities ultimately lend themselves to music-making in public performances, which may be informal student performances with peers during a class session or a presentation for the campus community (and beyond) in public spaces.

Chapter 5 examines the at-times contradictory nature of creativity in tertiary-level musical instruction, including the common lack of preparedness and comfort for many students to participate in creative activities that go beyond "reading the ink." The chapter illustrates how creative activities such as improvisation, composition, and arranging emerge from deep engagements within a particular musical tradition over time.

Chapter 6 considers the study of music and musicians for what it means, for its roles and functions, and its place in a culture's history and heritage. Included in the chapter are possibilities for cultural integration by teacher and students and through collaborations with other university departments and disciplines across the campus community. Suggestions for working in various on-campus resources are offered, all which enable the cultural background of various musical traditions to be equitably recognized and respected.

The final chapter addresses some overarching questions regarding the inherent challenges of teaching world music and with realistically implementing a WMP-infused framework into tertiary music programs. A summary covers the espoused benefits of the World Music Pedagogy framework into courses and ensembles and provides a review of ethnomusicological principles that help to ensure thoroughgoing and genuine experiences in the study of world music cultures. Practical suggestions for ensuring the impact of the WMP process within courses are described, particularly with an emphasis on realizing the goals of musical understanding, intercultural sensitivity, and global competence. Ultimately, the final chapter situates the WMP framework within tertiary music programs with attention to how ethnocentric conceptions of music teaching and learning can be replaced with more nuanced perspectives that support highly relevant and impactful instruction.

Teaching "episodes" are spread throughout the book. A set of learning experiences are provided for given selections via one of the five dimensions of World Music Pedagogy. These episodes provide step-by-step instructions for learning the music through audio recordings, video recordings, and online resources. However, episodes should be treated as suggestions rather than "recipes" for teaching, and instructors should remain flexible to their specific classroom contexts and the preferred learning processes of their individual students. In all, episodes are provided for 16 total selections, each of which is intended to demonstrate the practical ways in which a dimension may play out. Three of the selected recordings ("Time to Have Fun," "Dulce Sueño Mío," and "E Maru Rahi") are featured as Learning

Pathways throughout Chapters 2–6 to illustrate how world music may be taught and learned across the five dimensions. Of course, every featured world music selection can be developed into a complete Learning Pathway, and any musical work that is featured in just one episode can be expanded to all five dimensions of the instructional sequence.

WMP and the Road Ahead

The focus of *Teaching World Music in Higher Education* primarily refers to variations of world music culture courses, but these suggestions additionally apply to other common courses for undergraduate music majors and nonmajors on topics of music appreciation, musical foundations, and other introductory music courses. With opportunities to sing, play, dance, and create music in the style of selected musical works, students enrich their musical sensibilities even as they also come to a recognition of how music portrays and reflects the myriad people who likewise find music useful and meaningful in their lives. These guided experiences in the world's musical practices make conversations about cultural diversity and social justice concrete, providing a real antidote to uninspired and empty dialogue.

Certainly, designing a music program that centralizes cultural diversity requires the bravery to deeply question how *the way things have been* might advance to *the way things could (and should) be*. Undergraduate music studies are shaped by faculty who are genuinely committed to issues of diversity, equity, and inclusion and who are keen to ensure that music is learned and taught as a pan-human phenomenon. As music is a universally valued, culturally specific expression, the study of music in higher education—in all universities, colleges, and conservatories—should surely feature encounters in music that pay tribute to more of the world's musical practices. Even where Western European art music may continue as the principal focus of a four-year degree program, an understanding of music for its grand variety of expressions is invaluable to all students of our time.

We therefore ask university music faculty to inquire whether excellence in a singular musical culture, typically Western European art music, should be the only—or even primary—indicator of a university music program's success. We ask music faculty to consider the espoused benefits of world music studies for students who are extraordinary violinists, *bel canto* sopranos, and classical music theorists but are also voraciously inquisitive about music as a human celebration of culture and identity. But for all the talk surrounding the importance of cultural diversity in our field, it is meaningless without action. This volume aims to contribute to these discussions through an ardent and overdue call to action.

Glossary

Attentive Listening: The first dimension of the WMP process. Consists of directed and focused listening to music's elements and structures, guided by specific points of attention raised by the instructor's questions. See Chapter 2.

Creating World Music: The fourth dimension of the WMP process. The invention by students of new music in the style of a musical model through composition, improvisation, arranging, songwriting, and extending a piece beyond what is represented on the recorded model. See Chapter 5.

Enactive Listening: The third dimension of the WMP process. Involves performing the recorded work in which, through intensive listening to every musical nuance, the music is re-created by learners in as stylistically accurate a way as possible. See Chapter 3.

Engaged Listening: The second dimension of the WMP process. Includes participatory listening to the recorded selection through active participation by listeners in some extent of music-making (by singing a melody, patting a rhythm, playing a percussion part, moving to a dance pattern). See Chapter 3.

Episode: A set of learning experiences for a given selection via *one* of the five dimensions of World Music Pedagogy, each of which provides step-by-step instructions for learning the music through audio recordings, video recordings, and online resources. However, episodes should be treated as suggestions rather than "recipes" for teaching.

Integrating World Music: The fifth and final dimension of the WMP process but one that is imbued throughout all dimensions rather than existing as the conclusion of the framework. Involves the examination of music as it connects to culture and as it illuminates a prism-like grasp of integrated topics and interdisciplinary subjects as varied as history, geography, language and literature, the sciences, the visual arts, dance, and drama. See Chapter 6.

Learning Pathway: Specific to the World Music Pedagogy approach, Learning Pathways are used to describe plans for a complete instructional sequence through all five dimensions of the method (Attentive Listening, Engaged Listening, Enactive Listening, Creating World Music, and Integrating World Music).

Positionality: The conscious awareness of how an individual's social and political identities are constructed by their race, gender, class, and sexuality with respect to their ensuing perspectives and biases.

World Music Pedagogy: An approach that guides students through five dimensions of musical learning. They include Attentive Listening, Engaged Listening, Enactive Listening, Creating World Music, and Integrating World Music.

References

Campbell, P. S. (2004). *Teaching music globally: Experiencing music, expressing culture.* Oxford University Press.

Campbell, P. S. (2018). *Music, education, and diversity: Bridging cultures and communities.* Teachers College Press.

Church, I. M., & Samuelson, P. L. (2016). *Intellectual humility: An introduction to the philosophy and science.* Bloomsbury.

Hook, J. N., Davis, D. E., Owen, J., Worthington, E. L., & Utsey, S. O. (2013). Cultural humility: Measuring openness to culturally diverse clients. *Journal of Counseling Psychology*, *60*(3), 353–366. https://doi.org/10.1037/a0032595

Nettl, B. (2010). Music education and ethnomusicology: A (usually) harmonious relationship. *Min-Ad: Israel Studies in Musicology Online*, *8*(1), 1–9.

Sarath, E. W., Myers, D. E., & Campbell, P. S. (2017). *Redefining music studies in an age of change: Creativity, diversity, and integration*. Routledge.

2

Attentive Listenings for Cultural Awakenings

"[T]he approaches developed in ethnomusicology can underscore something already understood but rarely expounded, that oral (or more correctly, aural) transmission is the norm, that music everywhere uses this form of self-propagation, that in live or recorded form it almost always accompanies the written, and that it dominates the musical life of a society and the life of a piece of music."
—Bruno Nettl, 1983, p. 200

Dr. Berger enters the large lecture hall a few minutes before his first class of the spring semester. He cranes his neck upward and gazes at the hundreds of students seated in the large lecture hall before him. He has been teaching the undergraduate course "Music of the World's Cultures" for several years now and has come to expect the types of students he will likely encounter: The listless senior who needs one final humanities course to graduate, the exploratory freshman who doesn't know what she wants to major in yet, the sophomore music major who has been looking forward to taking a course with Dr. Berger for three semesters now. And countless categories of students in between—music majors, music minors, and students from an array of science, social science, humanities, and arts programs from across the campus. The majority sit silently as they fight off the residual morning sleepiness, while a handful of others engage in quiet conversation before the start of class.

Dr. Berger powers on his computer and rifles through his extensive music library. Precisely at 8:30am, he energetically greets the class: "Good morning, everyone! Welcome to MUS121: Music of the World's Cultures. In this course, as you might have guessed, we will be exploring music from all around the globe. Right now, I want you to think about the term 'world music.' What does it make you think of? What music does it include, and what music does it exclude? Better yet, who does it include and exclude?" The heads remain motionless and disengaged, but several hundred eyes are now looking up, tracking Dr. Berger as he paces around the room. "For example," Dr. Berger continues, "could we count this *as 'world music'?"*

He clicks play and an electronic pop beat fills the room. At first it sounds like any other recent American Top 40 hit, causing several heads to shoot up with an expression of puzzlement, presumably expecting to hear something a little less "familiar" to start off the semester. As the beat settles, the sea of heads becomes noticeably more animated. Pockets of students start moving in their seats along with the music, and much to Dr. Berger's surprise, a handful of Korean students in the back corner begin singing along with the lyrics: "Dollar Dollar! Haruachime jeonbu tangjin. Dallyeo dallyeo naega beoreo naega sachi!" *Several others follow suit.*

After a few minutes, Dr. Berger fades out the music, which is met with a mixture of disappointed groans and appreciative applause directed toward pockets of students who were bravely singing and moving along. "Well, I guess I shouldn't be surprised that you already know that song!" Dr. Berger shouts across the din in the lecture hall. "This group has won several international awards, and has taken the music industry by storm. They're celebrated for emerging as one of the top music groups in the world, and as far as I'm concerned, they're challenging the assumption that 'all the best music is made in America.' Does anyone know who they are?"

At least half of the lecture hall shouts in scattered unison, "BTS!" Among the laughter, a woman in the front row elaborates matter-of-factly, "They're also known as the Bangtan Boys, Behind the Scenes, and the Bulletproof Boy Scouts." She adjusts her glasses as she coyly points to a BTS sticker on her laptop computer cover.

Dr. Berger laughs appreciatively. "Yes, exactly! But now for the harder question, one that might take us a little more time to answer: What makes this music uniquely Korean? What I mean is, if not for the language of the lyrics, how would we know where this music comes from and what people it's meant to represent?" At this question, broad smiles transform into puzzled faces. Dr. Berger continues, "Don't worry just yet. Today we'll start with our first influential musical culture of the semester, the increasingly globalized phenomenon known as K-Pop." He continues, as students reach into their bags and pull out notebooks. "As we will soon find out, a vast and colorful history of instrumental and vocal music throughout South Korea can be traced back at least a millennium. So, today, we'll go from K-Pop to something we might call . . . K-Roots! Let's begin." Dr. Berger feels a twinge of newfound excitement for the start of the new semester—and to his novel introduction of the course.

Before diving into specific matters of the World Music Pedagogy approach, we might do well to first critically reflect upon how we think about musical diversity by comparing it to another human phenomenon—the culinary arts, for example. When it comes to food, there are those who consider themselves connoisseurs of cuisine, eating purely for pleasure rather than survival. They colloquially call themselves "foodies," otherwise known as gourmands or epicures. Foodies are known for immersing themselves completely into any culinary experience, focusing on the contrasts and complements of various flavors and textures, always working to take in every nuance with a heightened degree of awareness. When one talks with a self-proclaimed foodie, it is not uncommon for them to extemporize enthusiastically about the various cultural cuisines they've experienced over their lifetimes: Japanese sushi, Ethiopian injera,

Indian butter chicken, Greek moussaka, Vietnamese pho, and the list goes on. They will seemingly travel any distance to partake in these culinary-cultural experiences. They appreciate every form of cuisine, from street food to fine dining experiences at Michelin-star restaurants. They consider themselves cultural omnivores, and food is their medium.

If food serves as a suitable medium through which to experience another culture, surely music must be capable of the same. Yet, when we think of self-proclaimed "musical omnivores," we usually envision someone who indiscriminately enjoys rock, pop, jazz, classical, country, and hip-hop, perhaps—the musical genres that are pervasive throughout contemporary American culture. We typically do not think of someone who craves to consume music genres from the far reaches of the world, as open as they may passively be to them. They may not actively seek out Japanese *gagaku*, Balinese *gamelan*, Andean *sikuri*, Tanzanian *bongo flava*, Puerto Rican *bomba*, and Balkan brass band music—at least, perhaps not with the same fervor that a foodie would seek out meals from these same places. Can we imagine a foodie who only craves hamburgers, pizza, pasta, and other foods pervasive in American culture? We would likely not consider that person a foodie at all, for ridicule of being considered tragically "uncultured" in the culinary world. Why is it, then, that the same need not apply for our consumption habits when it comes to music? Is it possible to invigorate a society of *musical* omnivores who crave and yearn to ingest all the world's music as avidly as they seek out their favorite cultural dish?

Through the first dimension of the World Music Pedagogy framework, we seek for our students to not merely *listen* to music from near and far, but to develop an appetite for listening *voraciously*—toward wholesale consumption. Indeed, we seek for students to engage in attentive listening that ultimately leads to deep cultural awakenings.

More Than Just Music From "Far Away Lands"

In this chapter's opening vignette, Dr. Berger attempted to challenge students' assumptions of what "counted" as world music. He chose to kick off the semester with an example of something that is precisely a style with unmistakable global influences (and popularity among college-aged students). World music, as he presented it, envelops popular forms as it also encompasses art, folk, and traditional expressions. World music need not be exclusively associated with comparisons of distinct musical cultures that appear remote from one another, but can also encompass a multiplicity of musical commonalities that each contribute, separately and together, to a collective understanding of artistic expression globally (Taylor, 1997). Especially during the infancy of ethnomusicology, the field was primarily concerned with examining the world's musical cultures through comparative lenses, thus earning the name *comparative musicology* to represent the discipline (Nettl & Bohlman, 1991). However, as contemporary societies continue to converge and musical tastes further blend and integrate, the fields of ethnomusicology and world music studies have necessarily adapted by viewing the world's music not merely from a single, comparative lens, but from a more holistic, intercultural perspective. Further, the sprouting popularity of "global pop" music is an opportunity to explore this 21st-century stylistic pervasiveness.

BTS's Korean pop hit "Go Go" (Episode 2.1) directly explores these possibilities in the tertiary classroom. The introduction to the song is not particularly distinguishable from any other example of popular music throughout Western pop culture [0:00–0:13]. In fact, the very first words sung by BTS member Jimin ("Dollar, dollar") is a reference to American currency (South Koreans use the *won* as their national currency) as well as a symbolic homonym for the Korean word for "running" (*dallyeo*). However, in an intercultural fashion, several other English phrases are bounded by Korean lyrics as the group sings about the economic difficulties among South Korean youth. Layered atop a looping flute motif, the K-Pop band sings about the hedonistic desires of a generation that is unable to afford life's luxuries against the ironic backdrop of a celebratory dance club hit.

The decision to feature an internationally recognized K-Pop group, or some other popular music example, speaks to the instructor's necessary commitment to the relevant interests and priorities among typical students enrolled in an undergraduate world music course. It speaks to the potential to initiate the study of a musical culture with a contemporary selection and use a popular song as roots to the discovery of the multiple layers of a musical culture. To be certain, starting with globally influenced musical examples already close to the students' hearts (and perhaps already within their playlists) is not merely done to artificially produce "buy in" from the students. Rather, it allows them to utilize an intercultural lens to examine the deeper social messages of such songs as they engage critically with the contexts and purposes of various musical practices from around the world. Furthermore, by sharing a record-breaking hit from South Korea, the instructor explicitly communicates that while the U.S. might still be the most prolific producer of popular music, there are other producers that cannot be ignored within the global popular music scene. Indeed, BTS is not merely another boy band on the scene; they have experienced a meteoric rise as they became the first Korean group to win a *Billboard* Music Award in 2017 (and again in 2018 and 2019), as well as an American Music Award in 2018 and 2019 (among many other accolades).

There is an additional layer of interest that makes "Go Go" a particularly thought-provoking selection for a world survey music course. Beyond the emergence of Asian pop music within the global music sphere—which is just as central to our so-called conventional notions of world music as are the thousands of source recordings housed within historical archives—the music offers a gesture toward a more traditional South Korea as well. Specifically, the looping flute motif (Figure 2.1) could be interpreted to represent the sound of a traditional Korean instrument, the *sogeum* (Figure 2.2)—the smallest member of the transverse bamboo flute family in South Korea. Although it is unknown whether the song conspicuously incorporated the flute motif for such a symbolic purpose, it nevertheless would bear stimulating discussion among students. Facilitated by the instructor, speculating on the role of this instrument would encourage students to view the song within the larger context of global musical practices—in this case, the confluence of traditional and popular music in South Korean popular culture and society.

Figure 2.1   Looping flute/*sogeum* motif in BTS's "Go Go" [starting at 0:13]

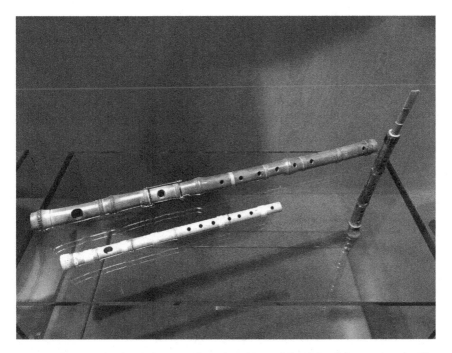

Figure 2.2   Two transverse bamboo flutes found in traditional South Korean music: The larger *daegum* and the smaller *sogeum*.[1] While the *daegum* has a characteristic "buzzing" quality created by a membrane, the *sogeum* does not, giving it a clearer timbre.

Episode 2.1: K-Pop and Interculturalism

Materials:

- "Go Go," BTS, Big Hit Entertainment.

Procedure:

1. Ask in advance: "Do you think this selection would be considered an example of world music? Why or why not?"
2. Play track [0:00–0:57] and field responses. Students in the affirmative might point to features such as the language of the song or the flute loop.
3. "Where in the world do you think this music might be from?"
4. Play track [0:27–0:57] and field responses.

5. Facilitate a brief discussion about K-Pop music, encouraging students to express what they may already know about the music and providing additional context as appropriate (3–5 minutes).

6. "What musical elements sound similar to American popular music?"

7. Play track [0:00–0:57] and field responses.

> **A:** Students may note the looping hip-hop style beat/groove or singing style/rapping.

8. Facilitate a brief discussion about the boy band BTS. Briefly discuss the international rise of the band both within South Korea and internationally (and especially in the U.S.).

9. "In what ways do you think this K-Pop song is *unique* from American pop songs?" (Anticipate/suggest 1–2 answers, also noting that other answers are possible.)

10. Play track [0:00–0:57] and field open responses.

11. Given the overall mood of the song, what do you think the vocalists might be singing about? (Anticipate/suggest 1–2 answers.)

12. Play track [0:00–0:57] and field open responses.

13. Provide early context about the meaning of the song. Through an online search, provide translations of the lyrics (on a projector or handout) to the class and discuss the possible relevancy of the lyrics to American youth culture (collectively or in small groups). If trustworthy lyrics cannot be found, instructors should consult several translations and compare any discrepancies.

14. "Now that we know a little more about the context of this song and its similarities to American pop music, let's ask ourselves again: Do you think this selection would be considered an example of 'world music'? How so or why not?" (Anticipate/suggest 1–2 answers.)

15. Play track [0:00–0:57] and field responses, leading toward a deeper discussion of what should constitute "world music."

Taking the Initial Dive Into WMP: Attentive Listening

The Attentive Listening dimension is the first step of the World Music Pedagogy framework. It is from here that brief sonic visitations will eventually unfold into extended activities in which students participate dynamically through playing and singing (and eventually full-on performing, composing, and improvising). It is for this reason that, for instructors, choosing the proper Attentive Listening selections can feel both thrilling and daunting at the same time.

Before diving into strategies for choosing quality repertoire, however, it is necessary to first distinguish how Attentive Listening, as conceived within the WMP framework, is unique from listening experiences that may be found within a more traditional world music survey course. Of the several texts commonly used for such introductory courses (see Appendix 2), most of which are written by working eth-nomusicologists in the field (who are typically also tenured at top universities where they teach similar courses of their own), listening materials are typically provided as supplemental materials to the text itself. They may be packaged with a link to an online audio/video library, a password to a companion website, or for older texts, a physical CD. Instructors who have used these texts before have likely become quite familiar (and comfortable) with the recordings, although they would acknowledge that they do not—and cannot—represent the entirety of musical practices around the world. Nonetheless, these recordings provide a certain confidence to world music course instructors because (a) they have been selected by experts in the field, and (b) descriptions of the recordings are usually articulated at length within the textbook. Therefore, such resources allow non-ethnomusicologists to tread the waters of world music with a greater degree of self-assurance.

Through Attentive Listening within the framework of World Music Pedagogy, the approach is not altogether different (as far as listening activities are concerned). However, there are several distinct contributions that the WMP approach offers. First, it opens the world of musical repertoire to the instructor's disposal. Rather than prescribing recordings in advance, it encourages instructors to use the vast array of resources available to plan musical activities of their own devising. Certainly, instructors can use the WMP approach in tandem with their preferred world music textbook with great success, but they can also forego the bounds of these texts and pursue cultures beyond these core sources. At first glance, this may sound to some instructors like the ripping away of a security blanket, which textbook recordings so effectively provide. However, as discussed in the following section, providing instructors with the agency to select their own musical experiences can be liberat-ing and need not represent a far departure from their textbook-curated selections. Perhaps the greatest benefit of this strategy is that it allows the course content to change from semester to semester, with instructors choosing to either retain their favorite tried-and-true recordings or select altogether new recordings to keep the material fresh and responsive to the students' identities and interests.

The second advantage that the WMP approach offers is that it uses listening examples not as ends in themselves, but rather as jumping-off points for further experiences in which students have the opportunity to create and perform the music on their own. In many world music survey courses, cultural "visitations" only go as far as a lecture on a particular musical culture, which would likely include the context of the culture's people, customs, history, and so on, followed by a handful of listening examples that feature the sonic elements and practices of that musical culture. Students thus learn highly contextualized material and are able to articulate how the contextual and historical factors of a given society informs the idiosyncrasies of that culture's musical tradition, including the unique sonic elements of that tradition. However, through the WMP approach, students take the music beyond this important step by actively singing, dancing, playing, performing, and creating the music of that culture—all of which falls under the broad umbrella of "active learning" in musically educating university-level students. Naturally, when taking such a hands-on approach to learning the material, students have the opportunity to develop an even deeper and more nuanced understanding of the music for themselves.

Finally, Attentive Listening moves beyond the passive listening experiences that are contained within many survey courses, and instead require that students actively respond to exploratory questions designed to help them explore the sonic structures of the music. As Episode 2.1 illustrates, questions are direct and to the point, and they encourage students to think critically about the music without first needing to know the correct answer—if one even exists. Of course, some questions may lead to the discovery of precise information, while others are intended to open minds to multiple possibilities. More about the specific characteristics of well-designed Attentive Listening questions will be discussed in the forthcoming section, "Focusing on Sonic Features."

Finding Quality Repertoire

Attentive Listening allows for free-spirited exploration—by both the instructor and the students—to identify musical selections that first and foremost pique collective interest. These recordings may very well be those contained within the instructor's textbook of choice, given the comforting assurance that they are considered "high quality" by the authoring ethnomusicologist. However, as these very authors would recognize, the featured recordings may often be bounded by strict copyright and fair use laws, which can affect the authors' ability to feature their first-choice record-ings, and/or result in limited samples of the chosen track (usually no more than 30 seconds). This may not be an issue in and of itself, since the WMP approach already suggests featuring short listening clips, but instructors wishing to use other portions of the textbook recording would be unable to do so. Furthermore, instructors using the same textbook recordings year after year may find that they become stale over time, potentially causing the instructor to present the material in a tired fashion over repeated semesters.

Auspiciously, other resources available at instructors' disposal feature a vast collection of recordings from around the globe. Smithsonian Folkways Recordings is an archive useful to both veteran and unseasoned instructors (and students) of world music, because musical collections feature downloadable liner notes that help in contextualizing the music historically, socially, and sonically. Audio recordings can be sampled, and the 30-second samples provided on the Smithsonian Folkways Recordings website are often sufficient for initial interactions with a musical exem-plar. The site includes quality tracks on particular topics (e.g., "Sounds of the Civil Rights Movement") or cultures (e.g., "Sounds of Haiti"), while archived videos feature culture bearers performing, teaching, and talking about their music. Other online archives are available as well, including the Association for Cultural Equity (which holds historic recordings, photos, and videos of the Lomax family), the Library of Congress, the Garland Encyclopedia of World Music, the Adam Matthew Digital Collection of Ethnomusicology: Global Field Recordings, and university-curated collections (e.g., UCLA, Indiana University, University of Washington). Additionally, ever-expanding databases of online music streaming services (such as Spotify and Apple Music) provide a seemingly endless selection of recordings, including popular/commercial, folk/traditional, and source/archival tracks—all for public consumption. Admittedly, streaming services provide limited context because they typically do not include liner notes or much contextual information about the musicians or style, but they can serve as a useful starting point for finding new music of interest.

Finally, YouTube is an unquestionably pertinent and viable resource for locating videos and recordings from various contexts. However, because YouTube operates through the dissemination of user-generated content, it must be handled thoughtfully and with care. Powerful videos can surely be found from users without a background or understanding in the musical culture they are featuring in their videos, and so their content should not be dismissed automatically. However, vetting the quality and authenticity of these videos with a culture bearer or expert is highly recommended. Better yet, it is recommended that videos be sought from recognized profiles curated by cultural heritage organizations or other trusted resources (e.g., archival establishments, academic institutions, culture bearers' profiles) in order to maximize the confidence instructors can place on these resources.

Focusing on Sonic Features

The Attentive Listening dimension usually begins with brief, repeated listenings of a single recording rather than extended listenings of the entire piece. This strategy allows students to focus on the specific sonic features of the music, with each listening guided by a single, specific question intended to orient students' ears toward the timbre, instrumentation, complexity, texture, melody, rhythm, or some other feature of the music. These repeated listenings—perhaps five, seven, or more at a time—give way to a more inductive recognition of the piece in a *gestalt* fashion. As Campbell (2018) wrote:

> it is the gateway to ever-deepening listening experiences, the initiation into the music, the first occasion for connection to sonic structures while also wondering about questions of who performs the music, when, where, why, and how the music sounds the way it does.
>
> (p. 114)

As the episodes in this chapter illustrate, the Attentive Listening dimension often begins with rapid *Ask-Listen-Respond* teaching frames. The instructor's first question might orient students' ears toward the instrumentation, with further questions directed toward the underlying rhythmic structure, the speculative uses and purposes of the music, and so on. Questions may additionally pique interest toward the larger sociomusical concerns of the piece—like the embedded social meaning of "Go Go" discussed in Episode 2.1. These early conversations initiate students' imaginings of the social, political, or ritualistic properties of the music—in a sense, their "cultural awakenings," which become the central concern of the fifth dimension, Integrating World Music (Chapter 6).

The WMP approach is considered "semi-sequential," so while it may not be necessary for every musical selection to progress through all five dimensions of the WMP approach, recordings that lend themselves to participatory musicking (Chapter 3), full-fledged performance (Chapter 4), and new creations (Chapter 5) are most desirable because of their holistic potentials. As such, selecting robust Attentive Listening examples may take some thinking ahead to determine the potential utility of recordings for later dimensions of the framework.

The three Learning Pathways described throughout this book illustrate precisely these possibilities. Each of these selections was specifically chosen because of one or more features that lent themselves provocatively to both intensive listenings and participatory musickings, as well as potentials for performing and creating/improvising/composing. Focusing on pieces that feature some sort of aural "hook" may help students grasp the notable structures of the music. This might be an engaging groove (e.g., Rahim AlHaj's "Time to Have Fun"), a repeated motif or ostinato, a catchy introduction/interlude (e.g., "Dulce Sueño Mío"), or a memorable vocal part (e.g., "E Maru Rahi"), for example.

On the other hand, the instructor may wish to begin with a musical example that lacks any sort of "comfortable" aural hook or otherwise orienting mechanism in the music. He or she may wish instead to *dis*orient the students' ears to accentuate the vast array of musical possibilities and approaches around the world—to demonstrate, perhaps, the broad-based interpretations of musical features like rhythm, melody, harmony, texture, and pitch (Wade, 2012). See, for example, Steven Friedson's commentary in the Faculty Feature at the end of this chapter.

Cultural Awakenings Through Attentive Listening Experiences

Two Nations Under One Sky: Iraqi *Oud* and Iranian *Santūr* (Learning Pathway #1)

For eight years during the 1980s, the countries of Iraq and Iran were at war. Iraqi *oud* player Rahim AlHaj vividly recalls the bloodshed, including his own imprisonment and torture after renouncing the violence of Saddam Hussein's regime. In 1991, he went into exile to avoid execution over his activism in the conflict, so perhaps it is not surprising that AlHaj might have struggled to envision a world in which Iraqi and Iranian civilians would one day get along again. He produced the album *One Sky* (2018) to celebrate this turning point for these past enemies, with the newfound Iraqi-Iranian bond symbolized through a collaboration with Iranian *santūr* (dulcimer) player Sourena Sefati. As AlHaj wrote:

> Our nations were sworn enemies, killing each other, but today an Iranian and an Iraqi are making music together. To establish peace in the world we need to learn to listen with open hearts to one another, to create more beauty together rather than more destruction. Let us share food and music; these simple acts create common ground. We all live under one sky.[2]

The featured track for Episode 2.2 is one of the most festive selections on the album, aptly named "Time to Have Fun." The piece features an upbeat invitation to celebrate through the use of a dance rhythm called the *khaliji* (present throughout the Arabian Gulf and Iraq). Regarding the groove of the piece, AlHaj commented, "if you don't feel moved to dance here, go find some children and dance with them." Note that pedagogically the questions precede the listening experience, thus directing learners to seek the answer through directed listening. There are five suggested questions, each one followed by listening and then discussions of possible answers. Many more questions, each preceding further opportunities to listen, help to focus ears and minds as they become increasingly familiar with the musical selection.

Episode 2.2: "Time to Have Fun" (Iraq/Iran) (Learning Pathway #1)

Materials:

- "Time to Have Fun," Rahim AlHaj Trio, Smithsonian Folkways Recordings.

Procedure:

1. Ask, "how many instruments do you hear?"
2. Play track [0:00–0:38] and field responses.

     A: Three instruments.

3. "Pick one of the instruments that you hear in this selection and try to describe it in your own words. Does it sound like a wind instrument, string instrument, percussion instrument?"
4. Play track [0:00–0:38] and field responses.

     A: Two string instruments [one plucked, one hammered]; percussion.

5. Display an image of the *oud* and *santūr* (Figure 2.3). Briefly discuss that both instruments can be found across the Persian Gulf in many forms and musical styles. Both instruments represent a long and diverse history of the lute family (*oud*) and dulcimer family (*santūr*) around the world.
6. "What function do you think this music might serve? What do you think the music attempts to communicate?"
7. Play track [0:00–0:38] and field open answers.

     A: The piece is related to dance and celebration.

8. "Throughout this section of the recording, does the melody appear to repeat or change each time it's presented?"
9. Play track [0:00–0:38] and field answers.

     A: It repeats.

10. "Close your eyes and raise your hand when you think you finally hear the melody change." *By directing students to close their eyes, they are encouraged to focus on their own assessment of the recording rather than raising their hands only by seeking agreement with peers.*
11. Play extended track [0:00–1:07].

     A: Students should raise their hands around 0:38.

Figure 2.3 Painting of a *santūr* and *oud* player by Ibrahim Jabbar-Beik[3]

A Tale of Tahitian Mourning (Learning Pathway #2)

From the very first sounds of "E Maru Rahi" (Episode 2.3), listeners might envision themselves on an "exotic" tropical island with Mai Tais, Polynesian dancers, and sunsets that melt into an infinite crystal-blue ocean. While the geographic location from where this song originates is indeed quite beautiful by any standards, such notions of a "simple life" devoid of worldly troubles paints an altogether one-dimensional portrayal of the daily lives of Polynesians living across the Pacific Islands. "E Maru Rahi" is a perfect example of a song that sounds careless and breezy on the surface, but actually tells the deeper story of familial loss and heartache through its mournful lyrics. According to the liner notes:

> This is the story of three brothers, one of whom has accidentally died while diving for mother-of-pearl in the lagoon of Takaroa in the Tuamotu Islands. The two brothers sing a song in memory of their beloved lost one who will never again gaze upon his country and family.[4]

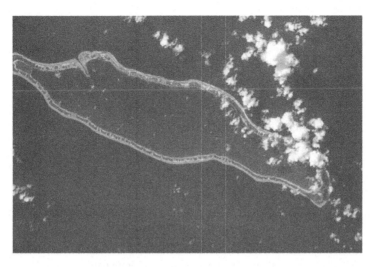

Figure 2.4   The Takaroa atoll, approximately 594 kilometers (370 miles) from Tahiti[5]

Takaroa (Figure 2.4) is an atoll (a ring-shaped coral reef that encircles a lagoon) in the Tuamotu Archipelago, about 370 miles northeast of the island of Tahiti. Pearl diving is pervasive around these Pacific Islands, and the dangers associated with this activity are equally understood. Pearl divers, often without protective equipment, descend to great depths and risk drowning, decompression sickness, and attacks from sharks or stingrays. Nonetheless, pearl diving is considered to be a central part of Polynesian culture (as well as of Latin American, Japanese, and Middle Eastern cultures).

Through an Attentive Listening of "E Maru Rahi," students begin by identifying the underlying rhythmic groove, the approximate instrumentation, and the possible geographic location of the music. These guided listening experiences will prepare students to actively sing and play the music on their own (Chapter 3).

Episode 2.3: "E Maru Rahi" (Tahiti)
(Learning Pathway #2)

Materials:

- "E Maru Rahi," Royal Tahitian Dance Company, Smithsonian Folkways Recordings.

Procedure:

1. "What instruments in this recording are providing the underlying groove or rhythm?"
2. Play track [0:00–0:54] and field responses.

   A: Ukulele, shaker.

3. "Is the groove in duple or triple meter?"
4. Play track [0:00–0:54] and field responses.

    A: Triple meter.

5. "What adjectives would you use to describe the mood of this song? Is it energetic or calming? Celebratory or mourning? Reflective or showy?"
6. Play track [0:00–0:54] and field open responses.
7. "How many musicians do you think are performing in this selection? Specifically, see if you can keep track of how many instrumental and vocal parts there are."
8. Play track [0:00–0:54] and field responses.

    A: There are at least 4 instrumental parts (1 ukulele, 1 bass, 1 shaker, 1 rhythm instrument) and about 3–4 vocal parts.

9. Play track again to check responses.
10. "Can you 'pretend play' along with the strumming pattern of the ukulele?"
11. Play track [0:00–0:54] and repeat as necessary.
12. "Given what you've heard so far, where in the Pacific Islands might you place this song? (Hint: If you listen closely, the singers will make reference to the island in the song.)"
13. Play track [0:00–0:54].

    A: Tahiti. (Note: The singers mention Tahiti at 0:49 in the song.)

Poetic Expressions of Puerto Rican Pride (Learning Pathway #3)

Over the past half century, the sounds of *jíbaro* have come to provoke deep cultural and national pride among the people of Puerto Rico. The music boldly celebrates the core of Puerto Ricans' rural roots with acoustic instrumentation, impassioned folk-like singing, and improvisatory lyricism. Originating from the mountainous terrains of the island, the music stands in stark contrast to the trendier and more ostentatious Puerto Rican salsa and *guaracha*, featuring several characteristic instruments supporting a *trovador* (vocalist): two ten-stringed guitar-like *cuatros*, a six-stringed guitar, a *guiro*, and bongos.

Perhaps the most distinctive feature of *jíbaro* music is the virtuosic treatment of the improvised lyrics, called *décima*. With the harmonic and melodic support of the instrumentalists, the *trovador* masterfully sings ten-line strophes of improvised poetry (further discussed in Chapter 5). For "Dulce Sueño Mío," the selection featured in Episode 2.4, the *trovador* sings an *aguinaldo* instead of a *décima*, using a *decimilla* (literally "little *décima*") of six syllables per line (rather than ten).[6] Episode 2.4 demonstrates the use of this selection with a lecture-style world music survey course and will focus student listening on the underlying instrumentation as well as the *trovador*'s lyrical patterns. By listening multiple times, the learner settles in to the music, progressively coming to terms with its structure in preparation for their further musical participation.

Episode 2.4: "Dulce Sueño Mío" (Puerto Rico)
(Learning Pathway #3)

Materials:

- "Dulce Sueño Mío (Sweet Dream of Mine)," Ecos de Borinquen, Smithsonian Folkways Recordings.

Procedure:

1. "Which instruments can you identify during the opening of this selection? Don't worry about identifying the exact name of it, but try to at least identify the timbre or the instrument family."
2. Play track [0:00–0:42] and field responses.
   > **A:** Two guitar-like instruments (cuatros); 1 rasp- or shaker-like instrument (guiro); 1 bass-sounding instrument (guitar); 1 percussion instrument (bongos); singer (trovador).
3. "What musical role is each instrument playing in this selection?"
4. Play track [0:00–0:42] and field responses.
   > **A:** Cuatros provide melody and harmony, guitar provides bass line, guiro and bongos provide rhythm.
5. "Pay attention to the singer/*trovador*'s singing. What language does he seem to be singing in?"
6. Play track [0:00–0:42] and field responses.
   > **A:** Spanish.
7. "Listen to the *trovador*'s words after he sings his introductory "le-le-la"s. Does it sound like he is repeating any lyrics?
8. Play new segment of the track [0:21–1:07] and field responses.
   > **A:** He repeats his first line as well as his last.
9. Post the lyrics of the first verse on the board or projector. "Listen to the lyrics again, and see if you can determine a pattern from what is being sung."

Sueño de mi vida

Porqué me despiertas

Cerrando una puerta

Y abriendo una herida

Hoy en mi se anida

Un mundo de hastío.

Y ya en mi plantío

Marchita una flor.

No me seas traidor

Dulce sueño mío.

10. Play track [0:21–1:07]; repeat as necessary.
11. Guide students to identify that there is a rhyming pattern at the end of each line.
12. "Can you write down the rhyming scheme that you see/hear in the first verse of the song? Use letters A, B, C, and so on."
13. Play track [0:21–1:07]; repeat as necessary.
14. Guide students toward uncovering the correct rhyme scheme: *ABBAACCDDC*.

Rhythm and Melody in Basque Country

Basque Country (Euskadi) is an autonomous community located in northern Spain. Partially linking the borders of Spain and France, the region is home to a rich diversity of linguistic and cultural identities. The music of Basque Country is typically associated with rural culture, but an assortment of musical styles and practices throughout the region extend far beyond such simplistic notions. Basque Country is particularly known for an internationally celebrated singing tradition (including both solo and choral settings), but Episode 2.5 features a captivating example of instrumental folk music. This particular song features the *txalaparta* (wooden idiophone), *txitsu* (endblown fipple flute), and *trikitixa* (button accordion). The piece begins with the *txalaparta* (usually played by two musicians) establishing a syncopated groove, followed by the *txitsu*, which lays the song's melody above. The result is an energizing interplay of a shifting rhythmic pulse with a singable melody, both blending together seamlessly until the melody is taken over by the *trikitixa*. As all three instruments blend together, the music drives toward an exciting conclusion, making for a compelling selection with which to involve students in the process of Attentive Listening—and eventually, participatory musicking (Chapter 3).

Episode 2.5: "Sigi-Sagan" (Basque Country)

Materials:

* "Sigi-Sagan," Juan Mari Beltran, *Elkar S.A.*

Procedure:

1. "Does the beat or groove of this piece feel symmetrical/even, or asymmetrical/uneven? What makes you think that?"
2. Play track [0:00–0:55].

    A: Asymmetrical or uneven. Students may point to one part of the beat feeling longer or more drawn out (although some students may not yet be able to articulate or identify specifically what feels "uneven" about the groove).

Note: Students may also struggle to feel the pulse until it is more clearly established at 0:30.

3. "How many macro (large) beats do you hear? How many micro (small) beats do you hear?

4. Play track [0:00–0:55].

   A: 3 big beats, 7 small beats.

   Note: This should lead into an Engaged Listening activity as students clap/ tap the rhythmic structure of the song (1,2–1,2–1,2,3) and identify the meter (7/8).

5. "Paying attention to the melody, what form do you hear for the first 30 seconds of this track? Let's indicate a letter for each 4-bar phrase."

6. Play track [0:00–0:30]. Indicate the measure number with fingers in the air to help students hear the breakdown of the form.

   A: AABB.

7. "Does this form continue as is (AABB) or does it change? What would we call the form up to this point?"

8. Play track [0:30–0:56].

   A: It starts out the same (AA) but then there is a new melody (CC). The form is currently AAABBAACC.

9. Continue steps 7–8 for the remainder of the recording (or as much as desired). Discuss how the "A" melody continually returns with new material between each repeated "A." This is known as *rondo form* in Western terms.

Recreational Music from the Central Region of Ghana

To young or inexperienced students, notions of "African music" are often quite misunderstood. It is common for students to conflate the practices of a singular musical culture with the entire continent, and to further exoticize their assumptions in a highly reductionist manner. Similar assumptions occur on a more micro-level, with students assuming that one musical practice within Ghana, for example, represents the entirety of musical participation throughout the country. They may fail to realize that hundreds of subcultures and languages can be found throughout Ghana, not to mention a vast diversity of musical instruments, ensemble types, rituals, and repertoires found across the region.

The music presented in Episode 2.6 represents the rich traditions of rural village music among the Akan people through a stirring combination of polyrhythmic drumming and call-and-response singing. "Akosua Tuntum" is a source recording of recreational music in the Assin area of central Ghana. The rhythmic groove (or *timeline*) is established by a set of four membranophones and four idiophones[7] that are variously known by different names throughout the region. The membranophones include the *dondo*, an hourglass-shaped double-headed drum played with a hooked stick; the *apenteng*, a goblet-shaped hand drum; the *pate*, a small, double-headed cylindrical drum (like a European side drum); and the rectangular square drum, which is struck with a wooden stick. The idiophones include the *afirikyiwa*, an iron vessel clapper; the *dawuruta*, an iron bell struck with a wooden stick; the *aggre*, or claves; and the *akasaa*, a rattle with external beats woven around a gourd.[8]

"Akosua Tuntum" earned its name from a woman whose singing was so admired by the Akan people that all recreational groups imitating her style became known by her name. "Akosua" is the name given to women born on a Saturday, and "Tuntum" means "Black." Episode 2.6 brings students' attention not only toward the layering of the instrumentation, but also to the call-and-response singing they will hear as well.

Episode 2.6: "Akosua Tuntum" (Akan Ghanaian Music)

Materials:

- "Akosua Tuntum," Akosua Tuntum Ensemble of Assin Enyinabirim, Smithsonian Folkways Recordings.

Procedure:

1. "From what part of West Africa do you think this music might originate? What clues might give you that impression?"
2. Play track [0:00–0:34] and field open responses.

    Note: Even in a more advanced class, encourage students to openly specu-late on this topic without fear of needing to have the correct answer in mind. This process of speculation invariably requires students to utilize their internalized knowledge of musical concepts (e.g., instrumentation, timbre, role of melody/harmony/rhythm) to inductively determine their best guess of the music's origin.
3. "What types of instruments do you hear, and in what order?"
4. Play track [0:00–0:34] and field responses.

    A: Iron bell, a higher pitched bell, shaker, voices, lower-pitched bell, drums, hand clapping.
5. "Within this segment, how many times do you hear a call-and-response pattern occur between the lead singer and the ensemble? Do the call-and-response patterns occur evenly or unevenly?"
6. Play track [0:00–0:34] and field responses. Repeat as necessary.

    A: 11; unevenly.

Extension (*Engaged Listening*):

1. "Can you sing the response "awe" along with the singers every time you hear it?"
2. Play track [0:00–0:34] and repeat as necessary.

facilitating Student-Centered Experiences With Large Classes

While readers may occasionally find themselves teaching world music courses in smaller, more individualized classroom formats, enrollments for undergraduate-level classes (especially with introductory survey courses) can easily rise well into the triple digits. In such contexts, determining realistic strategies for making the WMP approach truly student-centered and enriching can admittedly present some challenges. However, this is not to say that teacher-directed, lecture-only formats represent the only (or even the best) approach to teaching in such large-class contexts (Brookfield, 2017). Admittedly, detaching oneself from the relative comfort of teaching in a lecture format is not easy; planning interactive and stimulating experiences can be quite time-consuming. However, the benefits of enriching an otherwise one-directional instructional approach such that students become more involved and accountable for their own learning simply cannot be overemphasized. Beyond evidence from research, those university personnel with long experience in teaching lecture-style classes have substantiated how involving students directly through active participation and discussion have enhanced daily engagement, developed greater confidence on exams, and improved attendance—even in classes with hundreds of students. Naturally, the further along the WMP process the class journeys, the more students will be called directly into the music through responding, singing, playing, dancing, and creating.

Small Group Work

Large classes need not always mean full-class discussions. Asking individual students to engage in full-class dialogue can quickly feel ineffective with large class enrollments. Understandably, the majority of students will be unable to meaningfully contribute within the limited timeframe of the class, and often a handful of passionate students might commandeer the floor and preclude others from participating. Instead, breaking large lecture groups into smaller, more manageable units can help improve student engagement because students become able (and expected) to have their voices heard among smaller, student-directed groups. Thus, rather than seeking responses from hundreds of individual students, the instructor may instead seek responses from dozens of smaller groups, each representing the collective opinion(s) of the group members. This strategy also allows students who feel too timid to contribute a response in such a large and potentially overwhelming class to more confidently engage among a smaller group of peers.

An instructor can also instill accountability for student participation by conducting what is known in the educational community as "turn-and-talks" (also known to others as "think-pair-share"). Whenever discussion or feedback is desired, students can simply turn to a neighbor and share their thoughts for a moment or two. These brief moments can be built into convergent (closed-ended) questions or divergent (open discussion) topics. Knowing that the instructor will never hear from each individual student, turn-and-talks allow students to express their responses or opinions with an individual peer—compelling an interpersonal connection that is often lost in such large classes. The instructor (and TAs) could use this time to travel the aisles of the lecture hall, listening to students' responses. Furthermore, even online platforms such as Zoom allow for small-group learning to occur remotely, such that students can be directed to discuss concepts and share responses to questions using Zoom's "breakout rooms" or polling features. When the instructor takes the time to engage with several pairs of students as they are discussing their responses, and when he/she follows up the activity by asking small pockets of students what they discussed, the class quickly comes to understand their own accountability for engaging each other in sincere dialogues. Of course, this is a secondary benefit to a much more meaningful outcome: A stronger sense of understanding arising from actively grappling with the topic verbally, rather than passively receiving it from lecture notes, PowerPoint slides, or a textbook.

Checking for Understanding

Admittedly, with turn-and-talks the instructor rarely has the opportunity to hear responses from the majority of the class. Alternatively, one of the most popular methods of collecting and analyzing all students' collective responses is through the use of "clickers," which allows all students' voices to be heard (even if only through the selection of a multiple-choice response). The greatest benefit of clickers does not merely lie in allowing students to directly respond to instructor-presented questions, nor does it lie in the peripheral benefit of functioning as an attendance tool. Rather, its greatest strength lies in the facilitation of deeper discussions oriented around the students' shared responses. For example, with Dr. Berger's opening question regarding whether or not BTS's "Go Go" constitutes an example of world music, the instructor could utilize clickers to gauge students' opinions further. Indeed, the raw data of the students' opinions becomes a catalyst for deeper small-group discussion with surrounding classmates. Extending this activity further, students might position themselves on different sides of the lecture hall depending on how their opinions align with a particular issue (such as what "counts" as world music). Akin to a congressional debate, students from "each side of the aisle" could then argue their points, and clickers could be used as a voting mechanism—with an assigned task that, say, the class must arrive at a two-thirds majority.

Another popular medium for facilitating discussion is through the use of back-channel communication. There are several examples of back-channel hosting sites, including Google Classroom, Padlet, Mentimeter, Go Soap Box, and others. This technology utilizes multiple computers sharing a common, private network in order to maintain a real-time online conversation. These private chatroom-like conversations can be used to bolster a live in-class discussion occurring simultaneously. Since the use of computers and tablets is so pervasive among college students, embracing the technology (rather than fighting it) can significantly augment students' capacity for active participation. For example, in response to a question posed by the instructor, students can anonymously post their responses, request further clarification, or make a peripheral comment during class time. Because students can create their own anonymous identities on the site, they no longer face the fear of retribution or humiliation from suggesting an incorrect answer to a question (which invariably occurs when a student listening to a piece of Indian *raga* music, for example, mistakenly calls it "Egyptian" because of his or her inexperience with so-called "exotic" cultures). Additionally, students can post questions that they may otherwise feel foolish asking and can do so without raising their hand and waiting for the instructor to call on them. Instead, the instructor can choose a time during the lecture that is most convenient for the flow of the class and simply turn to the "questions" portion of the hosting site and answer questions in the order in which they were received. For clarification as to how such technology could be meaningfully integrated into classroom activities, the instructor might seek consultation with the campus I.T. learning specialist or designated center for learning innovation and design.

Stephen Brookfield (2017) notes that the use of back-channel technology in the classroom "is particularly good at surfacing power dynamics and taking the emotional temperature of hot-button discussions" (p. 107). Notably, Brookfield also warns that the rise of anonymity can also lead to an exercised lack of accountability, with students responding inappropriately to questions or peers' comments. Nonetheless, when handled thoughtfully and with ground rules in place, the benefits of utilizing such a rich technology certainly outweighs the potential drawbacks.

From Large Lectures to Small Seminars

Like larger lecture classes, special topics courses may be taught by faculty members in the ethnomusicology department, although for institutions that do not have such departments, instructors from music history, theory, music education, private studios, or other related subdisciplines may be asked to take on the task. These courses may be proposed and designed by the instructor-of-record in response to his or her teaching interest, requested by administrators to response to timely events (e.g., developing a "Music of the Refugee Crisis" course), or arise directly from student demand.

Special topics courses are expectedly smaller in size, allowing for greater individualized participation from students. Additionally, given their more advanced format, most enrolled students will likely have a somewhat stronger background in music (or the featured culture), enabling the instructor to ask more advanced questions about the music. They may ask students to isolate the harmonic progression, decipher the exact instrumentation, or identify sociocultural implications from the very start. However, for an introductory course, the questions one might ask can be easily "scaled back" to focus inexperienced students' ears to the sonic structures of the musical selection.

Faculty Feature: Listening for Soundscapes with Steven Friedson

Figure 2.1a   Steven Friedson

"Soundscapes are not just acoustical data. They're culturally shaped."

Steven Friedson is Distinguished Research Professor of Music and Anthropology and head of the ethnomusicology program at the University of North Texas. He is author of *Dancing Prophets: Musical Experience in Tumbuka Healing* (University of Chicago Press, 1996), and *Remains of Ritual: Northern Gods in a Southern Land* (University of Chicago Press, 2009), which won the Alan P. Merriam Prize for Outstanding Book in Ethnomusicology.

For the past 30 years at UNT, Professor Friedson has taught "Music Cultures of the World," an introductory ethnomusicology course for undergraduate students that functions as part of the university's core curriculum. Attracting music majors and nonmajors alike, enrollments for this course usually range between 100 and 130 students.

Q: Tell us about the students' first experiences in your "Music Cultures of the World" course. How do you approach their initial musical encounters?
A: I *don't* try to make it familiar. I want to make it *Other*—as Other as I can get it, in a productive way, to capture their aural imaginations. So, the first thing I do is Tuvan throat singing, which is *very* Other to the students. Not only do we learn about throat singing and its animistic approach to sound but, in the spirit of sound mimesis (Ted Levin's term), we try to sing a fundamental and forefront an overtone, which engages and, hopefully, awakens dormant musical bodies. I ask the class: "When is the last time you tried to make a new sound, just for the sake of making a new sound—when you were three or four?" We then try to do this collectively in class and most students can at least bring out one overtone, not that we necessarily do it like the Tuvans, for there are all kinds of ways to "cheat" by merely constricting the throat and lifting the back of the tongue. Are we going to become throat singers? Of course not, though some of my students have come up with surprising results. That's not the purpose of the exercise. It's to open ourselves up to exploring the sounds our body can make. Students really take to this, with just about all (according to feedback) trying it in the shower, in the car, or when walking down the street.

I also use that to talk about musical change. So, a lot of music was first learned by osmosis and then became more professionalized. For example, a young woman raised her hand in class and said that there's a heavy metal band from Mongolia called The Hu. And I turned to my TA and said, "great, go to YouTube!" So, we pulled them up and played their video. And I told them that the electric instrument they're playing in the video is similar to the Tuvan horsehead fiddle, the *igil*, and it's a traditional instrument that got electrified." So it opened up the discussion, and then we played a [more traditional] video with musicians throat singing and wearing traditional regalia. And I ask the class, "okay, how can we analyze this video clip, ethnomusicologically?" A student raised his hand and said, "they're singing into mics. It sounds like they're on a stage." *Professionalization.*

Q: How do you approach listening in your undergraduate courses?
A: First, we talk about soundscapes. And I ask, "what is *our* soundscape?" *Machines, traffic, trains.* For example, take trains. What did the sound of a train

used to mean if you were in the Deep South? *Freedom, escaping Jim Crow. . . .* What does it mean when you hear a train *now*? And everybody goes, "oh, we don't even pay attention to it." And I say, "that's my point!"

Another example: in Africa, if you don't honk your horn while driving, that's considered a *faux pas*. You've got to honk your horn to tell people to get out of the way or that you're going to pass. What happens in Texas? If you honk your horn at someone, you could get shot! So that's a perfect example of the same sound having an extremely different meaning in different cultures. Trying to get them to understand that soundscapes are just not acoustical data. They're *culturally shaped.*

Q: How do you incorporate active music-making into your large classes?
A: In every unit, the students make music. We throat sing, we sing a circle dance song from the Navajo, we do Ewe African drumming in class, and we all get up and dance. I tell them, "there are things I can't teach you; things that you've got to experience musically. In some ways the music is beyond description and words." And so they experience three and two together when making a rhythm in a composite with someone else. We also sing an ode to Ganesh, and I have them clap *tala* [Indian meter], emphasizing how it functions in Indian classical music. For example, I ask them, "what is a classical music culture? What makes it different? How is Indian classical music like Western classical music culture? What are the political implications of this?" And that's something else I get into with them, especially in India today with the politics of Hindu nationalism. And then we do a section on Bollywood as popular music culture and how it contrasts with Indian classical music culture.

As far as Ewe drumming, I'll bring bells and rattles into class and we'll get some people playing the timeline while the rest of the class plays on their desks. I've brought drums to class and had some people play. I've also brought Gideon [Alorwoyie; Ewe drummer and faculty member at UNT] into class and had the [African Drumming] Ensemble come in and play. It's just enough so that the students can hear how the different parts are talking to each other. So I tell them, "you've got to listen beyond what you're playing to have that experience."

Q: Do you incorporate any creative activities such as improvisation or composition into your classes?
A: For our unit on India, I have them invent a *raga*. I'll have a chart that shows the *melakarta* system of 72 scales. So I'll ask them, "what kind of *sa* do we want? What's the second note we want?" And then I ask, "what kind of ornament do we want?" And then as we go, I tell them, "there are certain rules in *ragas*, and in this *raga*, you can't go directly to the third note directly from the second. You've got to go to the fourth note first. Let's try some of that," and so on.

Attentive Listening Toward Participatory Musicking

The Attentive Listening dimension presented in this chapter merely scratches the surface for the potentials of the World Music Pedagogy framework. Perhaps given a lecture tradition in large university classes that emphasizes *passive* listening in most conventional lecture-style courses, the Attentive Listening dimension potentially risks falling back into inert, teacher-led listening experiences that can begin to feel lifeless. Thus, throughout the Attentive Listening dimension, instructors must remain ever aware of WMP's ultimate pursuit of facilitating *active* and *participatory* musical experiences for students. In this way, Attentive Listening exercises maintain their intrigue among students as instructors set the stage for the vigorous journeys of *participatory musicking*, to be presented in the following chapter.

Glossary

Attentive Listening: The first sequential dimension of WMP, which entails multiple directed listening experiences focused on structures.

Back-channel communication: A form of technology increasingly used in education by allowing students (and/or instructors) to share a common, private network in order to maintain a real-time online conversation. Some examples include Google Classroom, Padlet, Mentimeter, and Go Soap Box.

Comparative musicology: An early form of ethnomusicology that is especially associated with research in the late 19th and early 20th centuries. Comparative musicology sought to directly compare different traditional music systems from across the world (e.g., tuning systems). While ethnomusicology tends to take an anthropological orientation with deep interest in the experiences and views of cultural insiders, comparative musicology sought a more positivist approach influenced by acoustics, psychology, and music theory.

***Décima*:** A ten-line stanza of improvised poetry utilized in folk music traditions throughout Latin America. As *decimilla*, these become six-syllable phrases sung in Spanish language, in a semi-improvised style as part of Jíbaro music tradition.

Timeline: Also known as a "bell pattern," the timeline is the rhythmic structure underlying many forms of sub-Saharan African music.

Turn-and-Talks: Also known as "think-pair-share," this activity is used whenever the instructor wishes to promote small-group activities within the classroom. Students simply turn to their nearest neighbor and share their thoughts regarding a particular prompt.

Notes

1. Public domain. https://commons.wikimedia.org/wiki/File:Jeongak_Daegeum.jpg
2. Sonneborn, D. A. (2018). [Liner notes]. *One Sky* [CD], SFW40585.
3. Public domain. https://upload.wikimedia.org/wikipedia/commons/e/e4/Painting_santur.jpg
4. Monitor Records. (1974). [Liner notes]. *Royal Tahitian Dance Company* [CD], MON71758.
5. Public domain. http://eol.jsc.nasa.gov/scripts/sseop/photo.pl?mission=ISS008&roll=E&frame=17144
6. Sheehy, D. (2003). *Jíbaro Hasta el Hueso: Mountain music of Puerto Rico by Ecos de Borinquen* [CD]. SFW40506.
7. A membranophone is any musical instrument which produces sound through the vibrating of a stretched membrane. An idiophone is any musical instrument in which the entire instrument vibrates to make sound (e.g., xylophones, wood block).

8. Vetter, R. (1996). *Rhythms of life, songs of wisdom: Akan music from Ghana, West Africa* [CD]. SFW40463.

References

Brookfield, S. D. (2017). *Becoming a critically reflective teacher* (2nd ed.). Jossey-Bass.

Campbell, P. S. (2018). *Music, education, and diversity: Bridging cultures and communities.* Teachers College Press.

Lind, V. R., & McKoy, C. (2016). *Culturally responsive teaching in music education: From understanding to application.* Routledge.

Nettl, B. (1983). *The study of ethnomusicology: Twenty-nine issues and concepts.* University of Illinois Press.

Nettl, B., & Bohlman, P. V. (Eds.) (1991). *Comparative musicology and anthropology of music: Essays on the history of ethnomusicology.* University of Chicago Press.

Taylor, T. D. (1997). *Global pop: World music, world markets.* Routledge.

Wade, B. C. (2012). *Thinking musically: Experiencing music, expressing culture* (3rd ed.). Oxford University Press.

Listening Links

"Akosua Tuntum," Akosua Tuntum Ensemble of Assin Enyinabirim, Smithsonian Folkways Recordings. An *akosua tuntum* ensemble from the Assin area of Central Ghana, featuring call-and-response singing, membranophones (drums), and idiophones (bells and shakers). https://folkways.si.edu/akosua-tuntum-ensemble-of-assin-enyinabirim/akosua-tuntum/world/music/track/smithsonian

"Dulce Sueño Mío," Ecos de Borinquen, Smithsonian Folkways Recordings. A Puerto Rican *jíbaro* (folk music) featuring a *trovador*, two *cuatros*, guitar, *güiro*, and bongos and using a *decimilla* (ten lines, six syllables) poetic song structure. https://folkways.si.edu/ecos-de-borinquen/dulce-sueno-mio-sweet-dream-of-mine/latin-world/music/track/smithsonian

"E Maru Rahi," Royal Tahitian Dance Company, Smithsonian Folkways Recordings. A Tahitian song about three brothers, one of whom died while diving for mother-of-pearl in the Lagoon of Takaroa in the Tuamotu Islands. https://folkways.si.edu/royal-tahitian-dance-company/e-maru-rahi/world/music/track/smithsonian

"Go Go," BTS, Big Hit Entertainment. A 2017 K-Pop hit about consumerism and the economic hardships among South Korean Youth. https://itunes.apple.com/us/album/go-go/1284477237?i=1284478579

"Sigi-Sagan," Juan Mari Beltran, Elkar S.A. An instrumental Basque song in 7/8 featuring the *txalaparta* (wooden idiophone), *txitsu* (endblown fipple flute), and *trikitixa* (button accordion). https://music.apple.com/us/album/sigi-sagan/214808425?i=214808473

"Time to Have Fun," Rahim AlHaj, Smithsonian Folkways Recordings. An upbeat *khaliji* dance-style piece featuring *oud* (Iraqi lute), *santūr* (Iranian dulcimer), and percussion. https://folkways.si.edu/rahim-alhaj/time-to-have-fun

3

Participatory Musicking

Engaged Listening and Enactive Listening

"But if . . . an important finding of ethnomusicology is that the normal way to learn music in the world is by hearing it, then shouldn't we, who are trying to teach music as a universal value, be most concerned with this?"

—Bruno Nettl, 2010, p. 5

"[P]articipation to a degree was, in my experience, essential. My teacher was willing to have me play the role of observer, but he was not impressed; only when I indicated a desire to learn like his local students did I achieve some credibility."

—Bruno Nettl, 2005, p. 157

The lecture hall's silence is broken by the sound of a squeaky wheel from the back of the room. Students turn around and see their instructor, Malka, entering with a large metal cart. As the door slams shut behind her, Malka struggles to push the wayward cart down the center aisle. Students hop out of their seats to help their instructor with what appears to be a heap of ukuleles in soft, black cases. Malka thanks the handful of students now gathered around the cart. "Can you all help put these in that corner, the one with that sign that says Harmony*?" The students now notice four large signs placed in each corner of the lecture hall:* Melody, Harmony, Rhythm, *and* Dance.

Malka, now a PhD candidate in ethnomusicology, is the instructor-of-record for Music of the World's Cultures—a course that serves as both a requirement for freshman music majors and an elective for any interested non-music majors. She has struggled to keep the music majors engaged without leaving the nonmajors feeling left behind. It's also her first time ever teaching a class of this size—120 students—and she's been feeling clueless about how she might make the material more interactive for everyone. But while discussing the course progress during a meeting with her doctoral advisor, an idea dawns on her that might allow her to more creatively reach her students in an energizing fashion.

With the classroom materials now set in place, Malka begins playing the Tahitian tune "E Maru Rahi" through the lecture hall's speakers. The melody is contagious, somewhat repetitive, and after listening to it several times over the past two weeks, several students begin singing quietly, trying to match the phonetics of the lyrics as best they can. As they sing, Malka fires up the projector. The screen displays all 120 students' names listed under four categories: Melody, Harmony, Rhythm, and Dance. Malka points to the set of ukuleles under the Harmony sign in front of the lectern.

"I've gotten permission for us borrow the music education department's class-room set of ukuleles today. We have 30 in total. So, today we're going to get to play 'E Maru Rahi' for ourselves. As a class, we'll listen to the recording to guide our singing of the melody, as well as learning the ukulele harmony and shaker rhythm. We'll practice playing along with the recording for a while—at least until we feel comfortable playing it on our own. We'll even learn a simple Polynesian dance, all in groups of about 30. We'll rotate groups every 15 minutes so that everyone gets a chance to perform each part of the music within their centers. Our two TAs, Andreanna and Katerina, will both be in charge of certain centers: Andreanna will guide us through the dance, and Katerina will help with the melody and rhythm. I'll be teaching the ukulele part. It's going to be loud and chaotic as we work simultaneously in these separate groups, but sometimes, that's what mak-ing music is all about!" She continues to explain that once the parts are learned, they will be put together to form the whole piece—initially with but eventually without the recording.

Malka notices that some students can't seem to help themselves from showing a bit of apprehension, but she also feels an unmistakable energy buzzing throughout the space now. They'll all be on board soon, *she thinks to herself.* I've just got to remind them that there's no such thing as an unmusical person.

The Attentive Listening dimension presented in the previous chapter sought to whet students' appetites toward uninhibited and voracious musical listening. That stage is critical, but there is much more to come in the way of musical involvement that is both engaged and enactive. As students continue to deep-dive into extended listenings of a small handful of selections, the penchant for joining in with the recording in order to make the music for themselves arises naturally and should be opportunely embraced. Throughout the Attentive Listening phase, instructors may notice their students instinc-tively move their bodies to the groove, tap out the beat, or sing along with parts of the melody. Indeed, these are signs that curiosity is surfacing and meaningful progress is being made. The natural next step is the invitation to contribute their own music-making to the recorded models as they are listening and learning.

Traditional lecture-based courses feature a larger quantity of selections, thus imply-ing a preference by lecturers for breadth over depth (especially in introductory-level courses). In such "drive-by" situations, students might struggle to establish deeper engagements with a large number of musical selections. There can be simply too many cultures and too little time to do much more than listen to each selection and discuss its context (and for students, to desperately memorize whatever material they possibly can). The potential for actual *musicking*, a term coined by Christopher Small

(1998) to refer to actively engaging with music rather than passively interacting with it, is there awaiting realization through participation.

What if, instead of learning about as many different cultures as possible within a semester—only for it to be potentially forgotten in mere weeks—students became active *practitioners* of a smaller, more manageable handful of musical cultures? We might do well to consider: Would we rather have students who know *of* the major musical genres present in South India, including *kriti*, *varnam*, and *Ragam Tanam Pallavi*, for example? Or, might we prefer to have students who have actually *sung* a *kriti* while performing the *tala* (musical meter)? The former does not necessarily inspire a student to pursue further musical experiences that can become transformative in their lives; only the latter, even if only touched upon briefly, provides the space for experiences to potentially evolve into enduring curiosities and creative desires. Therefore, when talking about the importance of *participatory musicking* throughout this chapter, we are seeking those experiences that will potentially ignite an artistic fire within students: A fire to participate or perform for oneself beyond limited classroom experiences.

Understandably, switching focus from a wide breadth of musical cultures to a selective deep-dive of a few might cause critics to raise concern over the glaring issue of which musical cultures to feature. They would ostensibly argue that there could be no such decision that would not exclude a handful of "must-know" musical cultures. Yet, despite the validity of this point from certain perspectives, one could argue that any curricular model of world music, regardless of how expansive it may be, will always be exclusive of some musical traditions. Furthermore, we might better ask: Who gets to be the arbiter of which should be considered the "must-know" cultures? In short, educators will always be leaving something, or *someone*, out of their curricula no matter how expansive they may seek to be.

The next dimensions of the WMP process flow logically from the Attentive Listening phase by scaffolding listening activities into interactive participatory experiences. Through thoughtful listening, students by now have become so familiar with a handful of high-quality musical selections that their urge to make the music for themselves should be addressed. Indeed, this is the primary goal of the next two dimensions of the World Music Pedagogy framework: Engaged Listening and Enactive Listening.

"But I'm Not a Musician!" and Other Participatory Pretexts

Curiously, when students enroll in an introductory or survey-based music course, they typically (and often rightly) assume it will be offered in a lecture-based format: Music will be heard, analyzed, and discussed, but usually not actively made. Most students seem to rest comfortably within this format, grateful to never be asked to expose their musical vulnerabilities before peers—or worse, for a grade. Even music majors can get comfortable in a desk-chair during a lecture class, assuming that there will be no expectations of them beyond listening, note taking, and occasionally contributing to discussion. World Music Pedagogy breaks from the typical lecture-style tradition and offers ways forward to ensure that the unique learning opportunities enabled by performance are not missed in world music classes.

At least in academic settings, it seems, students not officially majoring in music often deny openly labeling themselves as musicians, as if there is some sort of prestigious aristocracy that separates musicians and non-musicians. However, their pretext really seems to communicate that they would not consider themselves to be musicians *within the eyes of the academic institution.* It is simply naïve to assume that students who are not actively studying music at the college or university level are necessarily non-musicians; yet we often suspect them to be so simply because they are not music *majors.* Actually, they may have had rich musical lives throughout their upbringings and may even continue to participate in musical activities. But because some are unable to read Western notation, or because they only dabble with composing beats and samples on their computers, or because they feel slightly more inclined toward the formal study of engineering than music, they often feel that their musical activities are not legitimate in the eyes of the university.

Therefore, it might be treated as a matter of ethics for instructors to expand their view of musicianship to include amateur singers in a community or church choir, trained pianists who instead choose to study medicine, musical hobbyists whose are fully self-taught using online tutorials, and so on. The teacher's first task should be to establish a musical climate of non-pretension in order to help students feel empowered to ultimately view themselves as valid musical beings—in whatever way this might be manifested—and thus, capable of genuine musical expression. Many of these students are just as much musicians in the college music classroom as they are in their homes and communities; they just need to be provided the opportunity to express themselves as such.

Yet participatory pretexts do not exclusively arise from those who do not call the music building home. When asked to perform beyond the comfort of their studios and ensembles, music majors might also experience a degree of discomfort as they engage with musical practices in unfamiliar contexts and idioms. They may feel flustered as they learn to alter their vocal tone or embouchure shape beyond their idea of a "desirable" sound, are expected to improvise as they perform, or experience the humbling reality that their musical expertise is, in fact, quite contextual. It is the position of the WMP approach, therefore, that students with *any* range of musical experience and expertise not only can but should engage in actively making music for themselves and with others.

Establishing a Climate of Musical Participation

It is certainly no easy feat for instructors to provide plentiful opportunities for their students to actively engage in musical activities, especially if these classes have not been taught in such a manner before. Given that most college-level courses run 10–15 weeks over the course of a term, there is arguably not much time to deeply cultivate a climate in which students feel empowered and safe to participate in such performative ways. Whereas public school instructors and community music facilitators often have the benefit of developing rapport with their student-musicians over an extended period of time, university faculty members typically only have a single term to develop these relationships. Of course, some university-level instructors might have the opportunity to go further by working with students from their introductory courses on a more intimate level, by recruiting them to continue their studies in upper-level world music seminars.

If participatory musicking is to be accepted as a core element of any course, it ought to be included into the very first moments so that students are immediately aware of the course expectations. Rather than using the initial class session to discuss the syllabus and possibly cover introductory material, as many first sessions may go, instructors would do well to organize an initial musicking activity that is immediately participatory and engaging for their students. The activity should allow for varying levels of participation so that students can self-select their level of comfort while participating—whether by simply stepping or clapping the beat, dancing ostentatiously to the groove, or fully singing their hearts out (for example, see Episode 3.4).

Regardless of how much time an instructor has to develop a participatory culture in their courses, it is important to first establish a common understanding that there should be several valid ways for students to actively contribute to musical activities. For many students, the opportunity to actively make music—rather than passively listening to musical selections through lectures—will be met with enthusiasm. For others, perhaps those who identify as more introverted in general or are fearful of making music with others, even the simplest participatory musical act might be met with a degree of trepidation. Therefore, it is crucial to allow students to participate in ways that they find most comfortable—especially early on in the term. For instance, perhaps students expressing some hesitancy will be given the space to simply clap or tap an ongoing ostinato while more adventurous students might sing the melody or attempt an accompanying dance. The layered and reinforced approach of the WMP framework could reasonably allow more fearful, self-conscious, or uncertain students to gradually manifest their participation in increasingly confident and animated ways.

Teaching faculty might also consider including a portion of the final grade to be devoted to participation—feasibly between 10% and 20%—so that students are aware of their expectations to engage in all musical activities from the very first class. However, a participation grade should always serve as an instrument of accountability and never as a threat for students who are hesitant to outwardly participate. It should be clearly communicated that there are several ways for students to validly participate. Arguably, to reify an expectation in which there are "right" and "wrong" (or "adequate" and "inadequate") ways of participating might risk inappropriately reinscribing value systems that perpetuate elitist ways of being musical.

Principles of Engaged and Enactive Listening

The second dimension of the WMP process, *Engaged Listening*, involves "the active participation by a listener in some extent of music-making (by singing a melody, patting a rhythm, playing a percussion part, [or] moving to a dance pattern)" (Campbell, 2018, p. 114). Here, salient musical components identified and learned throughout the Attentive Listening dimension provide the framework supporting a deeper focus in participatory activities. By the time students are prepared to enter into this phase, they are able to knowledgably discuss the core components of the musical selections, including the timbre, instruments, form, melodies, harmonies, rhythms, and more. For example, after identifying the *oud* and *santūr* in Rahim AlHaj's "Time to Have Fun," students' ears have simultaneously begun to recognize the repetitive melody, which they may organically demonstrate by singing along with the recording as it becomes more deeply internalized. Similarly, they may begin to sing the melody or tap out the shaker ostinato along with "E Maru Rahi" or "air play" along with the bass line of "Dulce Sueño Mío," thus demonstrating their readiness for more involved experiences.

As students continually grow familiar with the musical selections through active participation, they develop a greater awareness of the deeper musical nuances within the music—usually identifying subtler elements such as the particular style, the specific instrumental or vocal timbre, or the layering of the blend with greater attentiveness. At this point, students' participatory activities begin to shift toward the third stage of the WMP process, the *Enactive Listening* dimension. Arriving at this dimension rarely occurs on a fixed timetable. Depending on the musical culture or selection being featured, students may require several weeks (or more) within the Engaged Listening dimension, continually musicking with several distinct elements before feeling comfortable performing at a higher level. Once they have progressed to this point, the importance of listening deeply only grows further. As Campbell (2018) explained, "[p]erformance is the goal of this phase, or minimally an earnest effort to participate fully in recreating the music in accordance with the recorded model" (p. 116).

The episodes offered in this chapter demonstrate particular strategies for selecting musical concepts to feature more closely, such as the melodic contour, beat or rhythmic groove, form, and so on. These concepts, alone and together, comprise initial Engaged Listening activities that become further honed during the Enactive Listening dimension. Like the episodes featured throughout the previous chapter, these activities should not be treated as a prescribed "recipe book" of lesson plans or a detailed set of lecture notes, but as initiating techniques that may be expanded upon, altered, and developed with respect to one's unique teaching context.

Finding the Groove and Performing Rhythms

In many musical cultures, the groove or underlying beat/rhythmic structure of the music is central to the music itself. This is particularly true with participatory traditions that involve movement or dance, because the groove often functions as a sort of musical "glue" holding together other elements of the music such as the melody and harmony. After all, the groove is often the first element that students are able to identify within many musical examples—partially because grooves are usually repetitive by nature, and partially because they frequently tend to be the most energizing characteristic of the music. Often, the groove is quite straightforward, as is the case with each of the three Learning Pathway examples featured throughout this book ("Time to Have Fun," "E Maru Rahi," and "Dulce Sueño Mío"; Episodes 3.1–3.3, respectively). However, finding the groove might take more time if the metric pulse of the chosen selection is somewhat unfamiliar (or nonexistent).

Performing the rhythm or groove is often one of the first Engaged Listening activities that WMP practitioners plan, because in many cases the groove tends to be the most discernable (and memorable) element of the music. Furthermore, the rhythm and groove is an appropriate starting point because it allows students to dive into the texture of the music without much further information about the piece. That is, students do not need to first know what key the melody is in, which scale(s) it may use, what chords are accompanying it, or how to pronounce the lyrics. Instead, listeners can isolate a rhythmic groove and immediately re-create it for themselves by ear—whether by clapping or tapping a steady beat, playing the rhythmic groove in full, or creating an accompanying body percussion part.

Performing Melodies and Harmonies

While initial participatory activities might isolate the rhythm or groove, other selections will be more suited for immediate focus on the melody or harmony. This is especially the case in selections where the melody is so repetitive, memorable, or straightforward that it solicits the listeners' attention more immediately than the underlying groove. This may be the case with the memorable tango melody in "El Choclo" (Episode 3.5), for example.

Activities isolating the music's melody or harmony can be approached in several distinct ways, especially since the chosen music might feature any range of instrumental or vocal pieces. For example, with both instrumental and vocal selections, students might perform the primary melody by humming, whistling, or singing along on a neutral syllable. For vocal pieces utilizing lyrics, students might be prompted to sing either on a neutral syllable (*la* or *da*, for example) when the lyrics are unknown or unfamiliar, or sing the lyrics themselves when they are prepared to do so. In both instances, accompanying the singing with some sort of physical gesturing will help the instructor immediately see if students are adequately prepared to move forward—especially in larger classes where the instructor will not be able to aurally assess how accurately each student is singing. For instance, by asking students to both sing the melody and trace it in the air with the rise and fall of their hands, the instructor's aural assessment is supplemented visually, allowing them to assess which students are successful and which students appear to be unsure or unconfident.

When it comes to exploring the harmonic makeup of songs, students can be prompted to listen to when the underlying chords change within the music—even if they are not fully familiar with the basic functions of harmony from a music theory perspective. Many examples of folk music around the globe are excellent starting points because they are often intentionally straightforward to facilitate greater participation (Turino, 2008). Such musical examples feature non-complex chord progressions and a straightforward form that allow musicians to grasp the highly repetitive chord structure at their own pace. Irish *seisún* and Zimbabwean *Shona mbira* music are two clear examples of such harmonically accessible folk traditions.

Furthermore, the ukulele in "E Maru Rahi," and the *cuatro* in "Dulce Sueño Mío" both provide strong harmonic foundations to the music, outlining clear tonic (I), subdominant (IV), and dominant (V) chords for students to explore further. If students are unfamiliar with how chord progressions function from a music theory standpoint, they can nevertheless outline the general harmonic movement aurally, by gesticulating each chord change they hear within the selection (i.e., one finger on I chords, five fingers on V chords, etc.). More advanced skills might include outlining the roots of each chord on pitched percussion instruments (e.g., xylophones, metallophones) or playing the chord progressions on their own harmonic instruments (e.g., guitar, ukulele, piano).

Participatory Musicking With Learning Pathways

The three teaching episodes featured in this section (Episodes 3.1, 3.2, and 3.3), comprised of the book's three Learning Pathways, will detail both Engaged and Enactive Listening activities. These three episodes will help readers understand the distinctions between Engaged and Enactive Listening and will illustrate how a meaningful transition can be made between the two dimensions. In the section after, Episodes 3.3 and 3.4 will focus specifically on Engaged Listening activities with respect to a Mardi Gras Indian chant from New Orleans and a Uruguayan *tango criollo*, respectively. For these selections, questions from the prior Attentive Listening dimension will not be included, but the episodes begin with the assumption that students will already have had several exposures to the music through carefully crafted Attentive Listening questions (see Chapter 2).

Finally, Episode 3.6 will feature a Cameroonian Baka song for a more focused look at the structuring of potential Enactive Listening activities. Similarly, this selection begins with the assumption that students have previously demonstrated their knowledge of several musical concepts within the selection (Attentive Listening) and have already begun to engage with the music in some participatory manner (Engaged Listening). This episode will not present the Attentive or Engaged Listening sequences in full.

Episode 3.1: "Time to Have Fun" (Iraq/Iran)
(Learning Pathway #1)

Specific Use: Undergraduate introductory-level world music survey course

Materials:

- "Time to Have Fun," Rahim AlHaj Trio, Smithsonian Folkways Recordings

Engaged Listening

Procedure:

1. "Can you trace the *oud* and *santūr* melody with your finger? After you do so, describe how the A-section melody moves."
2. Play track [0:00–0:38] and field responses.

   A: It ascends and then descends several times within the A section.
3. "While you continue tracing your finger along with the melody, sing it on a neutral syllable (e.g., 'doo').
4. Play track [0:00–0:38].
5. Show students the notated melody on the board or projector (Figure 3.1).

   Note: For upper-level seminar courses, it might be preferable to have students transcribe the melody on their own or place it on their instruments by ear.
6. "Please sing along once again, using the following notation to help make corrections as you go."

   Note: It is important that students are able to demonstrate their internalization of the melody before being shown the notation, which reflects a "sound-before-sight" method. Because this music was likely composed/learned aurally between Rahim AlHaj and Sourena Sefati, it is recommended that students learn the melody in a similar fashion.

Figure 3.1 Melody to "Time to Have Fun (transcribed by W. J. Coppola)"

Figure 3.2 *Maqam kurd*

7. Play track [0:00–0:38].

8. Ask students to individually line up the pitches of the melody in order from lowest to highest (they should also omit the A-natural, as it represents a passing tone to the melody).

9. Discuss: "Just as most music in Western traditions are based upon a series of pitches, which we call *scales*, much of the music throughout the Middle East use what are called *maqams*. *Maqams* are similar to scales, but they tend to have different arrangements than our Western scales, and they don't always use the same types of pitches (for example, sometimes they might include microtones). Check with your neighbor to see what type of *maqam* you've discovered in this song. We'll give it a name later."

10. Show the scale on the board or projector (Figure 3.2).

11. "The *maqam* used in this particular example is called the *maqam kurd*. In this case, it is a *maqam kurd* starting on G."

12. Guide students toward an understanding that the scale's pitches indicate that the key signature would be Eb major, with three flats (Bb, Eb, and Ab). "However, we can't quite say that the song is in Eb major, because the song doesn't seem to rest on Eb as its 'home.' What pitch *does* appear to be the song's 'home' or resting place?"

    A: G.

13. "We place 'G' as the first and last note because it is the 'home,' or 'tonic,' of the song. In Western music, this is a special type of scale called a *mode*. If we are thinking about Eb major, but starting on the note G, which number mode would this be?"

    A: The third mode in Eb (Note: This might require assistance from visual cues of the Eb major scale for students to recognize this relationship).

14. Depending on the students' prerequisite knowledge, ask students to relate the scale to the mode used in Western notation (if not, skip to step 15). Ask, "does this *maqam* resemble a mode used in Western music?"

    A: Yes, the Phrygian mode.

15. Discuss: "In Western music, there's a special name for modes that start on the 3rd degree of the major scale. We call it the *Phrygian mode*. So, the Phrygian mode and the *maqam kurd* are actually the same scale. However, since we are studying this piece within the context of Middle Eastern music, we will refer to it only as the *maqam kurd*."

Enactive Listening

1. "Now, let's focus our attention on the percussion. Can you tap the beat along with the recording?"

2. Play track [0:12–0:38].

3. "Can you hear the basic pattern of low and high pitches in the percussion? Place the low pitches on your lap (or stomp feet) and place the high pitches in your hands (clap) or on the desktop."

4. Play track [0:12–0:38]. The pattern should be *low-low-high*.

5. "How many times does this *khaliji* pattern of *low-low-high* repeat during each phrase? What happens after?"

6. Play track [0:12–0:38].

    A: Seven times. After the seventh pattern, the percussion plays the eighth note figure along with the *oud* and *santūr* (see measure 8 of Figure 3.1).

7. Split the class into two halves. Have one half of the class sing the melody on a neutral syllable while the other half of the class performs the basic *khaliji* rhythm.

8. Play track [0:00–0:38]. Repeat as needed, and be sure to allow the class to switch roles.

9. "As an added challenge, try to tap/clap the *khaliji* rhythm while singing the melody. If you're not ready for that step, continue to perform only your role."

10. Play track [0:00–0:38].

11. Repeat without the recording. Immediately after, play the track again [0:00–0:38] and have students compare their performance with the recording. Repeat this step until the students feel comfortable performing it on their own.

12. Repeat this process for the rest of the recording, paying special attention to when and how the music shifts and continually comparing their performances to the recorded model.

Episode 3.2: "E Maru Rahi" (Tahiti)
(Learning Pathway #2)

Specific Use: World music special topics seminar (e.g., "Music in Polynesia," "Music of the Pacific Islands")

Materials:

- "E Maru Rahi," Royal Tahitian Dance Company, Smithsonian Folkways Recordings
- Ukuleles (or substitutes), shakers

Engaged Listening

Procedure, Melody:

1. "Can you sing along with the melody on a neutral syllable?"
2. Play track [0:00–0:54].
3. Post the lyrics on the board or projector. "Now, can you sing along with the melody with the lyrics? We will sing it several times through so you can hear how the lyrics fit the melody."

   E maru rahi e aue

   ua moe to tino

   e ita to mata

   e ite faaho e

   e ita to mata

   e ite faaho e

   to'u aia here

   o Tahiti rahi e

4. Play track [0:00–0:54] and repeat as necessary.

Procedure, Harmony:

1. "Now, let's focus on the harmony played by the ukulele. Can you 'air play' the ukulele part to try to figure out the strumming pattern?"
2. Play track [0:00–0:54].
3. While the strumming pattern is sometimes performed somewhat differently in an improvised manner, guide students toward the following strumming solution:

   Note: This pattern is more difficult to read through notation than it is to learn aurally. Instructors should consider using Figure 3.3 as a personal reference rather than providing it to the students.

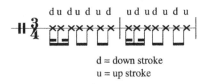

d = down stroke
u = up stroke

Figure 3.3 Strumming pattern to "E Maru Rahi"

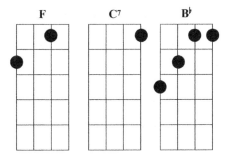

Figure 3.4 F, C7, and B♭ chords in "E Maru Rahi"

4. When ready, provide ukuleles (or guitars) to a handful of students. (Depending on how many are available, rotate the instruments so all students have an opportunity to attempt the activity. Refer to the activity in the opening vignette for one possibility.)

5. Guide students toward the two main chords of the song, F and C7 (see Figure 3.4). These chords are considered to be straightforward enough for unexperienced students to attain quickly. For more advanced students, also provide the third chord, B♭, and allow students to self-select their desire to attempt this more challenging chord. At this time, it is not important for students to be able to switch fluently between these chords, which is usually the most challenging aspect of playing the ukulele.

6. Split the ukulele-playing students into three groups: those playing only the F chord, those playing only the C7 chord, and those playing only the B♭ chord. For students with prior experience playing the ukulele, allow them to switch between all three chords on their own.

7. Displaying the below chord progression on the board, have students play along with the recording [0:00–0:54] on their instruments by playing only their respective chords (or self-selecting if they would prefer to play all chords):

Intro:	F	C7	F	C7
Verse:	‖: F	F	F	F
	F	C7	C7	C7

C^7	C^7	C^7	C^7
F	F	F	F
B♭	B♭	B♭	B♭
F	F	F	F
C^7	C^7	C^7	C^7
F	C^7	:‖	

8. "Now, let's continue playing the ukulele harmony along with the recording, but let's add the singing back in as well. Try to sing the lyrics while playing, or sing on a neutral syllable again if necessary."

9. Play track [0:00–0:54] and repeat as necessary (until students become more comfortable with singing and playing).

Enactive Listening

Note: Refer to the opening vignette of this chapter for a suggested strategy for incorporating the melody, harmony, and rhythm parts into a broader Enactive Listening activity.

1. "Now that we are becoming more comfortable with the singing and playing, let's focus once again on *how* the singers are singing the lyrics. How would you describe their singing style? Are they singing with an open sound? A forward sound? Let's see if you can match their timbre."

2. Play track [0:00–0:54]. The sound should be resonant and somewhat dark with a slightly forward tone.

3. Add the shaker rhythm back into the song. Provide shakers to several students and have them play along with the recording while singing (no ukuleles). Remind them that the rhythm is a fixed ostinato, or repeating pattern, so they should repeat the same rhythm once they've figured it out.

4. Play track [0:00–0:54].

5. Now, with all of our musical elements—the sung melody, ukulele harmony, and shaker rhythm—let's try to put it all together along with the recording.

   Note: Once again, the instructor may ask the ukulele-playing students to self-select their difficulty level with two considerations: (a) whether they should divide the chords (each group only playing one chord) or play all of the chords (switching between them), and (b) whether they should sing and play or just play (allowing the non-ukulele students to sing on their own).

6. Play track [0:00–0:54].

7. "Finally, let's try to play this whole section on our own, without the recording."

8. Perform as a group without the recording. Immediately after, play the track again [0:00–0:54] and have students compare their performance with the

recording. Repeat this step until the students feel comfortable performing it on their own.

9. Ask, "what else can we do to further bring our performance closer to the recording?"

   A: Add the sung harmony, add Polynesian dance, etc.

Episode 3.3: "Dulce Sueño Mío" (Puerto Rico) (Learning Pathway #3)

Specific Use: Undergraduate introductory-level world music survey course

Materials:

- "Dulce Sueño Mío (Sweet Dream of Mine)," Ecos de Borinquen, Smithsonian Folkways Recordings
- Instruments of students' choice

Engaged Listening

Procedure, *Cuatro* Melody:

Before this class session, request that students bring any instrument they may play outside of class (e.g., guitar, ukulele, melodica, wind instrument). For those without instruments, students can use a mobile piano app such as GarageBand.[1] Remember, many students enrolled in these courses may be active musicians outside of class, or may even be music majors. Alternatively, the instructor might provide pitched instruments such as xylophones or metallophones (which might be available for loan from the music education department).[2]

1. "Trace the *cuatro* melody with your finger, outlining separate arches for each 8-beat phrase."
2. Play track [0:00–0:21].
3. "Can you determine which of your arches were the same, and which were different? Let's listen again, and try to think of the melody's pattern in terms of As and Bs. What's the form?"
4. Play track [0:00–0:21].

   A: AABB' (Students might respond with AABB, but direct their ears toward the slightly different ending of the second B section).

5. "Since the introduction is just made up of two simple 8-beat sections, let's try to figure out how to play this melody. First, let's sing the melody on a neutral syllable."

6. Play track [0:00–0:21].

7. "Now, let's try to place these pitches on instruments. We'll start with the A melody together." In small/medium groups, allow students to use their own instruments to locate the melody. Use Figure 3.5 as a personal guide, but avoid showing it to students; encourage them to transcribe the melody fully by ear.

   Note: Although this may feel like an advanced activity, remind students that this is how folk musicians often learn to play what they hear in their heads, and they should use their instruments as tools to help them decipher and translate the music they hear. To facilitate this activity further, it is recommended that the instructor maintains an inventory of students' musical expertise and carefully divides groups so that experienced and inexperienced musicians are grouped together for more efficient facilitation of the activity. Most importantly, it is important to remain patient of each student's individual progress with this task.

8. Play track on a loop [0:00–0:10] and facilitate progress by working with individual groups throughout (as well as TAs that might be assigned to the class). Continue until most students are able to place the full A melody on their instruments.

   This step might also require students to return to step 5 (singing the melody) as needed. In fact, students should be encouraged to continually sing-then-play the melody to match what they sing to their instruments.

9. Repeat steps 7 and 8 for the B melody [0:10–0:21].

Figure 3.5 "Dulce Sueño Mío" *cuatro* melody (transcribed by W. J. Coppola)

Procedure, Sung Melody:

1. "Can you sing along with the melody on a neutral syllable?"
2. Play track [0:21–1:08].
3. Post the lyrics on the board or projector. "Now, can you sing along with the melody with the lyrics? We will sing it several times through so you can hear how the lyrics fit the melody."

    Sueño de mi vida

    Porqué me despiertas

    Cerrando una puerta

    Y abriendo una herida

    Hoy en mí se anida

    Un mundo de hastío.

    Y ya en mi plantío

    Marchita una flor.

    No me seas traidor

    Dulce sueño mío.

4. Play track [0: 21–1:08] and repeat as necessary.

Enactive Listening

1. Divide the class into three groups: vocal, instrumental, and rhythm: *Vocal* students will sing the *decimilla* [0:21–1:08]; *Instrumental* students will perform the *cuatro* melody [0:00–0:21] on instruments of their choice (see step 2 for more information); *Rhythm* students will perform the *guiro* melody with *guiros* and/or shakers [0:00–1:08].

    Note: while students should emulate the basic guiro *rhythm, they do not need to be concerned with performing it exactly as heard in the recordings, given the improvised nature of the* guiro.

2. With students, engage in a discussion about which instruments should be responsible for playing the *cuatro* part (see the "Embrace Approximations" suggestion under "The DIY of WMP" section at the end of the chapter). Allow students to decide between using pitched percussion instruments (metallophones/xylophones) and other available instruments.

3. Along with the recording, have students perform their respective *cuatro* (instrumental), vocal, and rhythm parts. Repeat as necessary.

4. When the instructor deems the class to be ready, fade out the music and have students perform without the recording.

5. Perform all three parts (separately and/or together) without the recording and compare their performance with the recording. Ask, "in what ways can we make our performance more similar to the recording?"

> **6.** Keep performing the recorded segment without the recording and continually compare to the recorded model.
>
> **7.** A new interlude is played at 2:05. Allow students to either continue playing the original AABB' melody for this section or learn this new melody by ear by once again following the Engaged Listening steps provided earlier.

Additional Engaged and Enactive Listening Exemplars

A Mardi Gras Indian Chant

Every year around carnival season, Mardi Gras Indians re-emerge in the public eye with highly ornate Mardi Gras suits[3] in celebration of the ancient tie between Black and Indian cultures in New Orleans (Smith, 2003). Much about these "Black masking groups" remains a mystery beyond carnival celebrations, yet the richness of their heritage extends far beyond carnival season. Nevertheless, these groups have remained a central feature of the annual New Orleans Jazz & Heritage Festival since its inaugural year in 1970. The White Eagles, featured here in Episode 3.4, are a long-standing Mardi Gras Indian tribe. They are presented here to highlight the necessity of considering cultural diversity not merely from an international perspective (which the very term "world music" problematically connotes), but domestically as well. Indeed, the characterization "world music" problematically implies a sense of "Othering" (see Chapter 7), and as such tends to ignore the vast cultural diversity that thrives *within* individual societies as well. Here, New Orleans Indians serve as an important reminder of the compelling degree of interculturalism between American Indians and Afro New Orleanians (which are themselves a culturally diverse mixture of African, Afro-Caribbean, and Creole lineages). In Episode 3.4, students participate in Engaged Listening activities to highlight the call-and-response nature of a rousing traditional Indian song, "Big Chief Got the Golden Crown." This episode picks up where plentiful Attentive Listening experiences would naturally leave off, thus ensuring that students are adequately prepared to dive into the participatory potentials of the music.

Episode 3.4: "Big Chief Got the Golden Crown" (New Orleans, U.S.A.)

Specific Use: Undergraduate introductory-level world music survey course

Materials:

- "Big Chief Got the Golden Crown (Live)," The White Eagles, Smithsonian Folkways Recordings
- Various percussion instruments (tambourines, cowbell, bass drum, bongos, buckets)

Engaged Listening

Procedure:

We recommend that the call, performed here by The White Eagles Big Chief Jake Millon, should be left to the recording and not re-created by the instructor or students for the sake of respect to the venerated role of the Big Chief. If the instructor wishes to perform (or have students perform) this role, it is important to (a) check with culture bearers about its appropriateness within the desired context (e.g., educational purposes only versus public performance), and (b) communicate with students the ethical matters that should be considered in this decision-making process.

1. Listen to the opening of the track to hear the context of the music and the Big Chief's introductory verses.
2. Play track [0:00–1:05].
3. "Sing the response, 'Big White Eagle got the Golden Crown' along with the music."
4. Play track [1:05–1:44 or until end of track, which repeats the response throughout].
5. Show video of The White Eagles rehearsing "Big Chief Got the Golden Crown" from the Alan Lomax Archive (available through a YouTube search). Encourage students to take note of the various percussion instruments being used in the clip: tambourines, cowbell, bass drum, bongos, buckets, etc.
6. Discuss: Mardi Gras Indian songs would usually be performed in a parade format, with members of the tribe playing various traditional roles, including "spyboys," the "first flag," the "wildman," and the "Big Chief" (the leader who chooses the parade route and decides which other tribes to engage with during the parade). When two tribes meet during a parade, a symbolic "face-off" occurs in which the Big Chiefs taunt each other, and the drumbeats of both tribes momentarily interlock before each group continues on their way. While these parades were sometimes violent between tribes in the past, today they have become peaceful and playful displays of symbolic competition, based primarily on the ornateness of the tribes' suits (Smith, 2003).
7. "While you sing the response ('Big White Eagle got the Golden Crown'), grab a percussion instrument and keep the groove going along with the music." Taking on the role as the Big Chief (terms of leading the processional; not recommended through singing), lead the class around the classroom/lecture hall. Following your lead, encourage students to continue singing the response as they move/step their bodies to the groove of the music and make their way around the space.
8. If desired, elect one student to fulfill the role of the "Big Chief," or have students trade off this role. Have them improvise their own calls.
9. Play track in full and repeat as desired.

Tango Criollo and the Bandoneon

Tango criollo, or Creole tango, describes a form of tango emanating from Argentina by working-class musicians of mixed Spanish and African backgrounds. Although the term *criollo* was used as a pejorative term, one of the best-known *tango criollos*, "El Choclo," is celebrated as one of the most popular tangos ever written. The composition is attributed to Argentinian Angel Villoldo, and its title translates to "The Corn Cob," purportedly referring to the proprietor of a nightclub who went by the same nickname. The recording included in the following episode is performed by Uruguayan bandoneonist René Marino Rivero. While many versions of the song have been performed by *orquestras típicas* utilizing a mixture of bandoneon, guitar, flute, piano, and violin, this version is performed as a solo bandoneon piece. As a result, while Rivero's recording is intended to be a celebration of dance music throughout Uruguay, it is performed here as a concert piece that is not intended to accompany dance or movement. Nonetheless, this virtuosic performance can be used as a memorable starting point for students to explore the vast world of tango music and its close relationship to dance.

Episode 3.5: "El Choclo" (Uruguay)

Specific Use: Undergraduate introductory-level world music survey course

Materials:

- "El Choclo," René Marino Rivero, Smithsonian Folkways Recordings

Engaged Listening

Procedure:

1. "The form of 'El Choclo' is very symmetrical. Can you alternate between raising your right and left hand for each 4-measure phrase? While we do that, let's figure out what the form appears to be."

   Be sure to model this action as well to clarify confusion regarding what constitutes a complete phrase.

2. Play track [0:00–0:25] and field responses.

   A: First phrase (A), second phrase (B), third phrase (A'), fourth phrase (C). The resulting form is ABA'C.

3. "Can you sing the melody on a neutral syllable?"

4. Play track [0:00–0:25] and repeat as needed.

5. "Let's treat each phrase as if it's part of a conversation. The right side of the room will sing the A sections and the left will sing the B and C

sections. Tango is a highly emotive art form. While this version of 'El Choclo' doesn't use lyrics, many lyrical verses have been added to the song over the years. Still singing on a neutral syllable, I'd like both sides of the room to engage in a conversation, communicating whatever emotion you think the song is trying to convey in a dramatized manner."

6. Play track [0:00–0:25] and repeat as needed.

Suggestions Beyond Engaged Listening:

1. *While we do not provide in-depth suggestions for this particular episode, the Enactive Listening dimension might include students learning a simple tango dance and performing it along with the recording (or other versions of the recording made for dance bands or* orquestras típicas*).*

2. *Following plentiful Enactive Listening activities, the Creating World Music dimension could be meaningfully utilized in following by asking students to compose their own lyrics to the melody, thus communicating their inferred emotion from step 5 through words and poetry.*

Cameroonian Baka Music

The Baka people are a semi-nomadic ethnic group located near the southeastern rain forests of Cameroon (bordering present-day Gabon and the Republic of the Congo). They have historically been known as a nomadic hunter-gatherer society, but many have now permanently settled in small, remote villages (largely due to issues of deforestation, which has impeded their ability to hunt and gather food). They have often been referred to as "pygmies," but they are simply referred to here as "Baka people" because the term pygmy is considered to be disrespectful given its reference to the short stature of the people.

Baka music is highly vocal, utilizing instruments exclusively for rhythmic accompaniment, if at all. The music is usually characterized by dense polyphony, created through multiple independent rhythmic lines that are bound by a common groove. Additionally, the use of disjoined melodic intervals (oscillating between the singer's head and chest registers) creates a unique yodeling effect called *yeyi*. In Baka communities, the women are responsible for singing while the men dance. The listening selection featured in Episode 3.6 is fully vocal, performed by 13 young girls and children. During the Engaged Listening phase, students will have kinesthetically performed the beat, sung emergent portions of the vocal texture on a neutral syllable (not yet concerning themselves with which parts belong to which singers), and isolated at least a few of the independently moving vocal parts. These precursor activities will enable the forthcoming Enactive Listening exercises, where students will continue to isolate the individual parts of the chant and perform it together, ultimately without the recording.

Episode 3.6: "Hut Song" (Cameroon)

Specific Use: Undergraduate introductory-level world music survey course

Materials:

- "Hut Song," Baka Pygmies, UNESCO Collection of Traditional Music

Enactive Listening:

1. "Find the steady beat and tap it on your lap/desktop/chest."
2. Play track [0:00–0:38].
3. "For now, let's focus just on the first voice in this musical texture—the eldest-sounding voice. Please trace the melody she performs as you hum along."
4. Play track [0:00–0:38].
5. "This pattern repeats every four measures. Continue to sing this part by itself, but at some point, I will fade out the music to see if we can keep it going on our own."

   Note: concepts such as "beat" and "measure" are not immediately tied to Baka music (nor is it relevant to much of the music in sub-Saharan Africa). However, using these terms slightly out of context will facilitate a smoother transmission process for most students. Nonetheless, it is recommended that the instructor communicate this distinction between how different cultures interpret concepts of time and periodicity.

6. Play track in full (the ostinato will repeat throughout the track). Repeat as necessary.
7. "Now, let's focus on the underlying vocal part, sung by the younger children. Focus on a part of your choosing and try to hum along with it. Note that you might end up singing a slightly different part than your neighbor, depending on which voice part you pull from the texture."
8. Play track in full. Repeat as necessary.
9. Divide the class into three uneven groups: Part 1 (large), Part 2 (medium), and Part 3 (medium). Along with the recording, have each section hum their respective voice parts, using Figure 3.6 as a guide if needed.

   Note: be sure to refer to Figure 3.6 only as a rough approximation for personal reference. In fact, there are likely more than three independent parts in the song; the notation simply approximates the salient voice parts emergent from the complex mixture.

10. Repeat step 9 without the recording. Have students compare their performance to the recording immediately after. Repeat until students are able to closely emulate as much of the recording as they can (including proper vowel sounds and vocal timbre).

Figure 3.6   Approximation of polyrhythms in "Hut Song" (in three parts) (transcribed by W. J. Coppola)

The DIY of WMP: Toward Immersive Cultural Encounters

The six episodes presented in this chapter merely represent possibilities for involving students in participatory musicking activities. In actuality, activities featured in the Engaged and Enactive Listening dimensions will rely upon the creativity of the instructor's "DIY" ("Do It Yourself") capacity, which can turn virtually any compelling piece into an appealing activity given adequate ingenuity and preparation. While more complex pieces might prove initially challenging in terms of establishing worthwhile musicking activities, the complexities of these works will slowly begin to melt away given enough focused listening. Indeed, it is worth recalling that the World Music Pedagogy framework is not a straight-and-narrow path; musicians may move forward and backward, quickly and slowly, and in whichever ways they see fit to develop a deeper familiarity with the music. To summarize, with whatever music the instructor chooses to feature, the following suggestions and reminders will help ensure success:

- **Maintain a rapid *Ask-Listen-Respond* teaching frame.** In order to keep students focused directly on a specific musical element, it is recommended that the musical "doing" or "thinking" occurs as quickly as possible. Maintain a teaching frame that consists of *asking* a direct question about the music, immediately *listening to* the selection so students can consider their response, and allowing students the time and space to *respond* to the question immediately after the listening. Often, teachers ask students specific questions about the music *after* they have already played the track, which fails to give them an opportunity to focus their attention toward the correct answer.

- **Ask only a single question before each listening.** Possibly in an attempt to save time, teachers often will ask students a heap of questions relating to a listening example, thus forcing students to split their attention toward several musical elements rather than concentrating on a single concept. Asking a single question before each listening example both (a) allows students to focus on one single concept at a time and (b) facilitates a greater overall number of listenings (thus promoting greater familiarity over time).

- **Focus on short, repeated listenings of an approximately 30–40 second clip.** The length of any listening example ought to be managed to facilitate better internalization and familiarity with the music. The recommended length of a single listening should be about 30–40 seconds, but some selections might require anywhere between 15 and 60 seconds depending on the melody or form. Listening to a short clip dozens of times will engender greater familiarity over time than listening to a full track only a handful of times.

- **Be mindful of the timing and proportion of "teacher talk."** Many teachers allow themselves to be bogged down with providing too much contextual information about the musical selection before students get to engage with the music itself. While it is suggested that the Integrating World Music dimension is opportunely imbued throughout the other phases of the framework (see Chapter 6), we also maintain that, to start, students should be provided only enough contextual information to understand the music's function and purpose within its musical culture. Additional points of context should be scattered throughout the rest of the framework, but never all at once in the very beginning.

- **Utilize liner notes, scholarly books, and culture bearers.** One of the distinguishing features of the WMP approach is that it allows practitioners with relatively little experience participating in or teaching world music a clear and practical strategy for doing so. It contends that music instructors need not necessarily become ethnomusicologists or world music experts in order to effectively teach these musical cultures in their classrooms. By utilizing album liner notes, accessing scholarly books on the musical cultures in question (e.g., the *Global Music Series* published by Oxford University Press), and partnering with culture bearers, teachers can effectively fill important gaps in their knowledge. While teachers need not necessarily be experts of musical cultures, it is nonetheless essential that teachers conduct as much personal research as possible to prepare themselves to competently teach the chosen musical cultures to students.

- **Embrace approximations.** It will often be the case that access to "authentic" instruments (that is, those that are considered original or true to the musical tradition) will not be readily available. However, rather than omitting certain cultures because of a shortage of authentic instruments, it is far more advantageous for students to participate in an *approximated* experience of that musical culture rather than not at all—as long as that experience is treated respectfully and the approximations are made explicit with students. Relevant examples have already been referenced in this chapter: For example, rather than simply excluding *jíbaro* because of a lack of access to *cuatros*, the use of ukuleles or guitars—*along with a brief discussion* regarding how the utilized instrument(s) are meant to serve as facsimiles—can offer students meaningful connections to the musical culture despite a lack of sonic accuracy. This is equally true for vocal traditions: In most cases, instructors should not simply omit exemplar selections because they are sung only by certain groups (e.g., children, women, elders) or because the vocal technique appears to be beyond the scope of possible student participation (e.g., *Khoomei*, or Tuvan throat music, which features overtone singing). In the case of the latter, students may not be able to realistically re-create the exact timbre of the singing but can nonetheless participate through thoughtful Attentive Listening questions or simple Engaged Listening activities (e.g., tracing the contour of the pitches, tapping an implied beat). For further discussion regarding the issue of authenticity in musical transmission, see Chapter 7 of this volume, as well as Schippers (2010) and Campbell (2004, 2018).

Faculty Feature:
Participatory Learning With Lois Hicks-Wozniak

Figure 3.1a Lois Hicks-Wozniak

"I find my job is part music but it's everything else. It's geography. It's sociology. It's anthropology. It's political science."

Lois Hicks-Wozniak is Adjunct Professor of Music at Marist College and SUNY New Paltz in New York State. An active saxophonist, she was a member of the West Point Band after studying ethnomusicology and performance at Florida State University and is now completing a graduate degree in music performance at Montclair State University. At both Marist College and SUNY New Paltz, she teaches introductory-level "Music Cultures of the World" courses. At Marist, her enrollment is about 20–30 students, all of whom are nonmajors (Marist does not currently offer a degree in music). At SUNY New Paltz, her courses run up to about 60 students, comprised of both music majors and nonmajors. After taking an intensive summer course on World Music Pedagogy in Higher Education at the University of Washington in 2018, Lois has been continuously working to further incorporate the principles of World Music Pedagogy into her college-level courses.

Q: How do you incorporate participatory activities into your "Music Cultures of the World" courses?
A: At different sections of the semester, students will clap out *adi tala* (Carnatic rhythm) and learn *sargam* (Indian solfege) syllables, for example. We'll also do some work with West African polyrhythmic ensembles. I don't bring in drums per se, but we make an attempt at figuring out the different rhythms. There are some fascinating resources out there that I use: In the Titon textbook [see Appendix 2], there is a demonstration recording that breaks it down. I also use www.thisworldmusic.com, which has *Agbekor* African drumming and dance from Ghana [among others]. On the website, you can take out different layers . . . so we could just concentrate on the *gankogui* (iron bell) or the *kagan* (high drum), and they can really get a sense of which drum is playing in two and which drum is playing in three. And at the end of our unit on music of the Caribbean, we get out of our seats and dance salsa, merengue, and bachata.

I also try to get the students thinking like an ethnomusicologist, so we're thinking about the music *in the culture*. We're thinking about everything that's in the soundscape. We're thinking about how the audience reacts to the music: *What is their involvement? Would you actually* count *the audience as part of the music?* We also have a concert attendance requirement, but I refer to it as *fieldwork* because they can't just let the music wash over them. They need to describe the music, but they also need to do things like look around at the audience: *What is the audience doing while they're listening to the music? How are the musicians interacting with each other? What are the things that they're observing?* Yes, we need to have a performance attendance requirement in these courses, but how can I make it more about "how would you approach this if you were an ethnomusicologist?"

Q: How do you actively involve your students in learning the material?
A: One thing I do throughout the semester that's similar to a "flipping the classroom" technique is that I have an essay and peer review assignment for the students to do on an online discussion board. I randomize students' names and divide them into groups. They have to find a video of a live performance of non-Western music, and they have to do some research. I ask them to describe the music and talk about everything that's in the soundscape. They have to read Tim Rice's "Conducting Research" chapter in *Ethnomusicology: A Very Short Introduction* [Chapter 3; see Appendix 2] as well as Bonnie Wade's chapter, "Thinking About Fieldwork" in *Thinking Musically* [see Appendix 2]. So, they read both of those and the last part of the essay is discussing how they would study the music as an ethnomusicologist. I ask them: *What do you think you would do? What would you focus on? For example, would you focus on how the children in the community would learn the music?* I have them select a topic or idea that they would hone in on, just to think about different things that they could do. So, they submit their essays and the other group peer reviews them. It's really about creating a conversation—at least between two people in the class, where one person has done research and they're sharing their ideas, and the other person is reading and providing feedback.

Q: Do you do any large-scale projects with your classes?
A: I do a partner project [as a final project]. I'm trying to create a collaborative experience, so I give the students four choices. The first choice is to create a PowerPoint presentation on a music culture that we haven't looked at or studied. They're asked to give facts not just about the music, but about the *culture*: Who are the *people*? Then they research the music, choose some listening examples, and explain the music.

The second choice I give the students is related to something regarding the rapper Residente, the lead singer of a Puerto Rican hip-hop group called Calle 13. According to the Netflix documentary *Residente*, he took a DNA test and discovered his ancestry, which was traced all over the globe. He was so inspired by this that he traveled to those places and collaborated with musicians from those areas of the world and created an album. So [for their projects], students can put together a concept album. They look at their ancestry, research the cultures, explain the music, and describe how they would put [a concept album] together. Maybe they even name their album.

The third option is a podcast. I don't make the students record it, but they curate a playlist as if they were a DJ at the campus radio station. They put a playlist together, and they outline their narration of the playlist. They pick one culture as if it were their one hour on the radio station to educate their colleagues about the music. So, they put together some [audio] clips and a narration of how they'd introduce and discuss each selection.

The fourth option is to write a social justice news article. There was a journalist who used to write for *The Washington Post* and he would write, for example, "The top 10 reasons why you should care about the Syrian Civil War." And he's explaining each aspect of what people need to understand about this situation. At some point, for instance point number 7, he might say, "we need to take a break. Here's some Syrian music to help you understand that we're talking about *people*." Because in the end, we're talking about people making music. So [their project] is to write an article about something in the world that's happening that they're concerned about, and then put music into their article. Make us care. Because these are *people*. And that's another theme in our class: all humans make music—this is *humanly organized sound*—all humans make music, are involved with music, experience music. It may be different, it may function differently in every culture, but we all do it. So, make us *care* about this issue *and* the music.

From Participating to Performing World Music

In some cases, the Engaged and Enactive dimensions of the World Music Pedagogy process will effectively be the "end of the line" for certain musical selections. Some selections might even be appropriate only for a brief visitation through Attentive Listening. Nonetheless, it is the hope that through the use of imaginative Attentive, Engaged, and Enactive Listening activities, students will eventually develop the penchant for performing these works on their own, or eventually imbuing their own sense of creativity over these musical experiences. Indeed, these next steps in the WMP process comprise the focus of Chapter 4 (Performing World Music) and Chapter 5 (Creating World Music).

Glossary

Enactive Listening: The third dimension of the WMP process. Involves performing the recorded work in which, through intensive listening to every musical nuance, the music is re-created by learners in as stylistically accurate a way as possible.

Engaged Listening: The second dimension of the WMP process. Includes participatory listening to the recorded selection through active participation by listeners in some extent of music-making (by singing a melody, patting a rhythm, playing a percussion part, moving to a dance pattern).

Groove: A rhythm that propels music and inspires listeners to move by dancing, clapping, or stepping.

Maqam: A particular set of pitches within a system of modes associated with many forms of Arabic and Central Asian traditional music.

Mardi Gras Indian: For generations, African Americans have dressed up as Native Americans for Mardi Gras parades in what has become a generally respectable form of cultural appropriation, and a tradition all its own.

Musicking: Credited to Christopher Small (1998), *musicking* involves "tak[ing] part, in any capacity, in a musical performance, whether by performing, by listening, by rehearsing or practicing, by providing material for performance (what is called composing), or by dancing" (p. 9).

Participatory musicking: Refers to the active involvement of listeners and learners who sing along, clap, dance, and play instruments to recorded (or live) music.

Tango criollo **(Creole tango):** A form of Argentinian tango dance music.

Yeyi: A yodeling effect in Baka vocal music featuring the use of disjoined melodic intervals by oscillating between the singer's head and chest registers.

Notes

1. In some institutions, it may be possible to rent a small classroom set of tablets with relevant piano/instrument apps pre-installed. Check with the music library about the availability of such devices at your institution.
2. F-sharp bars will be needed if using pitched percussion instruments.
3. See Claire O'Neill's (2012) NPR article, "The Mysterious World of the Mardi Gras Indians." for more information about the ornate suits of the Mardi Gras Indians as well as a slideshow depicting various tribes' suites prepared for Fat Tuesday annually. Additionally, be mindful of using appropriate terminology when referring to another culture's clothing; for example, avoiding the word 'costume' (which can be read as pejorative or patronizing) and use the culture's preferred term (e.g., suit, regalia, attire).

References

Campbell, P. S. (2004). *Teaching music globally: Experiencing music, expressing culture.* Oxford University Press.

Campbell, P. S. (2018). *Music, education, and diversity: Bridging cultures and communities.* Teachers College Press.

Nettl, B. (2005). *The study of ethnomusicology: Thirty-one issues and concepts*. University of Illinois Press.

Nettl, B. (2010). Music education and ethnomusicology: A (usually) harmonious relationship. *Min-Ad: Israel Studies in Musicology Online, 8*(1), 1–9.

Schippers, H. (2010). *Facing the music: Shaping music education from a global perspective*. Oxford University Press.

Small, C. (1998). *Musicking: The meanings of performing and listening*. Wesleyan University Press.

Smith, M. P. (2003). Buffalo Bill and the Mardi Gras Indians. In M. Gaudet & J. C. McDonald (Eds.), *Mardi Gras, gumbo, and zydeco: Readings in Louisiana culture*. University Press of Mississippi.

Turino, T. (2008). *Music as social life: The politics of participation*. University of Chicago Press.

Listening Links

"Big Chief Got the Golden Crown (Live)," The White Eagles, Smithsonian Folkways Recordings. A Mardi Gras Indian chant performed at the New Orleans Jazz & Heritage Festival, led by Big Chief Jake Millon. https://folkways.si.edu/the-white-eagles/big-chief-got-the-golden-crown

"Dulce Sueño Mío," Ecos de Borinquen, Smithsonian Folkways Recordings. A Puerto Rican *jíbaro* (folk music) featuring a *trovador*, two *cuatros*, guitar, *guiro*, and bongos and using a *decimilla* (10 lines, 6 syllables) poetic song structure. https://folkways.si.edu/ecos-de-borinquen/dulce-sueno-mio-sweet-dream-of-mine/latin-world/music/track/smithsonian

"El Choclo," René Marino Rivero, Smithsonian Folkways Recordings. A well-known *tango criollo* (Creole tango) performed on solo bandoneon. https://folkways.si.edu/rene-marino-rivero/el-choclo-2/latin-world/music/track/smithsonian

"E Maru Rahi," Royal Tahitian Dance Company, Smithsonian Folkways Recordings. A Tahitian song about three brothers, one of whom died while diving for mother-of-pearl in the lagoon of Takaroa in the Tuamotu Islands. https://folkways.si.edu/royal-tahitian-dance-company/e-maru-rahi/world/music/track/smithsonian

"Hut Song," Baka Pygmies, *UNESCO Collection of Traditional Music*. A polyphonic vocal song from Cameroon, sung by 13 Baka girls. https://folkways.si.edu/baka-pygmies/hut-song/music/track/smithsonian

"Time to Have Fun," Rahim AlHaj, Smithsonian Folkways Recordings. An upbeat *khaliji* dance-style piece featuring oud (Iraqi lute), *santūr* (Iranian dulcimer), and percussion. https://folkways.si.edu/rahim-alhaj/time-to-have-fun

4

Performing World Music

"One of my department colleagues at home, a man very much involved with the anthropology of music, when I asked him what it was that determined his area of interest, told me: "It's always the music first; you have to be turned on by the music, then the other interests begin to accrue." And indeed, the fact that, increasingly, ethnomusicologists have turned to participation and to the study of performance in their fieldwork leads them to feel about this music as their conservatory colleagues would feel about Chopin and Mozart."

—Bruno Nettl, p. 2, 2010

As a classically trained mezzo soprano, an experienced voice teacher, and a choral director, Carolina was hired three years ago at a small state college in the American Southwest. It is April, and she has just received her autumn teaching assignments: Applied Voice Lessons, the University Chorale, and to her surprise, a brand-new course in "World Music Cultures." The lattermost is a survey course intended to satisfy a recently implemented goal of global competence at the university. Having never taught world music before, Carolina feels both intrigued and intimidated by the task. She wonders to herself how a world music course will meet the university mandate, and whether it's possible to adequately incorporate a broad span of music (most of which she knows very little about) into the 30 class sessions she'll be teaching next autumn. Furthermore, because of her considerable experience in music as a performing art, she wonders whether a world music course might feature moments of performance as well. Then again, since she herself does not know music beyond Western art styles, she feels some angst as to how to facilitate performances of anything beyond her area of specialization.

With the full confidence of the department chair to fashion the course however she best sees fit, Carolina figures that she can make a go of it with the summer to load up on information. She borrows world music textbooks and recordings from the library and begins reading fervently on a geographic spread of music—in Bali and Mali, South Africa and South Korea, and in her own personal classification of music from the "lands"—Ireland, New Zealand, and Thailand. She's entranced by the interdisciplinary reach from music to geography, history, language, and cultural studies. She draws up a listening list for herself and scans the internet for videos to complement the readings she's selected. The instruments and ensembles are mind-boggling, but as a singer, Carolina is especially drawn to song styles and singing. She is captivated by many characteristic vocal timbres so distinctive in themselves and removed from the timbres and techniques she learned through her conservatory-style vocal training. Carolina is struck by the beauty of South Africa's isicathamiya *of Ladysmith Black Mambazo and the ornamental features in the Pakistani* qawwali *singing of Nusrat Fateh Ali Khan. She is drawn to the performances of women's choirs such as Philomela from Finland and Mystery of the Bulgarian Voices. She softly sings along to traditional singers from Kenya's Luo community, Ghana's Ashanti people, the Hebridean singers off the west coast of Scotland, and the Vietnamese singers of* vọng cổ. *Her ears fill with these new singing styles, and during her daily exercise routines, she finds herself singing along with the songs that stream through her earbuds.*

As she continues to probe the music of places previously unknown to her, Carolina challenges herself to tailor experiences that will work well for her students. She is leaning toward the development of a coursepack of book chapters and a playlist that will give accent to vocal-choral music of the world. She imagines that she must feature some of the world's great instrumental ensembles, from Japanese gagaku *and Javanese* gamelan *to Brazilian* samba, *Mexican* mariachi, *and the North Indian Hindustani trio of sitar,* tabla, *and* tambura. *But as a singer, Carolina is convinced that students enrolled in the world music course will benefit from some experimentation with vocal qualities themselves, taking trial runs of singing with the recordings, working their way toward culturally distinctive vocal expressions that they themselves can perform. She imagines that these same students will benefit from preparing brief and informal performances of a few songs—maybe African American gospel, Russian, and Samoan vocal works—in the lobby of the music building and at the faculty club. Moreover, she is toying with the idea of joining together her world music students with members of her University Chorale so that together they might provide for a program of diverse musical expressions for everyone within earshot.*

Inroads to Performing World Music

The potential to accurately perform music of another culture is a uniquely valuable avenue to the attainment of deep musical insights. For those who take seriously their capacity to learn by listening, and singing and playing with the recording, the world's musical expressions are conceivably open to them to ultimately perform for themselves, given plenty of care and sensitivity. Understandably, the more technically complex the music, the more listening time it will take to decipher it and to perform it in full. Then again, some musical works will unlikely be performed by students due to the complexity and the lack of time available to learn to perform it. Certainly, the advice of culture bearers can be sought to determine the appropriate performance strategy for a particular selection. Yet, most music is open territory for the possibility of learning it to the point of a public performance, particularly when respect is paid to the culture from which the music originated and to the musicians themselves, whose recorded models pave the way through imitation by learners to their full-on embrace of the music in performance.

Many academic music courses at the tertiary level, including music history, theory, and culture, tend to be "lecture courses," or small lecture-discussion seminars, such that they contain no elements of student performance. In keeping with the multidimensional World Music Pedagogy approach to learning culturally unfamiliar music, we posit that music majors as well students of other fields and disciplines are all capable of singing, dancing, and playing the music they study. The music that is listened to, and thus increasingly understood through immersion, can develop into performances that please the ears and pique the curiosity of their audiences. The WMP-fashioned performances may quite naturally run shorter in duration than the standard "concert performance," especially if only one or two selections are worked up for public sharing. As well, performances that emerge from world music culture courses may occur in a variety of off-stage and informal venues rather than in the "acoustically perfect" campus concert hall. Still, as a consequence of experiences in Attentive Listening, Engaged Listening, and Enactive Listening, music captured on recordings can lead the way to shaping performances by students for themselves, for their colleague-students, for invited guests, and for others who may wish to open their ears to the music of close and far cultures. World Music Pedagogy ensures that in university-level world music courses, acts of performance can be inserted into lecture courses, and that the performance of world music can provide an opportunity to go more deeply into music than lectures and student discussion otherwise allow.

Performances can run a wide gamut of venues, lengths, content, quality, and purposes. Expectedly, music learned via World Music Pedagogy is not likely to lead to full-length public performances of the caliber that emanates from ensembles that are expressly organized for such purposes. Moreover, while the stage image is the standard impression of what constitutes "a performance," with students in concert attire, lined up in standing formation on risers or sitting in predetermined rows of chairs with music stands, student performances of music from their WMP course are sometimes referred to as "informances" in that they are typically less formal and more akin to an informal "sharing." Yet, across all performance settings and situations, students gain greatly from opportunities to perform, enlightening themselves and others of a song from Tahiti or Tibet, or percussion music from China or Chuuk (a Polynesian island culture in the southern Pacific region), or guitar music from Spain or Senegal. When students put their fresh understandings of a musical culture on display, they further spread their knowledge of just how the diversity of humankind uniquely expresses culture through music.

Fostering a Music-Making Culture

Music is meant to be shared. Performing a Samoan *sa-sa* vocally and with stylistic gestures, a Croatian *kolo* (dance and instrumental music), or a Shona-style *mbira* piece of Zimbabwe on available instruments can have a lasting effect of capping students' deepest levels of musical understanding. Such performances might also turn out to be socially appealing to them and their audiences alike. These musical understandings grow out of course experiences, most of which are not intended to drive toward the ultimate "all-perfect" performance. Rather, experiences in a world music course may hover within the realm of the experimental and the exploratory, the increasingly active and interactive, and the live musical expressions that go along with the recordings. The opportunity looms large, too, that at the far end of the pedagogical sequence, students can be making music independently, without the support of the recording. This is the point at which learning turns the corner toward a live public performance.

Within schools and departments of music, performance is pervasive. It is usually the very point of studio lessons, to learn techniques and repertoire via the long-standing apprenticeship model with its 1:1 master-student arrangement, so to grow performance skills fit for public consumption in recitals. Performance is central to the nature of ensembles, and student members of the university symphony, wind ensemble, chorale, and jazz ensemble are working up repertoire in rehearsals that ready them for one or more campus performances, as well as off-campus performances at festivals, on field trips, and around the community. Musical study quite naturally leads to performance as an important means for students to demonstrate and share the skills and understandings they have acquired.

All musical study can be an adventure in performance, including the music featured in world music courses. Acts of music-making fit well within the world music classroom, be it a survey course or a capstone seminar, when learners begin to vocalize what they hear, tap out the rhythms, take a melody to a familiar instrument, or find the various parts that comprise a polyphonic texture. This music-making is informal, and can be fostered regularly when students are invited to listen, contribute components while listening, and eventually emulate what they hear in ways that are singable and playable. A music-making culture can readily be related to some of the processes that occur in the studio lessons and ensemble rehearsals of university's music program, and faculty charged with teaching world music courses can set expectations for students to "activate" the music they study—regardless of its origin and regardless of whether notation is anywhere in evidence within the musical culture under study. World music courses are in fact untapped occasions for fostering a musicking culture such that all students can learn more deeply when the opportunities are regularly presented there for them to make music.

Benefits of Performing World Music

What goes on in a world music class can seed a wide array of potential performance opportunities. Enrolled students can very well find themselves so completely immersed in music that they find themselves performing selections that emanate from Oaxacan *banda*, African American gospel, Brazilian *capoeira*, Celtic *sean nos*, or *kpanlogo* drum and dance music from the Ga of Ghana (Figure 4.1). As they listen ever more deeply, the music "becomes" them—it seeps into their voices, into their bodies, and out to instruments that are available to them.

While it may be of great value to listen analytically (if somewhat passively) to the works of master musicians from across the world, students can also learn the distinctive benefits of performing for themselves the music that is represented on these sanctified recordings. Beginning with a first hearing, the way to the performance of a Bulgarian choral song proceeds from an initial stage of hesitation and uncertainty to

Figure 4.1   *Kpanlogo* drum and dance music from the Ga of Ghana[1]

later stages of vocalizing the melody, singing the poetic verse, and eventually finding the harmony parts to sing—such that the full 40-second segment can be performed with and without the recording. Likewise, the way to performing Egyptian *maqam* begins with listening, then vocalizing instrumental parts, then finding the pitches on various available instruments, and then putting the parts together as they are combined on the recording. These accomplishments lead students to performing the studied music, as best as they can, always with opportunities to refer to the recordings of the cultural insiders and culture-bearing musicians.

If the benefits of world music study are undeniable, then the benefits of actually performing music from diverse cultures go even further. Consider the following, for example:

- One of the aims of 21st-century programs of music in higher education is a broader concept of musicianship (Sarath, Myers, & Campbell, 2017), one that encompasses music of many genres (e.g., art, popular, folk, and traditional) and music of many historical periods (e.g., early music of the European Medieval and Renaissance periods through the periods of the Baroque, Classical, and 19th-century "Romantic" era, and across the 20th and 21st centuries). It would seem only logical, too, that 21st-century students of music (including but not limited to music majors) would be given opportunities to try their hand at playing and singing a selected musical work out of Korea, Iran, the Andes, or the Himalayas. They will fine-tune their ears in the process of learning to perform the music, and they will find themselves with new techniques vocally and on their orchestral and wind band instruments as they take on the challenges of music beyond Western art forms. Such performance experiences benefit students in developing their musicianship beyond a single style, and from more than just one region of the world.

- Students who find themselves in the midst of learning to perform a challenging melody (i.e., a tune that does not follow the rules of music that are culturally familiar to them) will become enmeshed in a musical style that is different but equally logical to the music they know. Students will learn new musical "rules" in studying how music is structured in Bulgaria, Bolivia, Egypt, Haiti, India, Mali, the Philippines, and elsewhere. They will gain greatly from figuring out what the voice needs to do, or where the fingers need to go, in order to match the recorded performance of a new musical culture. There is simply nothing like the act of performing world music, puzzling out the details of one pitch to the next, as well as the durational values of a new kind of rhythm, particularly because the experience draws students into a more focused attention to the musical details. A commitment to performance details leads to genuine musical understanding at the deepest level (Patel & Demorest, 2013).

- There is an unmistakable social bonding that grows between musicians as a result of a performance (Tarr, Launay, & Dunbar, 2014). In rehearsals, at the moment of performance, and in the aftermath of a concert, musicians who perform together become a community of sorts. Likewise, when students learn the music of a particular style and culture, and they have learned by listening to recorded musicians, they grow an affinity to the artist-musicians. Often, students are then drawn to know more about the musicians, their cultural values, their traditional practices (and their innovations), their languages, their education and training, and the economies and political and social systems of their home communities. As a result of making music, students' curiosity is piqued as to the cultural identities of the musicians, and cultural understandings and appreciations develop.

- There is certain joy in the considerable accomplishment of having crossed cultures to learn a culturally unfamiliar music (Clarke, DeNora, & Vuoskoski,

2015). The journey is a rigorous one, and it's not unusual for students to wonder whether, at the start of the pursuit of learning a new musical work from an entirely unfamiliar culture, such music *could* ever be learned to performance level. There are the typical struggles by students of learning music by ear when notation has been their standard means of learning. There is the recognition, too, that even if notation were provided (or transcriptions were made), the challenges are in getting the ornamentations and embellishments, the stylistic nuances, and even the timbre of a musical work far afield from familiar musical practices. When these challenges are met, and even overcome, the joy of discovery is there, and the taste of success is very sweet.

Practicalities in Performing World Music

Beyond the philosophical stance that the world's musical expressions *should* be experienced through performance, there are still the practicalities with which to contend in ensuring successful performances with students enrolled in tertiary-level world music courses. There are considerations of time, skills, and access to instruments, among other matters, that challenge the potential of world music to be learned so well as to be performed.

Finding the Time

All learning takes time, and learning music is no exception. In fact, since music is a time art, then time must be found if music is to be reasonably learned to a level of performance. In the case of oral tradition music, which characterizes most of the world's genres, precious time must be devoted to enable the ear to "pick up" the melodies, rhythms, timbral qualities, and elaborations. While time has already been expended within the first three dimensions of World Music Pedagogy, a public performance requires additional critical listening in order to further refine and prepare the work. Especially when music is culturally unfamiliar, learners need time to dissect the sonic details that at first may seem unexpected, and this dissection happens via attentive, engaged, and enactive experiences with that 30- or 40-second segment. Expectedly, brief excerpts from longer musical works will need to be stretched through repetition, variation, and even the creation of new material in order to shape it into a desirable length for performance (see Table 4.1 and Chapter 5). Of course, the more complex the music, the more labor- and time-intensive the task of learning it will be. Wisdom has it that music of moderate complexity, and of some redundancy rhythmically and melodically (rather than the most complicated works), are often the best choices for performances by students in a time-limited world music course.

Preparations for a public performance by students in a world music course can involve students both within class and outside of class. With the support of a course website that contains selected recordings and videos, including the links to recordings that are provided for the music of this volume's episodes and Learning Pathways, students can independently practice musical selections and fine-tune themselves on the rhythms, melodies, and performance techniques that were acquired through course sessions. Small doses of class time can be spent in coordinating parts that were independently practiced and in determining just how the brief selection will be extended to become a complete 3- or 4-minute piece. Thus, a group performance of a world music selection is initiated via the WMP dimensions, which is then independently practiced by students and then rehearsed in the course prior to public performance.

Nurturing Vocal Skills

Many musical works of the world are vocally expressed, and because all students can sing (to some degree), these works represent a desirable entry point for students to begin the journey of performing world music. Granted, while some students will be more experienced singers, others will have had less singing experience or feel a bit more reticent to sing. The selection of vocal music is critical, and songs of small range, and with built-in melodic redundancy, may best fit the voices of inexperienced singers. Songs with a groove may draw even the most reluctant singers into performing them, and with familiarity comes a certain ease and even confidence in singing songs from culturally unfamiliar genres.

There are solo vocal works to highlight, as well as solo-chorus works, songs for unison voices, and songs in homophonic and various polyphonic textures. Learning a song out of Greece, Ghana, or Vietnam will require students' phonemic awareness for discerning and producing small units of sound that comprise the language of the song text. The WMP listening sequence does well to set students up for attending to melodic and rhythmic components as they mix with phonemes, including linguistic accents and the horizontal flow of phrasing. For songs with multiple vocal parts, additional attention is necessary for understanding how the parts fit together, how different pitches tune to one another, and how pitches and parts are timed to sound at the appropriate time. When time is severely limited for bringing songs to performance, selections can be of a simpler quality by way of unison songs, or songs with greater repetition in text, melody, and rhythm (including those in such structures as AABB, ABBA, and ABAB, rather than more through-composed selections). Other accessible possibilities include songs with a melody and accompanying drone, or songs using basic harmonies of only a few chords. More complicated harmonies can be learned by experienced singers, although even they will find themselves challenged in learning to sing certain polyphonic styles such as those found in parts of sub-Saharan Africa, in Eastern Europe, and in the Pacific Islands.

Applying Instrumental Skills

A different type of challenge arises when performing instrumental music of the world's cultures. First of all, can instruments from various musical cultures be located and adequately learned to play? Some instruments may be more easily found (and borrowed), as in cases of Latin percussion instruments, manufactured music education *djembes* and *dumbeks*, or xylophones, marimbas, and various drums and gongs in the percussion program. Sometimes a university's music program may have a steelband or a *gamelan*, or a local community may be willing to lend out their Filipino *kulintang*, Japanese *kotos*, Irish *bodhrans*, or Andean panpipes (called *sikuri* or *zampoñas*). Sometimes instruments can be made, too, as in the case of plastic bucket drums for playing *samba* rhythms, or PVC pipes for playing Australian *didjeridu*. There is great value in offering students opportunities to play traditional instruments (or facsimiles) from other cultures, and yet the downside is that it takes considerable time to learn to play, for example, a melody on Javanese *saron, gendèr*, or *bonang* (pitched percussion instruments of the *gamelan*).

Second, can available instruments be used to perform music for which no "original" instruments are available? Yes, and quite often this is the reality, so that when the challenges of accessibility to instruments cannot be overcome, substitutions can be made. Oboes can play parts meant for the Indian *shenai* and Chinese *suona*, violins play melodies that "belong" to the Iranian *kemanche* and Indian *sarangi*, trumpets and trombones can sound the music of animal-horn instruments from across sub-Saharan Africa, and guitars can play parts of every imaginable plucked lute from the Serbian *tambur* and the Afghan *rabab* to the Mexican *jarana* and the Vietnamese *đàn nguyệt*. Yet even the transfer of a Javanese xylophone's melody to a guitar, violin, or flute requires time to translate it from original sound to familiar and accessible instruments—time that is understandably at a premium in a world music course. If it is learned that enrolled students can barely recall their fourth grade recorder lessons, let alone their long-ago experiences playing in school bands or orchestras, decisions can go one of two ways: to capture a world music selection on the few instruments that students *can* play, or to focus on vocal-choral repertoire and percussion works that utilize various drums, shakers, sticks, and bells.

Venues and Functions for Performing World Music

On the campuses of most tertiary-level institutions, formal performances tend to take place in an acoustically designed recital hall or concert auditorium located either within the music building or in another specially designated campus space. These locations may be likely, too, for student performances of official department-sanctioned world music ensembles such as a *gamelan, mariachi*, or steelband. Public performances by students of a world music cultures course, however, may wind up elsewhere—due partly to the nature of the performance, the function of the music, and the brevity of the performance (or informance). Unless they are one of several components of a formal or full-length concert, performances emanating from a world music course will rarely happen in specially designated performance spaces but rather in venues around campus and in the community beyond the university.

Consider the intended function of a performance by students of a world music course. Is the purpose of the performance a chance to share with others music that is "new" or relatively unfamiliar? Is its intent the honoring of a given cultural community? Is its function the celebration of a holiday, or a national or regional event? Is it to offer an informance, or informal performance that is meant to be educational and entertaining? Is it an end-of-term event to communicate the accomplishments of students across a schoolwide set of studios, ensembles, and classes? Is it meant for visiting parents, on parents' weekend, or visiting siblings, on siblings' weekend? Is it an orientation of prospective students to the music program? Any of these functions can work well in featuring students of a world music course in performance.

Consider the campus venues in which students of a world music course may find themselves performing, informing, sharing, and celebrating the music they have learned. Within the music building itself, there is the classroom in which the world music course is taught, when students, faculty, and staff may be invited in to catch a performed piece or two in a very brief "program." Large rehearsal spaces such as the band room or the chamber music space may function also as performance venues, particularly if there is a need for sufficient space for dancing as well as singing and playing. Wide hallways, and particularly the lobby or atrium of a music building, can possibly make for fitting venues, too, and performances can be scheduled at the time of change of classes so to draw the largest audiences (and also to avoid the leakage of music into classrooms and studios in session). Weather permitting, and depending upon the nature of the music, the campus green and outdoor plaza can serve as venues; the music of percussion instruments carries better in the outdoors than do voices and stringed instruments. A sports arena may host a drumming group of West African music, a Korean *samulnori* percussion group, or a Mexican *mariachi*. With permission, the entryway of the campus library or the administration building may work well as a venue for a vocal-choral performance, as would a student cafeteria. Meanwhile, a smaller group of students on guitars or various lutes, or on recorders or other wind instruments, may fit nicely into the space of an on-campus coffee shop. There is typically room for performers, too, in the faculty club, and brief performances may be a welcome respite from faculty conversations about departmental policies and politics.

Traveling off-campus to community settings can be challenging to schedule for students with a full course load, including their ensemble rehearsals and other commitments to campus projects, jobs, or work-study arrangements. Still, an appearance by a class of world music students for a brief performance will be welcomed at various off-campus gatherings and is certain to strengthen campus-community relationships as well. There are those working in nonprofit organizations, government institutions, elementary and secondary schools, communities of worship, embassies and consulates, libraries, museums, and parks and recreation sites who would greatly appreciate formal or informal collaborations with colleges and universities. Organizations that support specific minority communities or that serve a more general public—such as the Boys & Girls Clubs, or the YMCA/YWCA—may encourage musical partnerships, and local senior centers, retirement homes, and hospitals are often enthusiastic about the opportunity to host a brief performance.

Community festivals may offer many performance opportunities as well, from those that celebrate a season (Chinese Dragon Festival in the summer and German Oktoberfest in the autumn) or a holiday such as Martin Luther King Jr. Day, Cinco de Mayo, and Rosh Hashanah. Cultural communities often appreciate attempts by young people to sing, play, and dance their music regardless of whether students identify with the particular culture. Music faculty know that it is often part of the university mission to maintain good working relationships with the "movers and shakers" of various communities, and certainly brief visits to these communities to perform world music "samples" can help to build campus-community bridges.

The Course as Launch to the Ensemble

As the academic world music course itself comes to a close, students may want something more to follow on their newfound musical experience. They may have enrolled in a world music course—as music majors, music minors, or students coming from other disciplines and fields across a university campus—for a broad array of reasons, from meeting a program requirement, to fulfilling their curiosity for the music beyond the concert hall, to learning more about specific cultures and traditions such as Korean K-Pop, Puerto Rican salsa, Intertribal powwow, Japanese *kabuki*, Irish *ceili*, Jamaican

Figure 4.2 Pakistani *qawwali* singer Abida Parveen and ensemble in concert[2]

reggaeton, and Pakistani *qawwali* (Figure 4.2). While some students have sought such academic world music courses with the expectation of attending as passive listeners to lectures, many are attracted to the possibility of some manner of greater musical involvement. While some students come with an intellectual curiosity of the changing roles and functions of music in historic and contemporary contexts, others are seeking outlets for their own creative musical expressions. As they move through a world music course into ever-deepening layers of understanding, they grow a level of comfort and competence with a musical work, genre, or culture that brings them onward to the point of performance. Students grow a respect for the music and musicians, and they develop a yearning to experience the music for themselves through the art of performance.

Performing world music in an academic course can easily have the "spin-off" effect of leading students to enroll in a university world music ensemble. Examples of full-term performance possibilities are present within some university music programs or through student services and clubs. Some universities offer elective courses in Ghanaian drumming (Akan and Ewe are standard practices), *mariachi*, gospel choir, Chinese orchestra, Andean panpipes, Caribbean steelband, Appalachian and Ozark old-time music, or Zimbabwean marimba (or "Zimarimba" groups). When faculty who teach world music courses arrange for the appearance of ensemble leaders as featured guests, they can develop an opportunity for these guests to perform, demonstrate, and engage students in the music of their ensemble (and even to recruit them to join these ensembles). Thus, as students tune in to the music and sample the performative nature of a musical work, the world music course becomes a launch point for the continuing involvement of students as performers in world music ensembles (see Solís, 2004).

Guidelines for Performing Recommended Selections

In all, there are 16 featured world music selections within this volume, each the focus of episodes in listening, participating, performing, creating, and understanding cultural meaning through music. Together, the selections comprise a sampling of music from diverse regions of the world, with the aim of offering a spectrum of the musical world for voices and instruments. They constitute an amalgam of cultural expressions from Africa, Asia, the Americas, Europe, and the Pacific region, including songs in various languages, percussion works, and pieces for various stringed and wind instruments. All selections are performable by students in world music courses to varying degrees, but of course the quality will depend upon the musical skills of the enrolled students, the time allotted for drawing students through the WMP sequence of experiences, and the choices that teaching faculty can make in organizing students for performance.

Suggestions for the performance of the 16 selections are provided in the following sections. The musical examples that comprise the three Learning Pathways are described in Performance Activities 4.1 (Middle Eastern fusion), 4.2 (Tahitian elegy), and 4.3 (Puerto Rican *jibaro* song). Suggestions for developing performance-ready experiences are offered by way of their associated recordings, the motivic material or harmonic outline, instrumentation for performance, and movement or choreography. Further performance suggestions, called "extensions," are intended as recommendations for developing the brief musical segments to performances of suitable length. Table 4.1 briefly charts the 16 selections as to suggestions for converting them from in-class experiences to complete, outright performances.

Performing Middle Eastern Fusion Music

Iraqi-American *oud* player Rahim AlHaj's collaboration with Iranian *santūr* player Sourena Sefati on the album *One Sky* features a particularly uplifting track, "Time to Have Fun," which uses a popular dance rhythm called the *khaliji*. In the spirit of interculturalism, AlHaj frequently performs alongside Western instrumentation including the guitar and string quartet. Students can adapt their newfound familiarity with the piece for use with multiple guitars, bass guitar, and hand percussion (Figure 4.3). With

Figure 4.3 Rahim AlHaj with *oud*, photographed by Michael G. Stewart[3]

parts learned "by ear" through Engaged Listening and Enactive Listening episodes, Performance Activity 4.1 offers further guidelines to full-fledged performances by students of various experience levels.

Performance Activity 4.1: "Time to Have Fun" (Iraq/Iran) (Learning Pathway #1)

Materials:

- "Time to Have Fun," Rahim AlHaj Trio, Smithsonian Folkways Recordings
- Guitars, bass guitar or double bass, available hand drums (e.g., *darbūkah*, *dumbek*, *cajon*, *djembe*), *oud* (if available)

Instrumentation:

1. *Melody*: Guitars (and/or *oud*) repeat the main ascending melodic motif in (refer to Figure 3.1).
2. *Accompaniment*: The bass provides root pitches, and a rhythmic pulse is provided by percussion instruments.

Motivic Material: This song is built on a repeated ascending melodic motif, outlined in measures 1 and 2 (see Figure 3.1), which is based in the Arabic *maqam kurd* (refer to Figure 3.2).

The form of "Time to Have Fun" consists of a 2-measure phrase played 3 times with minor variations, which is followed by a 3-measure concluding part, for a total of 9 measures before repeating (Figure 3.1).

Movement/Choreography: Have students search the internet for *khaliji*, to explore the nature of this Iranian-Iraqi dance in various Middle Eastern contexts. *Khaliji* is considered a joyful, celebratory dance, ideal for weddings and other pleasant events. The dance is sometimes performed by a single woman, but most often by groups of women in *thobe nashal* (or *thawb*), a richly embroidered and brightly colored beltless robe. This traditional dress, which is grasped and undulates in combination with long untied hair, makes intentionally wave-like graceful movements to express nature.

Khaliji dance is based on stepping the rhythmic pulse, with one foot ahead of the other, in a R-L-R, L-R-L floor pattern. Keeping the knees bent, the dancer playfully steps, and typically the back foot lingers on tip-toe while the front foot is placed in a flat position. Hair tosses and hand shimmies are characteristic features, as the arms are gracefully extended outward and enable the *thobe* (robe) to gracefully billow as the feet move. It is also relevant to know that in the Gulf states, men occasionally may also dance along with *khaliji* as well.

Figure 4.4 *Khaliji* rhythmic pulse using Western notation

Tek (L)		X		X		X
Slap (R)					X	
Dum (R)	X		X			

Figure 4.5 *Khaliji* percussion in TUBS notation

Figure 4.6 *Khaliji* bass rhythm in European notation

Performance Tips: The melody of "Time to Have Fun" can be accompanied by percussion playing a typical *khaliji* rhythm (see Figure 4.4), supported by a bass guitar (or substitute), as later indicated.

In the traditional Middle Eastern percussion pattern associated with the *khaliji* dance, the "dum" sound is a low thud, and the "tek" sound is higher and crisper, so that the slap gives an unmistakable accented "pop" to the rhythmic groove. Like tablature for the guitarist, world music drummers encountering non-European traditions tend to find the Time Unit Box System (TUBS) notation to be more intuitive, as illustrated in Figure 4.5.

The most elegant way to support this groove with a bass instrument (such as double bass or bass guitar) is to either only play downbeats or repeat a simple 3-note rhythm (Figure 4.6), all on the main root note of the piece (C).

To support the melodic motif, the previous figure can be played 7 times, followed by 2 measures of rest.

Rehearsal Tips: *Dumbek* and *darbūkah* are the ideal hand drums for *khaliji*, while *djembes*, congas, and *cajons* can serve as substitutes. It may help to have the *darbūkah* and bass players rehearse the *khaliji* groove together as a small group, since other instruments will rely on them to set the foundation for the entire selection.

Extension Suggestions: Increase the length of the piece through five repetitions:

1. Feature the full ensemble while dancers are off-stage or waiting at the periphery, with the bassist only playing the downbeat of each measure;

2. Repeat full ensemble with bass on the 3-note rhythm while dancers move in time, one by one reaching center stage and performing individual hair tosses;

3. Play hand drums, without other instruments, for the length of the segment, while dancers begin unison *khaliji* movement together;

4. Play hand drums and bass guitar on 3-note rhythm for length of segment, while a solo dancer is featured center stage;

5. Feature the full ensemble, softly, while dancers move in a circle facing each other;

6. Feature the full ensemble, at full volume, as dancers conclude and exit.

Performing a Tahitian Elegy

By the time they have reached the Enactive Listening exercises in "E Maru Rahi," students will already be mere steps away from developing a successful full-on performance of this emotive Polynesian piece—complete with ukulele, shakers, and singing. The element of traditional dance is an essential feature of Tahitian performance (Figure 4.7), much of which can be learned from tutorial videos available on YouTube and other websites. Some students may prefer to perform simple dance steps, while others may choose to sing and play instruments. Some improvisation, particularly on guitar and ukulele parts, is common in Polynesian music and can add character to the performance (see Chapter 5).

Figure 4.7 Polynesian dance rehearsal in studio[4]

Performance Activity 4.2: "E Maru Rahi" (Tahiti)
(Learning Pathway #2)

Materials:

- "E Maru Rahi" Royal Tahitian Dance Company, Smithsonian Folkways Recordings
- Ukuleles, guitars, bass guitar, percussion instruments (e.g., sticks, shakers)

Instrumentation:

1. *Voices*: The main melody is sung, along with homophonic harmonies that feature parallel thirds.
2. *Ukuleles*: Basic chords are strummed in a repeated pattern, as noted later.
3. *Rhythmic accompaniment*: Bass and percussion instruments offer rhythmic and formal support throughout the song.

Harmonic Outline: Instrumentalists can begin with learning the harmonic pattern for each four-measure phrase of the song (refer to Episode 3.2 for harmonic progression).

Note that the ukulele (and/or guitar) part is strummed with a distinctive rhythmic pattern. Refer to Figure 3.3 in Chapter 3.

Rehearsal Tips: Each supporting element of this song should be rehearsed and then combined for a full performance. The ukulele parts will require some practice, especially for the right hand, to attain precision in the repeated strumming pattern, but the chord shifts (left hand) are less difficult (see Chapter 3 for further suggestions for scaffolding this aspect of the performance). The vocal sound is open and relaxed, and with slow vibrato characteristic of Pacific Island singing.

Basic percussion parts can be added to support the song (Figure 4.8). Students with very little previous experience in percussion can use sticks to softly beat the ground in the same rhythm as the ukulele pattern, which may be doubled with shakers (e.g., maracas, egg shakers, rattles), while the bass guitar can

Sticks on ground	X			X	X		X		X		X	
High drum							X		X			
Low drum	X											

Figure 4.8   "E Mahu Rahi" percussion in TUBS notation

play a single root note on the downbeat of each measure. Optionally, during the final measure of 8-bar phrases, the bassist can "walk" either up or down the scale using quarter notes to reach the downbeat of a new section.

The vocal harmonies can be developed to encompass the root, third, and fifth of each featured chord in the progression. As the melody is learned by all singers, it is then possible to effectively divide the singers and have at least two groups of harmony singers on supporting parts, each singing group one third apart from the next. Note that major 6 chords are especially common in Polynesian music, and the 6th degree (e.g., D in the key of F) may optionally be added in some locations where a major chord is held for several beats, such as at the ends of phrases.

Movement/Choreography: Have students conduct an internet search for traditional Tahitian dance, so that they might attempt to incorporate stylistic moment into the performance (building from these efforts in Chapter 3). Note that knee-length skirts are essential attire for the dances, but they can be assembled from a variety of fabrics. In Tahitian tradition, *ami* is a dance step consisting of a wide and slow rotation of hips and pelvis. *Tumami* is a common form of *ami*, in which the pattern begins with the belly in a forward (rather than retracted) position. *Varu* is based on hip movements from *ami*, but often faster and in multiple directions that resemble a figure eight from the perspective of the dancer. Several suggestions for the *ami* dance follow:

1. Dancers must keep their feet fairly close together, their knees nearly touching, and maintain a straight back and still upper body. A common resting posture is to lift the elbows up and let hands rest suspended in the air in front of the dancer's chest (roughly perpendicular to the ground), where they look comfortable but do not distract from the main focus of this dance the movement of the hips.

2. Dancers should always have their knees slightly bent, never straight. This dance requires a wide range of hip movement, but this means moving from bent knees to *very* bent knees, and *never* to straight knees.

3. Forward knee movement enables hips to move in the desired way, side to side. By bending the opposite knee even further, the hip movement develops a deep and flowing shape.

4. Heels also need to be subtly lifted, higher and lower, for full mobility of the hips.

5. *Ami* requires a slow and wide circular movement of the hips, with knees pushing forward and back along with the hip rotation. The circular movement can be either clockwise or counterclockwise (in coordination with bending the opposing knee), and dancers should practice in both directions.

6. The balls of the feet generally remain stationary in *ami*, but dancers may gracefully shift to other locations as part of *broader* choreography.

Extension Suggestions: Increase the length of the piece through four repetitions:

1. Feature the full ensemble while dancers are off-stage or waiting at the periphery;

2. Repeat full ensemble, absent harmony voices (solo voice only), while dancers enter and take center stage;

3. All singers rest and only instruments play their parts, while dancers move close to the audience;

4. Softly repeat full ensemble, including all singers in vocal harmony, as dancers return to center stage;

5. Repeat full ensemble at full volume while dancers move away from center stage and conclude.

Performing *Jíbaro* of Puerto Rico

The *jíbaro* tradition represents an important aspect of Puerto Rican musical culture, especially its rich rural connections. After honing their skills in singing the song with the recording, students might choose to perform this rousing folk piece as they connect to Puerto Rican history and culture (further discussed in Chapter 6). Because *jíbaro* carries such a strong tradition of improvisation, students may be compelled to improvise (or compose) their own *décimas* (as further discussed in Chapter 5).

Performance Activity 4.3: "Dulce Sueño Mío" (Puerto Rico) (Learning Pathway #3)

Materials:

*   "Dulce Sueño Mío," Ecos de Borinquen, Smithsonian Folkways Recordings
*   Two guitars, bass guitar, voice, congas/bongos, *guiro*, drum set (high-hat)

Instrumentation:

1. *Voice*: The main melody is sung in unison; chordal harmonies can be added.

2. *Guitars*: Some students may be able to play the primary *cuatro* melody on guitar (or another melodic instrument, as desired). Others can play the primary harmony line that runs parallel to the melody. The majority of students can play the oscillating chordal harmonic accompaniment (G and D^7), which is less technically difficult. If the accompaniment becomes too

loud, students can strum without picks, while players of the melody and harmony lines can use picks for a higher volume and clarity.

3. *Rhythmic accompaniment*: The bass and hand percussion offer rhythmic and formal support throughout the song, often using syncopated patterns. This requires preparation to ensure accuracy with the recording; however, in the spirit of this improvisatory tradition, students should be encouraged to develop their rhythmic accompaniment within reason and stylistic appropriateness.

Instrumental Melody: Experienced *cuatro* players and/or guitarists can play the main melody, and then add harmony in parallel thirds. Refer to Figure 3.5 in Chapter 3.

Harmonic Outline: Note that although the melodic *cuatro*/guitar line to this song requires some technical competence, rhythm guitarists only need to know three chords to strum a basic accompaniment to this song (D^7, G, and C). The main challenge to their part is understanding that the first two beats are "pickups" to the first downbeat. Consequently, the easiest way to start the ensemble— in rehearsal or performance—is to establish the tempo by loudly counting off "*uno, dos!*" so the melodic guitarists know when to enter (on beat three) with their two-beat introduction (in 16th notes). Then the rest of the ensemble starts on the downbeat of the first complete 4/4 measure:

A section: (D^7) ‖: G | D^7 | G | D^7 :‖
B section: ‖: C | G | D^7 | G :‖

Movement/Choreography: *Jíbaro* music and dance are virtually inextricable from one another. Students can research various forms of *jíbaro* dance (especially through YouTube videos). *Jíbaro* dance consists of coordinated steps in pairs. Couples dance beside each other (rarely if ever touching), with women in long dresses and men in traditional suits and hats. The women often hold the opposing edges of their long dresses in each hand, while men sometimes move with their hands clasped behind their backs or make gestures with their hats. Couples frequently circle around each other with similar movements, or each couple takes turns moving in various directions together, and sometimes dancers form separate groups by gender and move in a circular "ring" pattern.

Performance Tips: The guitars and bass almost always play in syncopation against each other, which is characteristic of this style, but the underlying pulse is constant. Given the improvisatory nature of the music, particularly in the solo vocal part, students might find it more rewarding to revisit performance potentials after engaging with the creative activities detailed in Chapter 5.

A helpful way to support the *jíbaro* groove with a bass instrument (such as double bass or bass guitar) is to repeat a simple 3-note rhythm, playing the main root note of each chord twice, followed by a shorter leading tone as the third note in a transitional pitch to the root of each new measure (see Figure 4.9).

Figure 4.9   *Jíbaro* bass rhythm

Performance of this song can be especially rewarding for a class that includes at least one confident singer (or several singers who can take turns), some reasonably skilled guitarists, and several players of bass and percussion instruments.

Rehearsal Tips: Guitarists should rehearse together as a small group, since others will rely on them to set the foundation for the entire song. Congas players can perform quarter notes with a distinctive accent on beat four. On the drum set, a simple high-hat pattern of quarter or eighth notes can be softly sounded. The high-hat pattern can be all quarter notes, with a rather loose pedal on beats 1 and 3 (for a sustained sound), while beats 2 and 4 are tightly closed (for a short sound), occasionally adding faster rhythms as "fills" between sections (but without losing time).

Extension Suggestions: Increase the length of the piece through four repetitions:

1. Feature the full ensemble;
2. Repeat full ensemble, adding basic unison dance movements;
3. Feature the full ensemble, softly, without voice, as dancers develop and then conclude their movements;
4. Feature the full ensemble, at full volume to end the piece.

Implementing Performances in World Music Pedagogy

The following box illustrates how each of the recorded selections discussed across this book can lead to actual performances through the dimensions of World Music Pedagogy. Note that in this book, *extensions* refer specifically to strategies for lengthening a 30- or 40-second segment of music into a performable piece of 3 or 4 minutes. Additionally, the reference to *working groups* is the assignment of students to small-group work for the preparation of particular parts of a performance. In other words, where in the case of seminar of 30 students, there are suggestions for the division of the class into five working groups of six students, who may rehearse the parts for melody, harmony, and rhythm section, for example. Likewise, in a class of 100 students, there may be five groups of 20 students, for example. Expectedly, group sizes may be somewhat dictated by the number of available instruments (or other logistical matters), but the instructor's thoughtful planning will identify the arrangement of groups that will yield the most successful results.

TABLE 4.1 Recommended performance activities for selections featured throughout this volume

Title	Chapter	Culture Group/ Location	Suggested Working Groups	Extensions
Time to Have Fun	Learning Pathway	Iraq/Iran (Middle East)	3–4 groups: • Melody (guitar or *oud*) • Bass (bass guitar) • Rhythm section: hand drums (e.g., *darbūkah*) • Optional: *Khaliji* dancers	Repeat section (6 times): (1) Ensemble, (2) Ensemble/dancers, (3) Percussion/ dancers, (4) Ensemble/solo dancer, (5) Ensemble (softly)/dancers, (6) Ensemble (loudly)/dancers.
E Maru Rahi	Learning Pathway	Tahiti (Polynesia)	3–5 groups: • Melody (voices*) • Harmony (ukuleles) • Bass (bass guitar) • Rhythm (shakers, sticks, high/low drums) • Optional: Tahitian dancers *Voice parts may also be combined with instrumental parts/dancers*	Repeat section (5 times): (1) Ensemble, (2) Ensemble with solo voice as dancers enter, (3) Instruments and dancers only, (4) Soft volume with all voices, (5) Full volume as dancers exit.
Dulce Sueño Mio	Learning Pathway	Puerto Rico (U.S./ Caribbean)	4–7 groups: • Sung melody (voices) • Harmony (guitars* or *cuatros*) • Bass (bass guitar) • Rhythm (percussion: congas, bongos, *guiro*, drumset) • Optional: *Jíbaro* dancers *Guitar chords could be split between 3 groups for beginners*	Repeat section (4 times): (1) Full ensemble alone, (2) Ensemble with unison dance movements, (3) Instruments only (softly) as dancers conclude, (4) Full ensemble (with singer) to conclude.
Go Go	2	South Korea (East Asia)	5–6 groups: • Sung melody (voices) • Instr. melody (keyboards) • Flute sample (flute/*sogeum*) • Beat sample (computers) • Bass (bass guitar/keyboard) • Optional: K-Pop dancers	Repeat 4-measure (16-beat) phrase multiple times (see Figure 2.1): Twice with instruments only, twice with full ensemble (including sung melody), twice with only percussion and flute, twice with full ensemble and dance movement.

Sigi-Sagan	2	Basque Country (Southern Europe)	4 groups: • High idiophone • Low idiophone • Flute (or substitute instrument) • Keyboard (or accordion)	Repeat 4-measure phrase 4 times: (1) Percussion only, (2) Percussion and flute, (3) Full ensemble (soft), (4) Full ensemble (full volume).
Big Chief Got the Golden Crown	3	New Orleans (U.S.A.)	• Everyone sings response while improvising rhythms on their instruments • Have students trade off improvised calls • Mixed percussion (tambourines, cowbell, bass drum, bongos, buckets)	Call and response form (constant repeats) with improvised calls.
El Choclo	3	Uruguay (South America)	2–3 groups: • Melody (right hand of accordion/keyboard) • Harmony (left hand of accordion/keyboard) • Optional: Tango dancers and/or substitute voices (*a cappella*) if accordion/keyboard parts are too challenging	Repeat ABA'C form multiple times from first 25 seconds of recording. Play moderate tempo and volume. Repeat faster tempo and higher volume. Repeat slow tempo soft volume. Conclude with final repeat at fast tempo and strong volume.
Hut Song	3	Cameroon (Africa)	3(+) singing groups: • Layer the three vocal parts *a cappella*	Repeat 4-measure phrase (Figure 3.6) multiple times with 3 focal parts in different configurations: (1) Twice part 1 alone, (2) Twice parts 1 & 2 only, (3) Twice all parts, (4) Twice 2&3 only, (5) Twice 1 & 3 only, (6) Twice all parts soft, (7) Twice all three parts full volume.

(Continued)

TABLE 4.1 (Continued)

Title	Chapter	Culture Group/ Location	Suggested Working Groups	Extensions
Jarabi	5	Mali (Africa)	3–5 groups on xylophones, metallophones, or Zimarimbas: • *Kumbengo* (bass instruments) • Accompaniment (soprano/alto instruments) • Improvisers (soprano/alto instruments) • Optional: Latin percussion (see AfroCubism version)	Repeat 4-measure phrase (Figures 5.2–5.4) multiple times: (1) Bass alone, (2) Bass and accompaniment, (3) Full ensemble with melody, (4) Full ensemble with improvisation (soft), (5) Full ensemble with new improvisation (full volume), (6) Full ensemble with melody.
La Mariposa	5	Bolivia (South America)	4–5 groups: • Melody (flute/melodic instruments) • Harmony (guitars/ukuleles/*quenas*) • Bass (guitars) • Voices (with tambourines) • Optional: *Morenada* dancers	Repeat form (5 times): (1) Full ensemble, (2) Full ensemble (soft), (3) Harmony and bass parts only, (4) Melody and percussion only, (5) Full ensemble (full volume).
Flute and Drum at Sunset	5	China (East Asia)	Using GarageBand iOS app (or similar), perform student-composed *pipa* melodies (solo or ensemble) on digital devices (e.g., iPad/ iPhone). Add other Chinese instruments (*erhu* and *guzheng*) as desired	Students produce their own melodies, which can be developed further through an organized amount of repetitions.
Nihon Ettim	6	Uzbekistan (Central Asia)	Soloist and 5–6 groups: • Vocal soloist (alto or tenor) • Plucked strings (mandolins and/or ukuleles, acoustic guitars) • Bowed string melody (violas and/or cellos) • Bowed string drones • Bass ostinato (bass guitar or double bass) • Percussion (soft: padded mallets on large drums and/or wooden block) • Electronic keyboard (to cover any sounds missing)	Repeat slow 3/4 motif multiple times: 2× Bass ostinato drone, 8× with bowed string melody added, 1× Bass ostinato drone, 8× Full ensemble with voice.

Gula Gula	6	Sámi (Northern Europe)	Soloist and 5–6 groups: • Vocal soloist • Bass ostinato (bass guitar or double bass) • Plucked string ostinato (acoustic guitars and/or violins, cellos) • Percussion (frame drum or equivalent) • Flutists • Additional singers (optional, doubling vocal solo line and/or flutes)	Repeat motif (10-measure phrase) 6+ times: (1) Vocables only; (2) Vocables and solo drum; (3) Lyrics added with drum and bass; (4) String ostinato added (softly); (5) String ostinato (full volume); (6) Full ensemble with flutes also added.
Me He Manu Rere	6	Māori, New Zealand (Pacific Islands)	Soloist or in 3 groups: • Melody voice • Optional: Harmony voice (parallel thirds) • Optional: Accompanists (acoustic guitar, bass guitar)	Repeat melody four times: (1) Full ensemble, (2) Full ensemble with solo voice, (3) All voices *a cappella*, (4) Full ensemble.
Kuniburi no Utamai	6	Japan (East Asia)	4–5 groups: • Woodwinds (flute, oboe, bassoon) • Plucked strings (guitar, cello, violin) • Percussion (various drums, cymbals) • Drone (electronic keyboard, accordion, harmonica, clarinets) • *Bugaku* dance (optional)	Strictly copy first 2 minutes, learned by heart. This can be repeated once.
Deportees	6	United States (North America)	Soloist or in 3 groups: • Melody voice (can be *a cappella*) • Optional: Harmony voice (parallel thirds; can be *a cappella* with melody) • Optional: Accompanists (acoustic guitar, bass guitar)	Repeat entire form multiple times to cover all verses: (1) Solo guitar and solo voice, (2) Full ensemble (additional guitars and vocal harmonies), (3) Full ensemble instruments only (soft), (4) Full ensemble with voices (full volume).

Faculty Feature:
Jonathan McCollum on World Music Studies in a Liberal Arts College

Figure 4.1a Jonathan McCollum

"In performance, they are making music history come alive! My challenge has been to put history and culture in direct dialogue *with our contemporary lives and to make the broad study of music not only musically relevant, but also intellectually, politically, religiously (spiritually), economically, and even ecologically important.*"

Jonathan McCollum is Associate Professor and Chair of Music at Washington College in Chestertown, Maryland. Founded in 1782, Washington College is a private liberal arts college named for one of its founders, George Washington. Despite having a small music department, Washington College enjoys a strong reputation, particularly for the diversity of its music offerings. In the United States today there are over 500 liberal arts colleges—institutions which typically emphasize undergraduate teaching—many of which are situated on small or medium-sized campuses. Teaching for liberal arts colleges can be highly rewarding because such institutions place great emphasis on personalized instruction and often encourage innovative and interdisciplinary approaches.

Q: Can you tell us about your job, and what motivates your teaching?
A: At Washington College, I teach the Western music history sequence, as well as courses in world music. I also teach the Japanese music ensemble and the Indian music ensemble and use my experience as professional trombonist to direct the symphonic band and brass chamber ensemble. All three of the full-time faculty members in our music department have strong interests in world music and do some teaching of these courses. Only one of us actually has a PhD in ethnomusicology, so world music is my primary responsibility in addition to chairing the department. What most drives me as a teacher is that I am endlessly curious to keep learning, and I want to instill that kind of drive in my students, a deep curiosity to keep learning and to be creative.

Q: What are the main challenges you face with such a breadth of teaching responsibilities in a small department?
A: One of the challenges I face as a teacher at Washington College is in connecting performance with theory and history. As a professional performer myself, I understand the tremendous benefits performers gain by studying music history. For example, in my course Music of Asia, I typically focus on the music of China, Japan, and Korea. The course tackles an enormous breadth of history and musical styles. In my newly created Japanese Music Ensemble, we are putting the history and analysis that we had outlined in the Music of Asia course into action. Students are not only able to read about the music, but they are learning to read Japanese notation, to differentiate various breath and finger techniques, and to identify culture-specific aesthetics for musicality. In performance, they are making music history come alive! My challenge has been to put history and culture in direct dialogue with our contemporary lives and to make the broad study of music not only musically relevant, but also intellectually, politically, religiously (spiritually), economically, and even ecologically important.

Q: What kinds of further studies (or professional development) have you pursued after your degrees?
A: After completing the PhD, I continued to study *shakuhachi* (Japanese flute) until earning the Shihan, a kind of traditional master license, in 2015. My earliest degrees were in trombone performance, and I have continued performing professionally on trombone. I took additional courses in museum studies because I was interested in how we can represent and present culture in different formats, such as in performances and exhibitions. Now I am also pursuing a Master of Divinity in Zen Buddhism. While that might seem personal, it also directly relates to courses I teach. For instance, this semester I am teaching a course entitled Performing Japanese Buddhism, which is co-registered between philosophy and music, so that students can earn credits in either department.

This kind of course is often more likely to appear in the music program of a liberal arts college than in a large public or private university.

Q: You also lead an Indian Music Ensemble. How did that develop?
A: In the music programs, we wanted to develop some short-term study abroad options for students, so I discussed this with a composer colleague who had studied *tabla* in his own university experience, and we got the idea of introducing students to Indian music. Ultimately, our course was on the cultural life, religion, and music of North India. We brought students to India who studied directly with gurus there. Students later suggested, as a result of their short-term study abroad experience, that we form an Indian music ensemble when we returned, so we bought instruments from India, carried them on the airplane, and started the ensemble here at the college. Since then, we have been learning together. I have focused on coaching the melodic instruments, such as *sitar*, *bansuri* flute, and *harmonium*, while my percussionist/composer colleague teaches the Indian percussion instruments.

Q: I understand that you sometimes bring guest performers to your college. Can you explain how this benefits students, and how you obtain funding for it?
A: For about 60 years there has been a concert series at Washington College, but around seven years ago we decided to give it a broader musical palette than to feature only Western art music, which has been of great benefit to world music studies—and the ethnomusicology minor—at our college. One of the musicians invited recently was Rahim AlHaj (Figure 4.3), the notable Iraqi *oud* performer. It was amazing to hear his personal story of coming from Iraq, all the incredible challenges he faced, and it was inspirational for our students—many of whom come from privileged backgrounds—to hear from a musician of his caliber. At the pre-conference lecture, Rahim offered a lot of context for the music he would perform that evening, which made it so much more special for the students and audience members from the campus and local community.

Performance as the Culmination of Sustained Listening

While not every world music course will be stocked with student performances, we are suggesting that through the World Music Pedagogy approach, students are readying themselves to reproduce what they have learned by singing, playing, and dancing the music. Performing for the pleasure of public audiences extends naturally from experience and study. These performances need not always represent "perfected" renderings of the featured musical cultures, but they can reasonably include "working" performances as well as *informances*—performances whose primary goal is to *share* a musical culture with others rather than present it with strict and traditional performer-audience dichotomies. Whether performed in the comfort of the classroom or perhaps as an "opener" for another world music ensemble performance, in the student union, in the outdoor quad, or elsewhere, the act of performing world music demands a level of confidence and trust in the music that exceeds what the first three dimensions of the

WMP process provide. In essence, the experience of performing world music is greater than the sum of WMP's individual parts.

A musical performance may be viewed as a gift, something nurtured with care and lovingly shared with an audience. With performances in formal and informal settings, it is possible to frame the music-making as a unique event offered once, at a particular time and place, to a specific audience. All it takes is a few brief comments to remind the audience that a special gift has been prepared for their enjoyment, and it is theirs to accept.

Glossary

Available instruments: Those instruments that can be accessed by students (such as a personal flute, violin, or guitar, or instruments that are readily borrowed or loaned) in order produce sounds that are roughly equivalent to "original instruments" which are not readily accessible (such as a Japanese *shakuhachi*, a Persian-Iranian *kemanche*, or Middle Eastern *oud*).

Extensions: In WMP, a term used to describe particular strategies for repeating, varying, or otherwise lengthening a brief 30- or 40-second segment of music (often to 3 or 4 minutes), such that it fits well into a public performance or informances.

Informance: An event in which the principal aim of a performance is to inform (and to share musical expressions with) an audience rather than to present a perfect rendering of a musical work

Musicianship: The ability to perform music accurately and with sensitivity to the expressive nuances.

Working groups: In WMP, a term that refers to the assignment of students to small-group work for the preparation of particular parts of a performance.

Notes

1. Public domain (Creative Commons) "LAOC-KuluMele-65" by Knight Foundation is licensed under CC BY-SA 2.0.
2. Public domain (Creative Commons), licensed under CC BY-SA 2.0.
3. Provided with permission from Rahim AlHaj.
4. Public domain (Creative Commons) ("rhythm and emotion" by Pabak Sarkar is licensed under CC BY 2.0).

References

Clarke, E., DeNora, T., & Vuoskoski, J. (2015). Music, empathy and cultural understanding. *Physics of Life Reviews, 15*, 61–88. https://doi.org/10.1016/j.plrev.2015.09.001

Nettl, B. (2010). Music education and ethnomusicology: A (usually) harmonious relationship. *Min-Ad: Israel Studies in Musicology Online, 8*(1), 1–9.

Patel, A. D., & Demorest, S. M. (2013). Comparative music cognition: Cross-species and cross-cultural studies. In D. Deutsch (Ed.), *The psychology of music* (pp. 647–681). Academic Press.

Sarath, E. W., Myers, D. E., & Campbell, P. S. (2017). *Redefining music studies in an age of change: Creativity, diversity, and integration.* Routledge.

Solís, T. (Ed.) (2004). *Performing ethnomusicology: Teaching and representation in world music ensembles.* University of California Press.

Tarr, B., Launay, J., & Dunbar, R. I. M. (2014). Music and social bonding: "Self-other" merging and neurohormonal mechanisms. *Frontiers in Psychology, 5.* https://doi.org/10.3389/fpsyg.2014.01096

Listening Links

"E Maru Rahi," Royal Tahitian Dance Company, Smithsonian Folkways Recordings. A Tahitian song about three brothers, one of whom died while diving for mother-of-pearl in the Lagoon of Takaroa in the Tuamotu Islands. https://folkways.si.edu/royal-tahitian-dance-company/e-maru-rahi/world/music/track/smithsonian

"Dulce Sueño Mío," Ecos de Borinquen, Smithsonian Folkways Recordings. A Puerto Rican *jíbaro* (folk music) featuring a *trovador*, two *cuatros*, guitar, *guiro*, and bongos and using a *decimilla* (10 lines, 6 syllables) poetic song structure. https://folkways.si.edu/ecos-de-borinquen/dulce-sueno-mio-sweet-dream-of-mine/latin-world/music/track/smithsonian

"Time to Have Fun," Rahim AlHaj, Smithsonian Folkways Recordings. An upbeat *khaliji* dance-style piece featuring *oud* (Iraqi lute), *santūr* (Iranian dulcimer), and percussion. https://folkways.si.edu/rahim-alhaj/time-to-have-fun

5

Creating World Music

"Hold on, so literally any of these pitches will sound good?" Andy, a sophomore viola performance major experimented with his newly learned Dorian scale, running his fingers from "D" to "D" in two octaves but with all natural, "white" notes. As he played around on his viola, which now felt enticingly foreign, the discord in the room was growing as Professor Berton brought out three massive contra-bass xylophone bars, each of which Daniel struck with gusto. By now, Daniel had outlined the syncopated three-pitch bass line of the Malian tune "Jarabi" fully by ear, looping the same figure that they had been singing and playing for several sessions now. Daniel smiled widely as he wound his left and right arms up high and brought each down weightily, producing a dark and rich tone that resonated throughout the room. As Andy skeptically tested each of his viola pitches against Daniel's bass line, he realized that what he was playing didn't sound half bad—as long as he kept coming back to the pitch "D", as Professor Berton kept reminding them.

To Andy's right, a group of six classmates were chatting excitedly over a set of alto and soprano xylophones. Using her mallet as a pointer, Ashley and several other voice majors led her peers in playing a rhythmic loop that she had concocted fully in her own head. After a few moments, Kaitlin nodded along and placed Ashley's pattern higher on the xylophone, creating an ad hoc harmonic accompaniment that fit seamlessly with Daniel's bass line. Hearing the two parts finally lock in, the group of six began celebrating rowdily, dance stepping side to side and clicking their mallets on beat four as they continuously looped the pattern. The bass line was settled, the accompaniment was settled, and now it was time to jam on this infectious love song from West Africa.

Twenty minutes into class, the cacophony finally grew to order, the random commotion now only coming from a group of improvisers playing their primary instruments—a mixture of flutes, clarinets, trombones, and saxophones in the center of the room. Professor Berton raised her eyebrows toward Andy as an indication that it was his time to begin improvising. Andy smiled back with a nervous shrug. He knew that his training as a concert violist hadn't prepared him to make up his own music from scratch. He began to play, cautiously at first, somewhat unsure of how to approach this sudden moment of freedom. Then he looked up and recalled the instructions written on the board: Rhythmic or Melodic: Choose One! *Andy decided upon the former, relying on his strong sense of rhythm to develop an improvisation rather than trying to come up with an interesting melody on the spot, which he deemed impossible in this unplanned moment.*

Before he knew it, Andy's time in the spotlight had passed on to another player as they continued to jam over this kora *tune from Mali. His tunnel vision now widening, Andy was roused by the sound of applause and a classmate slapping him hard on the back. Three years into his viola performance degree, Andy had previously experienced plenty of moments in the spotlight. But this was a rare moment unlike any he'd experienced sitting in the orchestra. "I've been playing the viola for 15 years," he said to his classmate. "But I never got to do* anything *like that!"*

In the arts, it is seemingly taken for granted that everyone is creative. It is seen as impossible, after all, for an artist of any type to succeed without simultaneously tapping into their own human creativity. From that angle, there is an assumption that anyone found within the walls of a school of music, school of art, school of design, school of architecture, or other such academic stronghold of artistic expression must be inexorably creative. This is certainly the image from the outside, at least.

However, from inside the walls of the music school, "creative" is a designation that seems to be awarded quite differently. Seemingly, there are divisions of labor within the academic music scene, comprised of what we can artificially call the *creators* and the *re-creators*—or perhaps, the *inventors* and the *interpreters*. The latter usually personify performance, music theory, and music history majors who study and interpret an established canon of works, while the former usually refer to jazz studies, popular/commercial music, and composition majors who compose and/ or improvise daily. Within the conservatory model that is nearly ubiquitous among tertiary music programs, a harpsichordist might perform Bach's *Concerto No. 1 in D Minor* flawlessly but would not be trained to improvise her own fugue. On the other hand, a jazz saxophonist might improvise expertly over a standard like "Lester Leaps In," but would not be celebrated for re-creating Lester Young's legendary solo note-perfect as its own performance. The question of creativity becomes even more contentious once the two major subforms of artistic creation are considered: composition and improvisation. These musical activities are variously embraced and feared by musicians of all ages, and by the college years these beliefs about one's creative abilities become further self-actualized, for better or worse. In short, the specialized roles of conservatory-model music education and training has reinforced the expectations and identities of various "types" of musicians, effectively underpinning musicians' self-perceived notions of who is truly "creative" and who is not. Many missed opportunities for creativity have ostensibly arisen within modern music education, yet few would deny the importance of instilling creative skills and attitudes among musicians from all backgrounds (see Sarath, Myers, & Campbell, 2017).

What we see in higher education today is not how musicians were trained throughout history. At least with respect to the canon of Western European art music, early Renaissance and Baroque musicians would extemporize skillfully over a figured bass, using the *basso continuo* to invent new harmonic material on the spot—much like how jazz musicians use chord changes to invent new melodic and harmonic material today. This was not a specialized skill, either: all trained musicians were historically expected to interpret figured bass and improvise as a basic standard of performance skill. Indeed, famous anecdotes abound of such composers as J.S. Bach, Mozart, Beethoven, Liszt, and others improvising upon spontaneous themes, some of which later became their notated compositions.

Carol Gould and Kenneth Keaton (2000) have argued several reasons for this shift in training within the Western canon. Among them, they point to the development of the Romantic Period (ca. 1820–1900) and its ideology of the composer as the authoritative and solitary "hero," effectively decentralizing the role of the individual performer. Moreover, given romantic composers' subsequent desire for harmonic and formal complexity, it became further challenging for musicians to continue improvising over such intricate musical advances. It could also be added that the widespread distribution of sheet music throughout history further reinforced the role of musician as re-creator—especially as musical training increasingly focused on interpreting an established canon, note for note.

Of course, this history is specific to Western European art music, so how might it affect how students engage with musical traditions from elsewhere around the globe? Unsurprisingly, the musical cultures commonly featured in world music courses feature vastly different creative traditions—including who gets to create music, when it happens, what conventions it might follow, and how it occurs in practice. However, despite the keenness with which Puerto Rican *plena*, Zimbabwean *mbira*, and Carnatic *kriti* musicians might improvise, for example, it is reasonable to expect that many students of world music culture courses are products of a conservatory model in which improvisation and composition are hardly practiced, thus presenting a potentially uncomfortable task for many musicians.

Creativity from a Global Lens

Generally, Western musicians tend to think of composition and improvisation as two separate activities on opposing ends of a spectrum. However, this binary way of looking at original creation is largely based upon several assumptions, including the methods of transmission and preservation, the permanence of the creation, the timing of the creative act, and who is involved with the process. That is, at least in the Western canon, musicians assume that compositions are always notated while improvisations are not; compositions are fixed and unchanging while improvisations are spontaneous and unique to the moment; compositions occur prior to performances while improvisations occur spontaneously during the performance; and composing usually occurs individually and in private while improvisation occurs in group settings and before an audience. However, once musical performance is examined from a global lens, many of these assumptions no longer hold true (Nettl, 1974). Instead, musical practices come to light in which the acts of composition and improvisation become further blurred. In these contexts, compositions live and breathe as new generations of musicians interpret and change pieces to reflect contemporary society; improvisations become ossified into fixed works; fresh compositions materialize in group settings and in real time; and melodic and harmonic material for improvisation gets recycled and reused within and across genres. Rather than viewing composition and improvisation as dualistic ways of creating, the two activities begin to look more alike as one's view of music broadens (Wade, 2012).

Reigniting Creativity in Higher Ed Classrooms

As the fourth dimension of the World Music Pedagogy framework, Creating World Music assumes that students will already have had extensive experiences with a recorded model through plentiful Attentive, Engaged, and Enactive Listening activities. Students will by this point be able to articulate notable elements of the music, will have actively engaged with several aspects of the music, and will have worked toward re-creating the recording (in small portions or entirely) on their own. They may have performed the music they had learned by listening for themselves or in a public forum. They will also have briefly discussed contextual matters relevant to the music through brief visitations with the Integrating World Music dimension (presented in Chapter 6), which weaves throughout the entire WMP process. At this point, when the music is internalized deeply and the musical idiom is understood semantically, culturally, and ethically, students are prepared to begin imparting their fresh creative instincts into these culturally rich artistic excursions.

To understand the underpinning philosophy of this chapter, one might consider Randall Allsup's (2016) distinction between "closed" and "open" forms of music teaching and learning. On the one hand are closed forms—those which represent master-apprentice, fixed, canonized traditions. On the other are open forms, which refer to "hybrid, irreducible, often digital, often participatory . . . and sometimes open-source ways of making and doing music" (p. 48). Open experiences extend musically outward—from using traditional instruments and remaining genre-bound to using nontraditional instruments (for example, iPads and digital interfaces) and moving toward genre-free creations. These open experiences, often empowering and transformative, serve to be more far-reaching and long lasting than are closed forms of musical participation. When original creation takes precedence over re-creation, he argues, students become more central to a deeply organic, constructive process. Indeed, it is through the pursuit of these open forms that the Creating World Music dimension comes to life.

However, to avoid implying the existence of another false binary, there may indeed be situations in which a somewhat more "closed" approach to creativity might be warranted—particularly with traditions in which improvisational and compositional activities are uncommon or forbidden. In such cases, creative activities will honor the musical culture's original intent while creating something new, *as inspired by* the style of the original, deeply studied recording. Indeed, essential to properly realizing an open pedagogy within contexts sensitive to matters of cultural diversity is a recognition of the responsibility that one has in maintaining the integrity of the musical culture. Thus, while the pursuit of open forms undergirds the majority of this chapter, it ought to be accompanied with an associated degree of reverence for the musical tradition in question. After all, it might be considered improper to unabashedly engage students in improvisation exercises when a musical practice neglects does not utilize improvisation, such as Japanese *nagauta* (Kabuki dance music), or when it reserves the task for those who have truly earned the right (e.g., North Indian *sitar*, *sarod*, and *tabla* music). Nonetheless, while these concerns should be handled cautiously, they should not ultimately hinder instructors' creative goals for their course. Even within those practices where original creation is not normally practiced—or those in which it is not allowed or remains "closed off" to outsiders—musical material might still ignite the inspiration for *other* creative ventures to take place. For example, while *nagauta* is not an improvised musical form itself, the core concepts found within that practice (such as melodic treatment, rhythm, formal structure, and so on) might become the source of new creations separate and unique from the contextualized practices of *nagauta* music. The musical elements of this non-improvisatory practice, in other words, might become uniquely varied, sampled, quoted, or borrowed by students to develop a musical creation that is decidedly *not nagauta*, but is creative, exploratory, and unique all its own. Such a point will require clarification to the students, of course, and references to the origin-culture music and musicians may be an opportunity for comparative analysis.

Obviously, the best way to ensure that a particular musical culture accommodates original creation within its idiom is to conduct personal research on the held traditions and customs of that practice. Moreover, instructors may supplement their explorations by taking opportunities to participate in these practices for themselves, when possible. As discussed elsewhere, the diversity of many college and university communities (including surrounding neighborhoods) means that there may very well be opportunities for participating in many musical practices important to the local community; for instance, *mariachi* in central Arizona, Irish trad in Boston, Vietnamese *công đồng* in San Diego, and so on. In his chapter on improvising and composing within world music traditions, for example, David Hughes (2004) describes his experiences learning about the unspoken customs and rituals concerning creativity within several musical idioms—including who gets to participate in the process of original creation, when it occurs, and in what contexts it is deemed appropriate. Supplementing one's gaps in knowledge through conversations with culture bearers can often provide a robust understanding of the "inside practices" functioning at the very heart of many traditions. Finally, through the Integrating World Music dimension (Chapter 6), students can, in communication with the instructor, decide if, when, and how creative activities might be undertaken with respect and integrity. It is within the Integrating World Music dimension that students make deeper connections between the *sonic* properties of the music and the *social* meaning it carries within societies. In this respect, it is imbued throughout the entirety of the WMP process and not merely saved for the "final step." As such, elements of the Integrating World Music dimension could reasonably become the basis for determining how to best undertake creative activities within a situated culture.

Creating World Music: Strategies and Considerations

For some, the excitement of re-creating a musical culture for themselves will be closely followed by the desire to augment or transform what they hear with what they may be compelled to freely express from within. While this desire should be harnessed, it also cannot be rushed. To ensure that students truly understand the nuances of the artistic medium—including the rules and conventions that follow it—ample time within the Engaged and Enactive Listening dimensions should first be realized. This should typically include extensions of the pieces from brief clips to fuller pieces, as discussed in the previous chapter. It is possible that some students may have eventually found a degree of comfort through participatory musicking but might now balk at the request of creating something of their very own. Whether their discomfort stems from their conservatory-style training or an altruistic fear of doing another culture injustice, their fears should be reasonably quelled just like others' overzealous desires. We wish to promote a learning environment in which students engage readily and openly with the artistic opportunities before them.

Organizing successful creative activities in the classroom requires a great deal of facilitative preparation. As activities become more open-ended and inventive, students tend to further seek the comfort of parameters that allow them to better understand their degree of achievement. Much of this also lies in managing students' expectations of what constitutes a reasonably creative act—especially in an age of hypersensitivity to assessment. With prevalent images of creative mastery taking the form of John Coltrane, Rhiannon Giddens, Kim Duk Soo, B.B. King, Ala Farka Touré, Wu Man, and Anoushka Shankar, students may be stymied by the expectation that they too can create something meaningful and worthwhile. Therefore, several activities presented here will merely require students to participate on a small scale, with the expectation that their creative energies will expand once given the opportunity to express themselves in a well-supported and scaffolded environment.

Throughout this chapter are activities that seek to maximize artistic parameters while minimizing one's sense of creative abandon. For example, by choosing a selection with a repetitive pattern or ostinato, instructors can encourage students to simply alter or augment a basic figure—perhaps changing a single note or rhythm, extending the figure by several beats, or rewriting a new idea altogether. Students can additionally add a unique ornamentation to a melody, improvise a body percussion accompaniment, produce a new call-and-response pattern, or develop a unique way of organizing the song structure. Finally, for students who may consider themselves to be more *linguistically* creative than musically creative, composing new lyrics (in English or a relevant language) might be a more fitting early task.

Often, instructors neglect to pursue creative activities in their classes because of a perceived lack of time within a given term. However, most of the small-scale activities in this chapter will require mere moments to execute and would all the while reinforce the customs of the musical culture in an eminently memorable fashion. At the same time, investing time and space for more large-scale and open-ended activities further augments the learning experience as students work to assemble distinct musical features into fresh creations that are both similar to and different from the recorded model. Afforded the time and space, students might be asked to compose a brand-new melody from a scale, mode, or chord progression featured in the selection. They may be asked to improvise fresh ideas all their own in a stylistically accurate manner. Or, they may be asked to arrange a familiar folk song to feature a new instrumentation, fresh accompaniment, or unique form. Whatever approach an instructor finds most appropriate in a given context, it is critical that students have the opportunity to not only re-create culturally diverse music for themselves but to craft it anew in some appropriate and veracious fashion. For whatever level of creativity that students are pursuing within the dimension, regularly referring back to the recorded model can serve as a security blanket by allowing students to emulate and expand upon the recorded ideas. Furthermore, referring to the original recording as a symbolic end to the process beckons students back toward the music's origin and allows them to recall their reverence for the master musicians.

Motivic Composition

Many musical examples throughout this book feature melodies that are based on a repetitive motive. The primary melody in Rahim AlHaj's "Time to Have Fun," for example, utilizes the same motif at the beginning of each antecedent phrase (to use Western terminology), followed by a consequent phrase that continues within the *maqam kurd* (or G Phrygian mode). In Episode 5.1, students will compose and perform new melodies using the *maqam kurd* as the basis of their creation. There will be two possible levels of difficulty from which students may self-select, depending upon their level of prior knowledge and initial comfort with the task.

Episode 5.1: "Time to Have Fun" (Iraq/Iran) (Learning Pathway #1)

Specific Use: Undergraduate introductory-level world music survey course

Materials:

- "Time to Have Fun," Rahim AlHaj Trio, Smithsonian Folkways Recordings
- Instructor's and students' instruments of choice

Procedure:

1. After students are able to perform the selection confidently through various Engaged and Enactive Listening activities, divide the class into small groups of 4–8. Try to include at least one student who can read and write using Western notation, if possible. This student will act as the group's scribe.[1]

2. "Let's sing the main melody once through and assign letters to each 4-beat measure to figure out the micro-form of the melody."

3. Play track [0:00–0:38]. Hold up fingers for each measure to guide students who may not be familiar with concepts like "measure."

   A: The micro-form is ABAB'ABA'C.

4. "In small groups, we are going to compose brand-new melodies using the *maqam kurd* and the existing form of the song." Display the pitches of the *maqam kurd* (Figure 3.2) on the board.

5. "There are two different levels of participation for this activity, which you may self-select as a group. For Option 1, you will compose a completely

---

new melody. For Option 2, you may keep the 'A' motive and just compose new 'B' and 'C' motives."

6. To help facilitate the activity, have students write out their three independent motives separately before putting them in the order of the song's form. Provide the following parameters:

   • The A motive should lead melodically into the B motive;

   • The C motive should be 2 measures long (to make the full phrase 9 measures) and should end on the root of the *maqam kurd* (G);

   • Students may choose to honor or ignore the need to write slightly different motives for the A' and B' sections.

   Note: As presented, these steps are highly structured to give students the necessary parameters to feel comfortable with a potentially unfamiliar task. However, to be responsive to the students' level of comfort, the instructor should readily remove parameters as needed to allow students more creative freedom, as appropriate.

7. Have small groups perform their new compositions for the class.

8. Reincorporate the percussion part (learned during Enactive Listening) into these compositions.

9. If desired, have the class choose a handful of their favorite melodies and perform them as a class, creating an arrangement from these several motivic ideas.

Lyrical Composition and Improvisation

For vocal selections containing lyrics, students might find the process of composition much more accessible if they are asked to write new lyrics to accompany the melody of a piece—especially among those who might consider themselves creatively inclined in more verbal or linguistic ways. In this process, writing new lyrics can be approached just as one might approach poetry. Granted, in some cases it might be considered inappropriate to change the lyrics to a piece of music, especially if it is closely tied to a specific group, person, or spiritual event/figure (for example, some Lushootseed [Coast Salish] songs and songs from a broad spectrum of Indigenous cultures). However, it is often a perfectly acceptable practice in other musical cultures (for example, English ballads, which feature several verses that have been added and changed over time). As always, engaging in brief, personal research is essential before embarking upon any creative activities that depart from the typical practices of the home culture.

Episode 5.2 features an activity in which students use the Tahitian song "E Maru Rahi" to compose and perform new lyrics about a similar or different topic. Once again, prior to this stage, students will have sung the song with correct pronunciation and a stylistically correct vocal timbre and will have learned the basic harmony and strumming pattern of the ukulele part. These Engaged and Enactive skills are essential for facilitating the students' further success in composing new lyrics to the song.

Episode 5.2: "€ Maru Rahi" (Tahiti)
(Learning Pathway #2)

Specific Use: World music special topics seminar (e.g., "Music in Polynesia," "Music of the Pacific Island Cultures")

Materials:

- "E Maru Rahi," Royal Tahitian Dance Company, Smithsonian Folkways Recordings
- Ukuleles (or substitutes), shakers

Procedure:

1. This activity involves students writing new lyrics to accompany the "E Maru Rahi" melody. As the instructor, decide whether students should be asked to use the existing topic of the song (the loss of the singers' brother) or an entirely different topic (to be decided by the class).

2. In small groups (or individually), have students compose poetic verses regarding their topic, in English. If using the existing topic of the song, students might tell the story of how the brother died, how the family mourned his loss, or about the spirit of the brother, for example.

3. Optional: Have students first count the number of syllables in each phrase and compose their poetic verse with the same number of syllables. (If this step is not desired, students can conduct the same activity but will slightly change the rhythm to fit the new lyrics.)

   E maru rahi e aue (8)

   ua moe to tino (6)

   e ita to mata (6)

   e ite faaho e (6)

   e ita to mata (6)

   e ite faaho e (6)

   to'u aia here (6)

   o Tahiti rahi e (7)

4. Have a small group of students play ukuleles and shakers as each group's newly composed verse is displayed on a projector.

5. While the instrumentalists are playing the harmonic accompaniment (Episode 3.2), have the rest of the class sing the new lyrics using the original melody.

Episode 5.3 creatively extends the Engaged and Enactive activities in which students have thus far re-created the recording as closely as possible. Yet, because *jíbaro* is an improvised tradition, the truest essence of participating within the tradition emerges within the Creating World Music dimension. In this episode, students participate directly in the rich *jíbaro* practice of *décima* improvisation. In order to further facilitate success, this activity has been adapted into a composition activity given the distinct difficulty of spontaneously improvising *décimas*.

Episode 5.3: "Dulce Sueño Mío" (Puerto Rico)
(Learning Pathway #3)

Specific Use: Undergraduate introductory-level world music survey course

Materials:

- "Dulce Sueño Mío (Sweet Dream of Mine)," Ecos de Borinquen, Smithsonian Folkways Recordings

Procedure:

1. "Describe the content of the *trovador*'s improvisation. What is he singing about? How does he communicate his ideas? Through imagery? Metaphor? Literal depiction?" Review the Spanish/English lyrics of "Dulce Sueño Mío" for the sake of understanding the content about which the *trovador* sings.

2. Play track [0:21–1:08] and field responses.

    A: He sings about unrequited love. He communicates it through poetic metaphor and similes.

3. As a class, collectively decide upon a single topic for use in a new *décima*. Topics are often philosophical (e.g., love, freedom, nationalism) but can also be about a current events topic or other context-specific topic.

4. In small groups, have students compose 10-line *décimas* (in English or Spanish) following the proper rhyme scheme of *ABBAA CCDDC* and 8 syllables per line.

    Note: While décimas *would traditionally be improvised spontaneously, allow students time to compose their* décimas *and appreciate the difficulty of the trovador's task.*

5. Once each group has written their full *décima*, have them speak it aloud with a clear, even rhythm (no pitches yet). Students should repeat this until a clear rhythm develops from their chanting of the words.

6. Have students create a harmonic backing with *cuatros* (or instrumental facsimiles) and percussion instruments. Use a non-complex harmonic progression (such as oscillating I–V^7 chords) to allow students to focus on successfully improvising melodies that fit the harmonic progression.

    Note: The focus here is not on re-creating the harmonic background of the original recording, but to create something new using the tradition of décima *improvisation. Thus, using a simple I–V⁷ allows students to main-tain focus on the lyric-writing aspect of the activity rather than harmonic or melodic concepts.*

7. Cue students to continue chanting their non-pitched lyrics as a separate small group performs the harmonic progression in a loop. Encourage students to begin taking note of where their lyrics might be taking them melodically. Repeat as necessary.

8. Display each group's newly composed *décima* verse on a projector or white board.

9. While the instrumentalists are playing their invented harmonic accompaniment, have each small group perform their *décima* using either (a) an improvised melody or (b) the melody from the original recording.

Full-fledged Improvisation

Throughout Western Africa, the Mandé people are known for their rich popular and traditional music expressions. Mandé music is deeply tied to deep histories preserved and shared by West African historians, storytellers, poets, and musicians called *griots* (also known as *jali/jeli*). These revealed figures possess deep spiritual and social connections within Mandé culture and frequently perform on the *kora* as their instrument of choice. The *kora* is a lute- or harp-like string instrument with 21–25 strings and a large gourd resonator (see Figure 5.1). Musicians play it by sitting with the instrument facing them, using both hands to pluck open strings that each represent a distinct pitch. The *kora* is widespread across West African countries such as Mali, Senegal, and The Gambia and represents a core part of Mandé popular and traditional music.

One of the most-recognized pieces heard throughout Mali and neighboring countries is a love song called "Jarabi." Among Malians, the song serves as a metaphor for the love of their country, their culture, and the Mandé people. It was written by *kora* master Toumani Diabaté (see Figure 5.1), who himself came from a long line of *griots*. Possibly the most fascinating aspect of "Jarabi"—and the reason it is featured here in this chapter—is how compellingly the song blurs the lines between traditional notions of composition and improvisation. In fact, while the tune does have its own identifiable melodic theme (see Figure 5.4a), the tune is most immediately recognized by its iconic three-pitch bass line (see Figure 5.2). The bass line and harmony function as a *kumbengo*, or cyclical phrase that provides the rhythmic and harmonic accompaniment of the music. This *kumbengo* persists throughout the entirety of the tune, which Diabaté manipulates in a masterful recording of virtuosically improvised themes.

Today, "Jarabi" has become a standard piece of repertoire not only for *kora* players, but for musicians spanning several genres and categories—particularly those that consistently seek to blur the boundaries of musical culture and style, such as jazz musicians, Afro Cuban musicians, and contemporary classical musicians. Indeed, there are now countless versions of "Jarabi" to be found across several genres. Some are performed at bright, energetic tempos while others are more meditative

Figure 5.1   Toumani Diabaté and the *kora*[2]

and unhurried; some are performed by solo *kora* while others include an ensemble of instruments from around the globe; some feature lyrics while others are purely instrumental; some seek to maintain the tune's Malian flavor while others boldly mix intercultural flavors. But what connects just about every version of "Jarabi" most immediately to listeners is the *kumbengo* and its memorable bass line.

In Episode 5.4, "Jarabi" is used as a tool for engaging students in improvisation, regardless of prior experience or musical knowledge. Given the highly improvisatory nature of this piece, the Enactive Listening dimension will likely be but a brief point of arrival for students. Instead, the Creating World Music dimension is where a piece such as this will truly come to life. The focus of Episode 5.4, therefore, will be for students to begin improvising over "Jarabi" as they further pursue an "accurate" representation of the musical experience. This particular tune was chosen not only because of its aesthetic appeal, but also because of the straightforward nature of the *kumbengo*, creating an accessible climate for improvisation across a wide range of experience levels.

Improvising With "Jarabi" From Mali

This episode opens by suggesting that students expand beyond Diabaté's masterful recording and explore other ways in which musicians have interpreted the song over the years. After all, most composers, arrangers, and improvisers would readily agree that many of their artistic ideas come from plentiful listenings of recordings and performances by esteemed peers and venerated masters performing the same or similar pieces. The boxed text titled "Reinterpreting 'Jarabi'" initiates this process of comparative listening with the intention of developing creative ideas for improvisation or arranging.

Reinterpreting "Jarabi"

Many versions of "Jarabi" have been performed and recorded based on Toumani Diabaté's original work. In small groups or as a full class, have students listen to these various versions and articulate what makes each interpretation unique. Encourage students to explore versions of the tune beyond this list as well (however, caution students that several available recordings titled "Jarabi" appear to be unrelated to Diabaté's original). This process is often how composers, arrangers, and improvisers explore new possibilities for their reimagined works. As such, this activity will become an important introduction to Episode 5.4.

- "Jarabi," Toumani Diabaté, *Kaira.*

  The "original" recording of "Jarabi," performed by Diabaté on solo kora. *This is the version that is recommended for use during the Attentive, Engaged, and Enactive dimensions.* Available at https://music. apple.com/us/album/jarabi/1325146150?i=1325146977

- "Jarabi," Sona Jobarte, *Fasiya.*

  This version is performed by the first woman kora *player (also granddaughter of Master Griot Amadu Bansang Jobarteh and cousin of Toumani Diabaté). Jobarte plays the* kora *with vocal improvisation, alongside Femi Temowo (guitar) and Robert Fordjour (percussion).* Available at https://open.spotify.com/track/3PHDLlBp2ryGBOtzAN5 Wzb?autoplay=true&v=T

- "Jarabi," AfroCubism, *AfroCubism.*

  This version features an intercultural fusion of Malian and Afro Cuban styles. It features Diabaté singing the story of Jarabi, performed with balafon *(West African xylophone), guitar (featuring Eliades Ochoa), and Cuban percussion instruments.* Available at https://music.apple.com/us/ album/jarabi/1467800044?i=1467800055

- "Jarabi," Sousou & Maher Cissoko, *Adouna.*

  Performed by Swedish guitarist Sousou and Senegalese kora player Maher Cissoko. This vocal version begins with a contemplative and

> *unhurried tempo before diving into an up-tempo groove for an inter-
> weaving improvisation of* kora, *guitar, and voice*. Available at *https://
> music.apple.com/us/album/jarabi/299492658?i=299492662*

* "Jarabi," Tunde Jegede & Derek Gripper, *Mali in Oak.*

  > *This purely instrumental version is performed by a Nigerian-English* kora
  > *player (Jegede) and American jazz guitarist (Gripper). Both the guitar
  > and* kora, *which are timbrally similar yet aesthetically distinct, inter-
  > weave contrapuntally through an elaborate improvisation.* Available at
  > *https://music.apple.com/us/album/jarabi/1209563317?i=1209563817*

Once students have opened their ears to the multitude of ways musicians might interpret a standard such as "Jarabi," the creative process may truly begin to take shape. For this particular teaching episode, students will use pitched percussion instruments such as xylophones, metallophones, or Zimarimbas to perform the *kumbengo*, which will serve as the basis for the students' improvisation. Like in previous episodes, it would be reasonable to expect that departments within the school or department of music (likely the percussion, music education, or ethnomusicology departments) would have access to these instruments for temporary loan. If not, creative substitutes can also be utilized, including students' primary instruments or iPads and other technological options. Because "Jarabi" has served as a creative palette for countless musicians across many genres, Episode 5.4 likewise explores the creative potentials of an intercultural approach and does not seek to remain purely Malian in character. For the sake of clarity, the activity outlined in the episode will extensively use the AfroCubism recording as a guide for beginning improvisation, particularly because it highlights the intercultural nature of a composition that blends both Western African and Afro-Caribbean styles. However, students might choose any version of the tune upon which to base their creation, or perhaps even pursue a version that is entirely independent of any previous models.

Episode 5.4: Improvising with "Jarabi" (Mali)

Specific Use: Undergraduate introductory-level world music survey course

Materials:

* Various recordings of "Jarabi" (see "Reinterpreting ' "Jarabi'" box)
* Xylophones, metallophones, or Zimarimbas, or other pitched instruments

Setup:

* 3 instrumental sections:
  (1) bass instruments, (2) alto and/or soprano instruments, (3) soloists (mixture of alto/soprano instruments), all fitted with natural bars (C, D, E, F, G, A)

Procedure:

1. In small groups or as a full class, use the box "Reinterpreting 'Jarabi'" to conduct an analysis of various versions of the song with different artists, genres/styles, instrumentations, and interpretations. Discuss what was unique and similar about each recording, and begin sharing possible ideas for how a class creation of "Jarabi" might sound.

2. Discuss: "What each of these versions share in common is the three-pitch baseline, which functions as the music's *kumbengo*. First, we need to learn this basic *kumbengo* on our instruments." Using the bass bars (or bass xylophones/metallophones/Zimarimbas; hereafter referred to as xylophones only), guide students toward playing this part by rote (see Figure 5.2).

   Note: Obviously, only a handful of students will be able to play these instruments at a given time. However, for the sake of learning the patterns, students can play the figure on any xylophone or "air play" the shape of the pattern on their laps or desktop while chanting the pitches aloud.

3. "If we refer to some of the other recordings of 'Jarabi,' we would hear more harmonic elements of the *kumbengo*. For example, in AfroCubism's version, a *balafon* (West African xylophone) plays a repeated figure above the bass line. Since we have xylophones here with us today, let's start with learning this figure to add to the bass line. Later, we can create a new accompaniment that might come to us as we're exploring other possibilities." See Figure 5.3a–c for three options with performing this accompaniment, depending on the desired level of challenge.

4. "Now, let's improvise! Let's recall from our Enactive Listening phase that the pitch "D" is our 'home,' so we can improvise using any of the natural (or 'white-note') pitches, as long as our ideas more or less return back to D."

   Note: Technically, this tune utilizes the pitches of the D Dorian scale, but it is not necessary to define the scale as such since this term would not be used in the context of griots teaching or learning this tune.

5. With or without the recording (preferred without if students can maintain the *kumbengo* on their own), encourage students on instruments to begin improvising collectively at first, while other students loop the complete *kumbengo*.

   Note: By asking students to improvise collectively first, they are able to first practice and experiment with various ideas without social pressures or expectations (which is often a primary fear among students when asked to improvise).

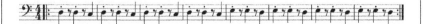

Figure 5.2   Bass line of "Jarabi"

a. Simple accompaniment in two parts (Level 1)

b. Full accompaniment in three parts (Level 2)

c. Full accompaniment in two parts (Level 3)

Figure 5.3a–c   Possible accompaniment patterns (based on AfroCubism's version of "Jarabi")

6. After a moment, cue students to improvise individually (without stopping the *kumbengo*). Encourage students to maintain the lyrical integrity of the song by playing simple yet expressive melodic ideas (rather than attempting to play randomly or busily). Alternatively, encourage students to focus on fewer pitches and play with more attention toward creating an interesting rhythm.

    Note: Students can raise their mallets in the air to indicate an interest in attempting a solo so that the instructor chooses willing students rather than "cold calling" students who may be momentarily uncomfortable with the task.

7. Be sure to rotate students so everyone has an opportunity to improvise and/ or perform the *kumbengo* parts.

a. Diabaté's original melodic theme to "Jarabi"

b. Interlude featured in AfroCubism's "Jarabi"

Figure 5.4a–b   Possible interlude cues or backgrounds for soloists

8.   The main melody (Figure 5.4a), which likely would have been learned during the Engaged and Enactive Listening dimensions, can be utilized as a background or cueing interlude for the next soloist to begin improvising. To include backgrounds or soloing cues, students may choose from several possible options:

(a)   Accompaniment instruments perform Diabaté's original melodic theme (Figure 5.4a) as a background or cue behind soloist (bass line continues);

(b)   All instruments perform a pre-composed interlude in unison. For example, borrowing one of the themes used in another recording, such as AfroCubism's interlude (Figure 5.4b);

(c)   Students can compose a new background or interlude cue entirely.

Arranging Folk Songs

When it comes to creating original music, composition and improvisation are usually thought to be the primary options for musicians. However, improvisation may at times present too complex a challenge for students who are expected to spontaneously invent new ideas within a relatively unfamiliar musical idiom. At the same time, a musical selection may not lend itself appropriately to original composition given, for example, because of the import or sanctity of the music to that musical culture. Alternatively, arranging is an activity in which musicians are tasked with reconceptualizing a preexisting work through creative changes to the instrumentation, harmonization, melodic presentation, structure, timbre, tempo, style, or other musical component. Arranging music is very common practice in musical genres such as jazz and Trinidadian steelpan music and is decidedly different from orchestration, which typically seeks to maintain the integrity of the original composition rather than impose fresh creative choices on the work.

"La Mariposa" is a Bolivian folk song that features the *quena*, an Andean flute made of wood or cane, and the *charango*, a small guitar-like instrument traditionally made from an armadillo shell with five courses strings. "La Mariposa" sings of the *morenada*, a traditional Bolivian dance also known as the "Dance of the Black Slaves," which is believed to date back to a time when enslaved Africans were brought to Bolivia to work in the mines of Potosí. In Episode 5.5, students will practice the craft of arranging with this well-known Bolivian folk song. After learning to perform the song with instruments and voices, and perhaps learning to perform the *morenada* dance during the Engaged and Enactive listening dimensions, students will work in small groups to develop and present a fresh arrangement of the folk song using any combination of instruments and voices at their disposal.

Episode 5.5: Arranging "La Mariposa" (Bolivia)

Specific Use: Undergraduate introductory-level world music survey course

Materials:

- "La Mariposa (The Butterfly)," El Grupo Jatari, Monitor Records
- Assorted instruments of instructor's and students' choice

Procedure:

1. "Let's listen to the entire recording of 'La Mariposa' and figure out how El Grupo Jatari presented this folk song in terms of instruments, voices, form, and other musical features."

2. Play entire track.

3. Break down the entire recording with students, as follows:

   Song Form, first time (AABBB'B')

   A: Solo quena *(Andean flute);* charangos *(guitar-like instruments) play stop-time pattern*

   A: Quena *with* charangos *playing in time*

   B: Quena *with different* charango *strumming pattern; ululating voice*

   B: Quena *with same* charango *pattern; no ululation*

   B': Quena *with same* charango *pattern; rhythmic whistling*

   B': Quena *with same* charango *pattern; no whistling*

   Second time (AABBB'B')

   A: Solo quena *with* charangos *playing in time; some ululating voice*

   A: Quena *with* charangos *playing in time; some rhythmic chant*

   B: Voices singing lyrics (no quena*); same* charango *strumming pattern as first time*

B: Same

B': Voices singing lyrics (no quena*) with clapping and stomping*

B': Same

Third time (A only, looping)

A: Quena *and voices singing neutral syllable "lai"; same* charangos *pattern; tempo increases as music fades*)

4. Manually create small groups of 6–8 students, seeking to include different levels of experience and representation of primary instruments (for those who play one) within each group. Provide a selection of instruments, pending availability: guitars, ukuleles, xylophones (or other chordophones/idiophones), etc.

5. Acting as a facilitator, have each group come up with their own arrangement of "La Mariposa" using any combination of instruments and/or voice. Each arrangement should incorporate their unique choices about the style, harmony, melody, form, dance (using the original *morenada* dance) and so on.

6. Have each group perform their arrangements for the class.

Employing App-Based Technology

Until now, the majority of musical experiences outlined throughout this book have asked students to participate through singing, playing an instrument, or joining in a movement or dance. The underlying understanding here, as discussed in Chapter 3, is that any experiences using instruments will likely require approximations or instrumental facsimiles: ukuleles for *cuatros*, guitars and wind instruments for *ouds* and *santūrs*, xylophones and chordophones for *koras*, and the like. Taking an "approximation" approach certainly provides a manageable entry point for students to readily engage in musical experiences without being burdened with the near-impossible task of obtaining a wide variety of "authentic" instruments. Nonetheless, students employing this approach inevitably must forego the experience of creating the unique musical timbres for themselves or experiencing the tactile realities of playing the original instruments. Alternatively, another possibility might be to place a priority on re-creating the authentic *sounds* of the original instruments in real-time using technological substitutes such as mobile apps. Understandably, this would come at the expense of more true-to-life human interactions with instruments (which is gained, albeit imperfectly, with instrumental substitutes). In other words, with the latter focus, students still may not be able to experience the precise feeling that comes with playing these world instruments, but they would at least appreciate the sensation of creating music that closely resembles the genuine sounds from that culture.

Arguably, deciding between these approaches becomes a matter of balance between *timbral* imperfection and *experiential* imperfection. After all, there might be certain musical cultures in which the timbres of certain instruments are deemed so central to the musical culture that to replace them with substitutes would be to lose the very essence of that tradition—the shimmering resonance of a *gamelan angklung* ensemble or the timbre of a Mongolian *morin khuur* (horsehead fiddle), for example. It is in these cases that technological alternatives might reasonably supplement a more holistic experience. Ultimately, it is the instructor's role to decide, through research and conversations with culture bearers, what approaches and activities one should pursue with particular musical practices.

Here, we focus on one specific technological tool that could provide stimulating experiences for students: the inclusion of tablet- and app-based technology in the music classroom. It can be reasonably expected that app-based learning tools would be at many instructors' disposal, even if they may not have previously considered such possibilities before. Indeed, many colleges and universities now offer students iPads or tablets as part of their enrollment, and other institutions have invested in classroom sets of tablets that may be reserved and rented from the library on a per-use basis. Even if these options are not offered to students or faculty, instructors might require students to download one or more mobile apps to their personal devices (iPads, iPhones, Androids) given the present ubiquity of students with smart phones. (However, alternative options should be made available for students who do not own smart phones to avoid propagating social divisions of "haves" and "have nots" in the classroom. While instructors should certainly be sensitive of students' possible lack of affordability or access, they should nonetheless explore possible creative modifications.) With a tablet or mobile device, most relevant world music instrument apps can be downloaded free of charge.

Composing With Digital *Pipa*

This section somewhat ironically advocates for the use of app-based technology with an instrument that considerably predates modern technology: the Chinese *pipa*. Granted, it might seem strange to apply a 21st century technology to substitute a 2nd century traditional instrument, especially as most musicians think about the benefits of such technologies for more modern means, such as sampling, beat creation, and recording. Nonetheless, influential app-based technologies such as Apple's GarageBand have come to recognize the potentials in offering hands-on experiences with world music instruments as well.

For the sake of clarity, we will discuss these pedagogical possibilities with respect to one particular mobile app, Apple's GarageBand for iOS, although this is certainly not the only app that offers world instrument samples. In addition to offering various instrumental effects across a variety of keyboard sounds, guitar/bass sounds, and drum sounds, the app now offers an entirely new category of world music instruments (see Figure 5.5a). At the time of this writing, the currently offered "world" music instruments all curiously come from Asian cultures, but it might be reasonable to expect that this collection will continue to grow over time. Some of these instrument samples are automatically included while others can be downloaded from the sound library within the iOS app (at no charge). Users can currently access the following instruments: Chinese *pipa*, *erhu*, and *guzheng*, and Japanese *koto* and *taiko*. Episode 5.6 features a compositional exercise using the Chinese *pipa*.

As one can imagine, GarageBand's *pipa* interface is far from authentic (Figure 5.5b), given the size of an actual *pipa* in relation to the size of a tablet or mobile screen. As such, it is imperative for any app-based activities such as these to be reinforced with videos, images, and demonstrations of the "true" instruments. However, the interface is quite realistic and comprehensive in terms of the offered

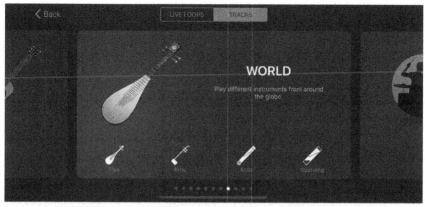

a. Apple GarageBand world music instruments (iOS)

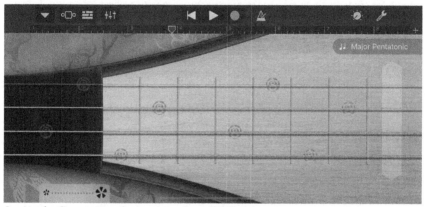

b. Apple GarageBand *pipa* interface (iOS)

Figure 5.5a–b   Apple GarageBand world music instruments and *pipa* interface

effects and techniques that *pipa* players would truly perform—including plucking (*tan* and *tiao*), harmonizing (*fen*), tremolo (*sao* and *fu*), string bending, portamento, and so on. Finally, when selecting an instrument such as the *pipa* or *guzheng*, the digital fretboard is automatically set to the major pentatonic scale (which may reflect a stereotypical view of Chinese music) although this setting can be easily changed. However, this setting does simplify the interface considerably, allowing students to experiment with the sounds of the *pipa* using an agreeable series of pitches (rather than providing the actual fretboard with its full division of semitones). Additionally, the interface can be switched from playing individual notes to complete chords (and choosing the "autoplay" option will automatically create a harmonic accompaniment).

To prepare students for the compositional activity that will take place in Episode 5.6, allow sufficient time for students to freely navigate the app on their tablets or mobile devices. They should be comfortable with changing the key, scale type, and chords/notes selection and should understand how to perform various effects on the instrument. Once they have gained familiarity with using the app and can explicitly recognize the ways in which the technological substitute differs from the "true" instrument, they are ready to use the app to create their own compositions based on Chinese classical music.

"Flute and Drum at Sunset" is a traditional Chinese song, performed here by solo *pipa* to depict a soothing landscape of the Xunyang river (part of the Yangtze River). The piece was adapted from the poem "The Moonlit Night on a Flowered Spring River." Before diving into this musical experience, students should first come to recognize the reverential ways in which music has traditionally been treated in Chinese society. Especially from the view of the philosopher Confucius (551 BC–479 BC), music (*yue*) is central to the pursuit of human virtue, and anyone partaking in musical activities should approach them with sincerity (*chang*), benevolence (*ren*), and kindness (*shan*). To make music with others is to express one's common humanity with others, and so musical participation becomes a highly revered social act in this context. Central to the integrity of a composition activity with Chinese music, therefore, is for students to engage in the creative process with respect, open-mindedness, humility, and benevolence toward one another. For a detailed discussion about the nature of music teaching and learning from a Chinese perspective, see Fung's (2018) *A Way of Music Education: Classic Chinese Wisdoms*.

Episode 5.6: Composing *Pipa* Music (China)

Specific Use: Undergraduate introductory-level world music survey course

Materials:

- "Flute and Drum at Sunset," Noble Band, *Best of Chinese Traditional Musical, Vol. 5* (Noble Music Co.)
- iPads/iPhones or other tablets/mobile devices

Procedure:

1. On a projector, display the artwork *Pipa Player at the Bank of Xunyang River* (Figure 5.6). Available at https://g.co/arts/5NP8zkHS4eM7CpZc9.

2. "This artwork is called *Pipa Player at the Bank of Xunyang River*. Can you find the *pipa* player in this work as you listen to the full track? Once you do, try to picture the imagery she is trying to portray through this song."

   Note: A high-resolution display of the artwork will likely be necessary for students to see the pipa player.

   Answer: The *pipa* player is located on the second, smaller boat in the bottom, left part of the image. She is almost fully obscured by the trees and the riverbank.

   Discuss: "Isn't it interesting that this artwork is titled after a *pipa* player, yet she is barely visible in the image? Why do you think this might be?"

Figure 5.6 *Pipa Player at the Bank of Xunyang River* (Suzhou embroidery)

3. Listen to the full track [0:00–6:03] and have students jot down the ways in which they might depict a similar landscape of the Xunyang River.

4. Using the *pipa* interface on Apple's GarageBand for iPad or iPhone (or alternative app), have students set the key to "E" and the scale to "minor pentatonic."

5. In small groups, have students create original compositions for *pipa* using the same imagery as "Flute and Drum at Sunset" (the Xunyang River). As a group, students may choose to write a solo *pipa* piece, compose for a polyphonic ensemble of *pipas*, or include other Chinese instruments such as the *erhu* and *guzheng*. The instructor should act as facilitator throughout, allowing students to create their works in an open-ended, constructive manner.

6. Have groups discuss/present their compositions and perform them for the class.

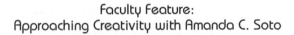

Faculty Feature:
Approaching Creativity with Amanda C. Soto

Figure 5.1a Amanda C. Soto

> *"When students have an understanding of what they're playing and where it came from, it's going to mean something different to them, and their playing relationship is going to change. I think that's a pretty powerful thing."*

Amanda C. Soto is Associate Professor of Music Education at Texas State University, where she embodies the interdisciplinary spirit between the fields of music education and ethnomusicology through her teaching and research. At Texas State, she teaches undergraduate courses in music teacher preparation and a specialized World Music Pedagogy course for both undergraduates and graduate students, and she is an instructor for the Smithsonian Folkways World Music Pedagogy Certification Course at the University of Washington in Seattle. Beyond her work with WMP, her research interests include children's musical culture and identity, technology in music education, social justice, and

Mexican and Mexican American music and culture. Her work has been published in the fields of both ethnomusicology and music education.

Q: How have you incorporated technology into your approach to teaching world music?

A: I had written a grant several years ago to get iPads so we could teach world music through technology. I got a classroom set of iPads and created an entire unit, which was probably about a third of the course, where we learned to use technology to teach world music and to apply it to the process of World Music Pedagogy.

There was a series of classes where we started using several of the mobile apps to play certain instruments, like *gamelan*, steel pan, *angklung*, Latin percussion, Chinese *guzheng*, Middle Eastern drums, and so on. We worked with various ways of interacting with the apps on the iPads, too. Sometimes, the apps functioned as an actual instrument, and sometimes the app drew us into listening to different drum patterns for certain musical styles. I've been featuring apps with the students for about three years now, and it's been really fun and exciting.

Q: What is your rationale for using technology such as iPads to teach world music?

A: Most music education departments have access to a classroom set of instruments such as xylophones, metallophones, recorders, and hand percussion. So, when teaching world music in my music education classes, I'll use those instruments to move us beyond the listening and into musical participation. We'll play a *gamelan* piece on the xylophones and metallophones. We manage to get a sense of the musical form of the piece by playing it, but students are not really experiencing the actual timbres of the *gamelan* instruments (nor do they learn the damping techniques of *gamelan* instruments or the full effect of the interlocking drum rhythms and patterns). On the other hand, the iPad and some of the mobile apps allow for opportunities to perform world music with the sound of timbres that are close to the sound of real instruments. Sometimes, we can listen to a selection and progress to the iPads for fully playing the selection. If students move beyond performing the selection they've learned from the recording to the point of Creating World Music, the sounds produced on technology like iPads can stimulate their creative flow and motivate them to compose or improvise. The sounds they produce can often sound a little bit more substantial than playing on classroom instruments.

Now, will technology ever replace real instruments? Of course not. Even though the iPad *is* a real instrument, it's not *the* instrument that is featured on the recording of music from Ghana, or Mexico, or Japan. So, you have to figure out what your goals are for teaching a certain musical style or selection, or a certain instrument, and how you're going to use the technology. Because all the apps out there have different purposes and different ways that students will interact with them. You've got to make that judgment call to see what would be most appropriate for your goal. Sometimes, we might just listen to the timbre and figure out the different tones on the instrument, and then with those tones we can create something else. But of course we recognize that playing the music on the iPad is not how the instrument is played (the instruments are far smaller on an iPad than in a real *gamelan*).

You can get a set of iPads for a reasonable price, or you can borrow them. iPads are relatively inexpensive, accessible, and portable, and you don't have to pay $10,000 or $15,000 for a steelpan ensemble, for example. Students can take some satisfaction in playing many styles of world music on iPads.

Q: Have you been able to explore the Creating World Music dimension in your teaching? What has that looked like?
A: Yes, I have, and it was awesome! We had three sessions with *gamelan*, listening to a *gamelan* selection, then working what we heard onto classroom xylophones. Then, Gordon Jones, the *gamelan* specialist at Texas State, took us into the dimension of Integrating World Music, and then we learned to play some patterns on xylophones. We talked about the cycle of the music, and then we went to the *gamelan* room and transferred what they had played on classroom xylophones onto actual *gamelan* instruments. Once students understood the way the parts all work together, they made the transfer on to the *gamelan*. We returned to the classroom to the xylophones, played the *gamelan* we had started there, and then I challenged the students to create a new piece based on the underlying musical patterns they had learned from the recording and had played. So, about 20 minutes later, the students were ready to play their newly created composition (still in the style of the original work), worked out democratically and rehearsed until it coalesced. They were really proud of themselves! It was a really beautiful representation of WMP. The dimension of Creating World Music dimension can take a while and it's challenging if it's not sequenced well or the experiences aren't put into context.

Q: And how well would you say the students understood the structures and concepts of the music while they were creating?
A: At the very end, they understood the logical structures of *gamelan* music, to the point that they had gone from listening to playing to creating a new musical work all together. They did it all by themselves, and they were surprised that they moved from something that was really challenging and felt so foreign to something that they actually *understood* and were really eager to learn more about and participate in.

Q: Has using World Music Pedagogy affected the way you teach generally?
A: I really think World Music Pedagogy is appropriate for teaching *in general*, and I think that the components (of listening, participating, performing, creating, and integrating) can be applied to teaching *any* music. If we throw out the 'world' and just keep 'music,' it's a pedagogical sequence that makes sense. That's one of the issues I raise to my students, suggesting that they consider that whether

they're teaching orchestra, or band, or other performance ensembles or classes, the WMP dimensions are workable for getting more deeply into the music, for listening more, for bringing contextual and cultural meaning to the music. The result is that the music then has more meaning and is much more powerful.

And when students have a thorough understanding of the music, by listening repeatedly, by learning to play it by ear, by knowing what the music signifies in the culture, it's going to mean something different to them than if they're playing an arrangement of some world music genre from notation, and that's a powerful thing.

Interesting, too, is that I recently asked my music education students to evaluate the different pedagogies, like Orff, Kodály, Dalcroze, and World Music Pedagogy, through the lens of Culturally Responsive Teaching (CRT), a pedagogical approach that recognizes the importance of including students' cultural references in all aspects of learning. And of all of the pedagogies, World Music Pedagogy was one of the best for addressing a lot of the issues relevant to CRT, such as the importance of students' cultures and identities.

The Pinnacle of Artistic Expression

When we have found the capacity to tap into the depths of our artistic being, doing so through the mores and customs of a once-unfamiliar musical world, creating music that is fresh, unique, and possibly heard never before, then we have arguably found ourselves at a pinnacle of artistic creation. We need not compose symphonies, suites, and rhapsodies to feel legitimized in our pursuits of self-expression. We need not maintain impenetrable walls between one musical culture and another. We need only find ourselves so engrossed in and captivated by our musical excursions that we both can and *must* express ourselves through these once-distant artistic expressions. When we do so, we come to understand that the music, the culture, and the people whom it represents are not static and ageless, but dynamic and animate.

Glossary

App-based technology: With the recent popularity of smartphones and other digital devices have come a vast array of software applications, commonly known as "apps," that serve convenient functions, many of which are specifically designed for music-related tasks.

Creating World Music: The fourth dimension of the WMP process. The invention by students of new music in the style of a musical model through composition, improvisation, songwriting, and extending a piece beyond what is represented on the recorded model.

***Décima*:** A ten-line stanza of improvised poetry utilized in folk music traditions throughout Latin America. As *decimilla*, these become six-syllable phrases sung in Spanish language, in a semi-improvised style as part of *jíbaro* music tradition.

Griot: Also known as a *jali*, the *griot* is a form of hereditary musicians common across West Africa (especially Mali, The Gambia, and neighboring states). Many preserve local history in their songs, which are often performed on voice to the accompaniment of the *kora*.

Lyrical composition: In WMP, lyrical composition is an approach to Creating World Music that consists of writing new lyrics to accompany the melody of a preexisting piece.

Motivic composition: In WMP, motivic composition consists of the construction of new melodic variations loosely based on the central motif at the root of a song.

Notes

1. Again, while AlHaj likely wrote this piece by ear, it might be preferable for students to write their compositions down using Western (or other, even "invented") notation so that it can be recalled and performed later in the class.
2. This image is licensed under the Creative Commons Share-Alike 2.0 Generic License. https://commons.wikimedia.org/wiki/File:Toumani_Diabaté.jpg.

References

Allsup, R. E. (2016). *Remixing the classroom: Toward an open philosophy of music education*. Indiana University Press.

Fung, C. V. (2018). *A way of music education: Classic Chinese wisdoms*. Oxford University Press.

Gould, C. S., & Keaton, K. (2000). The essential role in music performance. *The Journal of Aesthetics and Art Criticism, 58*(2), 143–148. https://doi.org/10.2307/432093

Hughes, D. W. (2004). "When can we improvise?": The place of creativity in academic world music performance. In T. Solís (Ed.), *Performing ethnomusicology: Teaching and representation in world music ensembles* (pp. 261–282). University of California Press.

Nettl, B. (1974). Thoughts on improvisation: A comparative approach. *The Musical Quarterly, 60*(1), 1–19. https://www.jstor.org/stable/741663

Nettl, B. (1996). Ideas about music and musical thought: Ethnomusicological perspectives *Journal of Aesthetic Education, 30*(2), 173–187. https://doi.org/10.2307/3333198

Sarath, E. W., Myers, D. E., & Campbell, P. S. (Eds.). (2017). *Redefining music studies in an age of change: Creativity, diversity, and integration*. Routledge.

Wade, B. N. (2012). *Thinking musically: Experiencing music, expressing culture* (2nd ed.). Oxford University Press.

Listening Links

"Dulce Sueño Mío," Ecos de Borinquen, Smithsonian Folkways Recordings. A Puerto Rican *jíbaro* (folk music) featuring a *trovador*, two *cuatros*, guitar, *guiro*, and bongos and using a *decimilla* (10 lines, 6 syllables) poetic song structure. https://folkways. si.edu/ecos-de-borinquen/dulce-sueno-mio-sweet-dream-of-mine/latin-world/music/ track/smithsonian

"E Maru Rahi," Royal Tahitian Dance Company, Smithsonian Folkways Recordings. A Tahitian song about three brothers, one of whom died while diving for mother-of-pearl in the lagoon of Takaroa in the Tuamotu Islands. https://folkways.si.edu/royal-tahitian-dance-company/e-maru-rahi/world/music/track/smithsonian

"Flute and Drum at Sunset," Noble Band, Noble Music Co. Solo piece for Chinese *pipa* (lute) depicting the landscape of the Xunyang river (part of the Yangtze River). https://music.apple.com/us/album/flute-and-drum-at-sunset-pipa-instrumental/11806 71917?i=1180672084

"Jarabi," Toumani Diabaté, Hannibal Records. A popular Malian *kora* love song that has been widely recorded by artists spanning multiple genres and categories. https://music.apple.com/us/album/jarabi/1325146150?i=1325146977

"La Mariposa (The Butterfly)," El Grupo Jatari, Monitor Records. A Bolivian folk song about a dance called the *morenada*, featuring the *quena* (Andean wooden flute) and *charango* (small guitar-like instrument). https://folkways.si.edu/el-grupo-jatari/la-mariposa-the-butterfly/latin-world/music/track/smithsonian

"Time to Have Fun," Rahim AlHaj, Smithsonian Folkways Recordings. An upbeat *khaliji* dance-style piece featuring *oud* (Iraqi lute), *santūr* (Iranian dulcimer), and percussion. https://folkways.si.edu/rahim-alhaj/time-to-have-fun

6

Integrating World Music

"As citizens of the world, we know that musical experiences, musical exchanges, have often been in the vanguard of intercultural understanding."
—Bruno Nettl, 2010, p. 7

"Where's Gabriela?" Dr. Parroco asked. The small class of second- and third-year music majors looked around at each other, shrugging. No one had seen her lately, they said. Noah, an indifferent student in the back of the room, muttered something about never being able to understand Gabriela when she spoke. Dr. Parroco ignored the microaggression momentarily, instinctively wanting to come to the defense of Gabriela's soft and kind nature. Gabriela's English had improved by leaps and bounds since she'd begun her university studies, but her thick accent was noticeable still seven years after her family's move north from Mexico to Texas. Gabriela seemed wedged between two worlds, yet felt a full resident of neither. Dr. Parroco could see that pride in her rich Mexican heritage pulled Gabriela in one direction, while an inescapable feeling of being Othered tugged her the other way. Lost in reverie for an instant, Dr. Parroco then turned to the content of her "World Music Cultures" course session, powering on the projector as the music of Pete Seeger filled the room. She announced the topic: "Protest Songs as Markers of Social Movements."

The answer to the question of Gabriela's whereabouts became known later that afternoon. Along with two other student DREAMers—undocumented children of immigrants who were brought to the U.S. as minors—Gabriela was unable to provide sufficient documentation of her conditional permanent residence status, and in the swiftness of a surprise raid in her neighborhood early Sunday morning, she was detained along with her mother and brother.

In the next class meeting, Dr. Parroco channeled her own sadness and frustration through music, using Mr. Seeger's words as a substitute for her own. A simple banjo accompaniment played behind Seeger's words: "You won't have your names when you ride the big airplane. And all they will call you will be 'deportees.'" Dr. Parroco shared the origins for Seeger's rendition of "Deportees," also called "Plane Wreck at Los Gatos" after a 1948 plane crash near Los Gatos Canyon, California. Woody Guthrie had written the song in response to his view of the racist mistreatment of the 32 deceased passengers, 28 of whom were migrant workers who were being deported back to Mexico. Dr. Parroco offered contextualization of the migration of farm laborers from Mexico to the U.S. and of the bracero program that had been initiated in the 1940s to provide for decent living conditions of migrant workers. She clarified that the individuals who had died in the crash were on their way back home to Mexico at the close of their agreed-upon work, but that Guthrie's concern was that there was no respectful recognition of them as individuals, with individual names, in the national news reports on the crash. One especially eloquent student exclaimed, "We should think of this music as both a time capsule and a tool for transformation to come. Given the current circumstances, maybe this song could live in both the past and the present."

And so, the old protest song was given new life when only a week later the 12 students of the world music course found themselves standing on the steps of the city's detention facility along with a few hundred other students and the local news media. Noah, once disinterested in the back of the classroom, now stood at the front of the crowd holding a banjo in his arms and strumming the introduction to "Deportees," calling for other protesters to sing along in unison. Dr. Parroco proudly stepped up next to Noah, joining the singing, and marveling over the matter of the revival by her student of an old Woody Guthrie song. Her students had taken on an integrated study of the song, its lyrics, and the incident that had inspired it. They had joined their new understanding with a realization of Gabriela's plight, and they had initiated their need to be heard and to convert their sense of injustice to social action. In taking a stand on social justice, they had found an immediate relevance of a world music course session that was making its way far beyond the sonic analysis of a song's melodic structure.

Integration and Music

How might an understanding of the world's musical cultures be enhanced through interdisciplinary studies? How might faculty facilitate student learning through the integration into their world music courses a spread of themes that are relevant to the music, musicians, and musical cultures? From an ethnomusicological standpoint, music is best understood as it relates to culture in all its many dimensions. Within university settings, music has been shaped into a discrete subject for specialized musical study, nearly as if music is not inextricably connected to many other aspects of cultural life. From an ethnomusicological standpoint, however, context is critical in knowing music, as are the backstories of musicians and their music. Calls for social justice also raise the reality of music as more than sound alone but also linked to the cultural identities of those whose lives are wrapped into the origin and ownership of the music. Chapter 6 continues the vision of World Music Pedagogy to include numerous possibilities for the integration of information and insights about featured musical cultures within lecture courses, lecture-discussion capstone courses, seminars, and performance ensembles.

The WMP approach is thus grounded in the belief that music is most fully learned when it is contextualized and studied from an interdisciplinary perspective. Music consists of much more than merely attractive sounds, since it expresses the most profound of human ideas and is used as a prominent vehicle to create meaning in human life. Songs are vehicles that reflect people's lives, their behaviors and values. At the tertiary level, the multidimensional contexts and meanings of music are greatly enhanced through integration with other disciplines and fields. Suggestions for working with on-campus resources and academic disciplines such as anthropology, sociology, the visual and media arts, international studies, and gender and sexuality studies are noted, as well as ways that such initiatives may serve to enhance learning while also amplifying the holistic experience of a globally infused music program.

Importantly, the "Integrating World Music" dimension interweaves fluidly among the other four dimensions of World Music Pedagogy rather than existing only at the end as a curricular apex of the framework (refer back to Figure 1.1a). It is not the pinnacle, the finishing point, or the "final frontier" of the pedagogical process. Rather, the integration of topical themes should imbue all aspects of the teaching and learning process, from start to finish. By sprinkling this dimension throughout the WMP process, instructors maintain the identity of the approach as rooted in deep listening and participatory learning, while also reminding students of the music's source, its cultural context, and the broader meanings and practices with which it is associated.

An organic way of thinking about the contexts of musical traditions from an interdisciplinary perspective is provided by the *Cultural Prism Model* proposed by Patricia Shehan Campbell (2004). The following is a depiction of how it applies to specific music examples relevant to higher education. Figure 6.1 illustrates the kinds of questions that may be categorized in terms of this model.

Musical Beginnings: *Who created the music? When and where was it created? How old was the creator when the piece was created? What inspired the creation of the piece? Who first performed it? How was it performed: As music with expectations for quiet listening, dancing, marching, or background to social conversations?*

Musical Continuities: *Who performs it now? What qualifications do performers of the music have? Does it always sound the same, or is there flexibility within the tradition to personally interpret it, vary it, transform it? Are there recordings of the piece? Who teaches it? How is it learned? How do audiences respond to the music? Are there social norms for these responses?*

Musical Meanings: *Are there particular social or cultural themes to the music? What use or function does it fulfill? Do historical and contemporary performances of it demonstrate different meanings? Do particular groups of people, as defined by age, gender, ethnicity, religion, socioeconomic status, nation, or religion, identify with this music?*

Figure 6.1 Questions from Campbell's Cultural Prism Model (Adapted from Campbell, 2004).

Historical knowledge is necessary in order to address the first component, *musical beginnings*. Consideration of the functions of music in society is useful for addressing the categories of musical "continuities" (or *actions* in contemporary life) and "meanings" (*interpretations*). Classroom discussions of these questions can also be developed in relation to Alan P. Merriam's (1964) classic "Ten Functions of Music" that music fulfills within society: (1) emotional expression, (2) aesthetic enjoyment, (3) entertainment, (4) communication, (5) symbolic representation, (6) physical response, (7) enforcing conformity to social norms, (8) validation of social institutions and religious rituals, (9) contribution to the continuity and stability of culture, and (10) contribution to the integration of society. More recently, Martin Clayton (2016) proposed four functions of music in cultures: (1) regulation of an individual's emotional, cognitive or physiological state, (2) mediation between self and other, (3) symbolic representation, and (4) coordination of action.

In order to have a robust understanding of music of the world's cultures, students do well to develop *interdisciplinary* understandings of music that result from their professor's integration of cultural matters on the people, their histories, and their local conditions. This is one of the ultimate objectives of World Music Pedagogy, stemming partly from its ethnomusicological underpinnings, and is easily fitted alongside student experiences in listening, performing, and creating music. Well-planned activities of Integrating World Music that require students to interact with questions of musicians and their cultural circumstances are important, as straight-ahead lectures might instead lead students to "zone out" rather than seek out the significance of the music for understanding a broader culture. The complexity of such activities can range from merely asking a provocative question and pausing for responses to having students debate, map out concepts, and develop their own presentations. A wider variety of pedagogical actions, including the weave of interdisciplinary understandings, is ideal for university students, in addition to lectures and textbooks.

Disciplines as Lenses for Integrating World Music

In higher education, the interdisciplinary study of music provides a wide-angle view of ideas that enhance and enrich learning. World Music Pedagogy calls attention to the balancing of closely detailed study and the further afield study of the musical work, the musicians, and the musical culture that promises enlightened meanings and interpretations. Even the natural sciences contribute to a fuller understanding of music across the world: Physics includes the subfield of acoustics, which offers important insights into ideal ways, across multiple cultures, of designing musical instruments, performance spaces, and sound recording equipment and studios. Chemistry offers important insights into which materials are suitable in instrument construction, as well as how human physiology (including brain chemistry) might be affected by music. Biology offers insights into reasons why music has been necessary to human evolution—for mother-infant interaction, language development and communication, sexual selection, and social organization. Computational science, including "big data" analytics, aids an understanding of music as it is increasingly produced, disseminated, consumed, and analyzed though the use of digital technologies.

Beyond the natural sciences, the social sciences offer a panoramic window on music's meanings in human society. Psychology contributes insights on the mechanisms of music perception and cognition, as well as on music's relationship to identity, role in social organization, and use for individual emotional regulation. Prominent sociologists in the history of that field, including Max Weber and Theodor Adorno, wrote extensively about music in social life and across social classes, which continue to be important topics among sociologists today as well. Anthropology is the social science field most strongly connected to ethnomusicology, providing insights on musical behaviors deemed important to cultural groups, with attention to cultural meaning, norms, and values. Economists also express interest in music as a component of the culture industry and offer insights on the role of music in leisure-time involvement. Additionally, political scientists have frequently examined the role of music in mass movements and as a powerful force in driving or reflecting sociopolitical change.

In the humanities, philosophy is a prominent field in which well-known scholars from as far back as Plato and Confucius (who was himself a *guqin* [plucked zither] player) have thought deeply about music for its acoustical properties and social purposes. Religion and ritual studies are relevant, too, in that much of the world's music is grounded in sacred beliefs and practices, and even secular music may brush at the edges of the moral principles that are embedded in a culture's code of beliefs. Today, music philosophy is a thriving field all its own, and philosophers are increasingly drawn to questions of music's needs, uses, benefits, and aesthetics in world cultures. The field of history has also tended to embrace music as a prominent topic, and its role in historic eras and movements has been examined by many scholars worldwide. The integration of literature into meaningful study of music is evident in the study of literary depictions of music-related stories, the culturally favored myths and morals that are portrayed in poetry, and the even the extent to which song lyrics are composed or spontaneously created in the course of performance.

Likewise, there is study of music's integration with the visual and performing arts. Music is inextricable from dance and drama (including opera and musical theater), of course, but its impact is vivid in the visual arts as well. For example, Jackson Pollock famously listened to jazz as he painted his iconic "splatter paintings," stating that jazz was "the only other creative thing happening in the country." In short, engaging with music through as many interdisciplinary lenses as possible is endlessly beneficial for gaining the most meaningful understandings of music as a global human practice.

Interdisciplinarity and the Ethnomusicological Approach

Teaching world music well compels faculty to think ethnomusicologically. This entails their taking an interdisciplinary approach to understanding human music-making as a global phenomenon. Surely, there is musical analysis to consider, with attention to cultural-specific treatment of pitch, rhythm, form, and instruments and their associated performance techniques, and yet learning music of the world's cultures is enriched and more meaningful when attention is drawn to the musical culture's historical developments, its social structures and norms, and its political and economic processes.

Along with efforts by teaching faculty in music to integrate ideas from assorted disciplines, and by individual students to delve further into cultural meanings through assignments beyond class, there is also much to gain from interdisciplinary collaboration with faculty in other departments—from A (Anthropology) to Z (Zoology). Some universities have established centers of study—for example, the centers for

African Studies, South Asian Studies, Indigeneity, and Near Eastern Studies. While there's much to be found online, there are also university librarians whose task it is to work with faculty and students in gaining hold of relevant material beyond familiar territory and into peripheral fields that can contribute to interdisciplinary insights. An ethnomusicological approach to the study of the world's music cultures presses the case of understanding music's cultural milieu.

Integration and World Music Pedagogy

The dimension of Integrating World Music can be best understood through further exploration of the three works that have been building, one dimension at a time, into full Learning Pathways across the chapters. In all cases, these fields of information presented here encompass geography, history, the social sciences, laboratory sciences and mathematics, world languages, as well as the visual and performing arts. Apropos to Integrating World Music is an understanding that interdisciplinary excursions are best developed in a continuous stream of small insights that appear across the sequential dimensions of Attentive Listening, Engaged Listening, Enactive Listening and Creating World Music.

Episode 6.1: "Time to Have Fun" (Iraq/Iran)
(Learning Pathway #1)

Materials: "Time to Have Fun," Rahim AlHaj Trio, Smithsonian Folkways Recordings

Geography

There are approximately two million Arab Americans, with over 215,000 immigrants from Iraq and nearly 400,000 from Iran. Students can explore for information on Iran and Iraq using the search functions on such websites as CIA World Factbook and National Geographic.

Sample discussion questions:

1. How and when were the current borders developed in the region in which Iran and Iraq are situated?

    A: 1639 Zuhab Treaty with Ottoman Turks.
2. What is the strategic importance of such countries as Djibouti, Qatar, and Kuwait in relation to the larger Gulf States?

    A: All have access to sea and oil.

History

Students can seek out information on some of the world's very earliest known musicians, many of whom lived in present-day Iraq and Syria, from the period 2300–970 BCE: Enheduanna (ca. 2300), Dada (ca. 2040 BCE), and Risiya (fl. ca. 1790 BCE). They can explore examples from the Golden Age of Islam (600–850 BCE), including Barbad (ca. 600 CE), Jamila (715 CE), Ibrahim al-Mawsili (742–804 CE), Ishaq al-Mawsili (767–850 CE), and Ziryab (ca. 790–850 CE). Ziryab was an accomplished African musician who had a profound on European music in medieval times. Students can also explore important 20th-century musicians such as Wadi al Safi, Fairuz, and Umm Kulthum.

Sample discussion questions:

1. Where do you think our knowledge of these earliest known musicians come from?

   A: Archaeology, ancient writings.

2. What was the Golden Age of Islam, how was it important for music, and how did it ultimately impact scientific development in Europe?

   A: This is the historical period spanning the 8th–13th centuries, a time of the development of robust music theory by Al Farabi, and scientific methods by such figures as Avicenna and Averroes.

3. How did music of Iraq and Iran change in the 20th century?

   A: Relevant processes include westernization, standardization, and application of technologies.

Social Sciences

Students can learn about the "Translation Movement" of the Islamic Golden Age, which enabled innovations in math and science to be introduced to Europe through translations into Arabic, and ultimately to Latin. They can further explore the contributions of Avicenna (one of the earliest known proponents of music therapy), Averroes (who reintroduced Aristotle to Europeans), and Al Farabi (one of the world's first prolific theorists of music, who had a major impact on both Middle Eastern and European thinkers of later generations).

Sample discussion question:

1. How did Avicenna, Averroes, and Al Farabi impact European science?

   A: Their works were translated into Latin, and became standard textbooks for courses in medicine, mathematics, philosophy, astronomy, and musicology when these subjects were first established at the universities of Paris and Oxford. These works inspired Roger Bacon, Leonardo of Pisa (Fibonacci), Thomas Aquinas, Johannes Kepler, Galileo Galilei, and many others.

Laboratory Sciences and Mathematics

Some of the greatest mathematicians of all time were associated with Iraq and Iran.

Students can explore this important legacy from the age of Al-Khwarizmi (ca. 780–ca. 850), to the Golden Age when Avicenna (ca. 980–ca. 1037) lived in Baghdad, to Jamshid al-Kashi (ca. 1380–1429), and eventually Maryam Mirzakhani (1977–2017), winner of the 2014 Fields Medal for achievement in mathematics.

Sample discussion question:

1. How have Iraqi and Iranian scholars contributed to the global advancement of mathematics at various points in history?

    A: Global popularization of "Arabic numerals"; invention of algebra by al-Khwarizmi; mathematical concepts directly borrowed from Arabic sources, including algorithm, average, degree, and zenith.

World Languages

Iran is home to many influential poets, particularly Mevlana (Mevlevi), known to Europeans as Rumi (1207–1273). His poems continue to be popular all across the Middle East, in Arabic, Turkish, Farsi, and other languages. The typical graduate of Iranian schools can recite hundreds of poems that were memorized as an essential part of the educational system. Select some of Rumi's poetry to explain to the class. Locate recordings, including by video, of these poems recited in the original languages (Farsi and Arabic).

Sample discussion question:

1. Can you identify and interpret some poems by Rumi, referring to both the original language and English translation?

    A: See "This Marriage," "Gone to the Unseen," and selections from Masnavi Book I.

Episode 6.2: "E Maru Rahi" (Tahiti)
(Learning Pathway #2)

Materials: "E Maru Rahi," Royal Tahitian Dance Company, Smithsonian Folkways Recordings

Geography

Students can explore for information on French Polynesia and Tahiti using the search functions on such websites as CIA World Factbook and National Geographic. Around 200,000 people live in the Society Islands, an archipelago of French Polynesia in which Tahiti is the major island.
Sample discussion question:

1. How do geography and landscape impact the materials available for construction of musical instruments, and how is this reflected in Tahiti?

    A: Tahiti's traditional instruments include *ihara* (struck bamboo percussion), the *vivo* (nose flute), and the *pu* (conch trumpet).

History

Reliable resources can aid in telling of Tahiti's "discovery" and colonization by Europeans. Tahiti has been long associated with dance, and Tahitians know that there is great beauty in how these ensembles attain unified gestures with harmonious singing and instrumental accompaniment.
Sample discussion question:

1. What factors have contributed to the evolution of an eroticized image since the earliest colonial contacts?

    A: See Captain William Bligh's Mutiny on HMS Bounty and Paul Gauguin's paintings of Tahiti.

Social Sciences

Notable industries and products associated with the island economy of Tahiti are pearls, coconut products, vanilla, and tourism. Students can locate and watch videos about pearl diving in Tahiti, then read about the hazards of the pearl diving profession. Students can search online for articles about the perils of pearl divers. They can explore, too, the place of music and dance in Tahiti's cultural tourism.
Sample discussion questions:

1. What notable risks are faced by pearl divers?

    A: Drowning, oxygen deprivation, sharks, and stingrays.

2. How can cultural tourism have both positive and negative impacts on traditional island communities?

    A: Increased income streams, commodification of both nature and culture.

Laboratory Sciences and Mathematics:

Some low-lying regions of Tahiti are no longer above sea level. Governments of the Marshall Islands (and the Maldives) have even begun seeking to negotiate options for evacuation of the human population within a few generations. For reference, students may consult the Majuro Declaration from the 44th Pacific Islands Forum summit (2013) and further developments since that time.
Sample discussion questions:

1. Is it possible to calculate how much longer each of these islands is likely to last before evacuation of the human population may become necessary under current rates of climate change?

    A: Debatable; many calculations exist, but the exercise of exploring this timely issue is the primary point rather than arriving at an absolute answer.

2. Is climate change represented in any musical examples from Tahiti or the vicinity?

    A: Yes, it is a common theme in popular songs, such as "Pate Pate" by the Polynesian band Te Vaka.

World Languages

Many words in Tahitian are similar to Māori and other Polynesian languages. The dissection of a song text can offer culture-specific insights or universal principles that are understood by people of many cultures. See the translation of "E Maru Rahi" for a launch to discussion.

E maru rahi e aue (Great tenderness and how)

ua moe to tino (lost is your body)

e ita to mata (and your eyes)

e ite faaho e (and see how that)

e ita to mata (and your eyes)

e ite faaho e (and see how that)

to'u aia here (my beloved)

o Tahiti rahi e (is tucked nearby)

Episode 6.3: "Dulce Sueño Mío" (Puerto Rico) (Learning Pathway #3)

Materials: "Dulce Sueño Mío" (Sweet Dream of Mine)," Ecos de Borinquen, Smithsonian Folkways Recordings

Geography

Students can explore for information on Puerto Rico using the search functions on such websites as PuertoRicoReport.com (welcome.topuertorico.org) and National Geographic. They may try to solve some free online quizzes (locatable via common internet search engines) such as "Do You Really Know Puerto Rico?" and "Puerto Rico History Test."

Traditionally, Puerto Rico has been famous for sugar cane and rum production. Note that today pharmaceuticals manufacturing is by far the largest specialized industry in Puerto Rico, followed by biotechnology and medical device manufacture.

Sample discussion question:

1. How is Puerto Rican rum made?

    A: Through a complex distillation process that is explained on the websites of famous rum makers.

History

Students can explore the island's past as a Spanish colony (1493–1898) and its transition to its current designation as an unincorporated U.S. territory (1898—present). The earlier Arawak and Taino indigenous populations were overtaken by the Spanish during a long colonial period (1493–1898) and the arrival of enslaved Africans. The late 19th century saw the struggle of Puerto Ricans for autonomy, and the Spanish-American War, which led to the country's establishment as an American territory and commonwealth.

Sample discussion question:

1. What were some of social and economic changes in Puerto Rico as an American territory?

    A: The island agrarian culture was rapidly developed into a modern economic society, with the sugar, tobacco, and coffee industries leading the way. Schools, hospitals, roads, and communications reflected the American influence.

Music History

Leonard Bernstein's *West Side Story* depicted the Nuyorican (Puerto Rican diaspora in U.S. mainland) community as part of its plotline, which also served as the conceptual basis for some of that well-known musical's complex rhythms. Some Puerto Rican and Nuyorican (New York-based) musicians became well-known for establishing salsa and Latin jazz styles, including Tito Puente, Willie Colon, and Tito Rodriguez (who also interacted with great Cuban and Cuban American musicians such as Celia Cruz, Perez Prado, Machito, and Xavier

Cugat), and later came such popular stars as Ricky Martin, Daddy Yankee, and Luis Fonsi. However, *jíbaro* is the traditional *folk* music of Puerto Rico's rural Hispanic population (rather than the popular style of salsa), and famous *cuatro* virtuosos include Edwin Colon Zayas and Yomo Toro.

Sample discussion question:

1. What are some of the musical subgenres and styles attributed to Puerto Rican (and Cuban) musicians since the early 20th century?

     A: Examples include salsa, cha-cha-cha, son, rhumba, and merengue.

Social Sciences

There is a difference between a U.S. state and a U.S. territory, the latter of which is Puerto Rico's current status. Referendums have indicated that the vast majority of Puerto Ricans would like the territory to become a U.S. state.

Sample discussion question:

1. What are the potential gains and challenges for Puerto Rico were it to become a U.S. state?

     A: Greater political power is given to residents of states rather than to territorial residents. The shifting of language could prove challenging, since Spanish rather than English is the preferred language of the territory.

Laboratory Sciences and Mathematics:

Puerto Rico's economy has gradually shifted from an emphasis on agricultural products to pharmaceutical production and biotechnologies. However, the region still struggles with high unemployment.

Sample discussion question:

1. How do major economic indicators—such as gross domestic product (GDP) and purchasing power parity (PPP)—of Puerto Rico compare with the wealthiest and poorest U.S. states?

     A: Puerto Rico is one of the poorest parts of the U.S., where wages are low and jobs are not available for all citizens.

World Languages:

Spanish is among the most widely spoken languages in the world. Unlike English, spelling and grammar in Spanish is relatively consistent with few exceptions to basic rules.

Sample discussion question:

1. Are there alternative ways of translating the lyrics to "Dulce Sueño Mío"? Spanish-fluent students can be called on for deciphering various interpretations and metaphors used. Note the approximate translation of the Spanish lyrics to "Dulce Sueño Mío" that can be displayed by projector (see Chapter 2).

    Dream of my life

    Why wake me up

    Closing a door

    And opening a wound

    Today in me it nests

    A world of weariness.

    And already in my plantation

    Withered a flower.

    Don't be a traitor

    Sweet dream of mine.

Interdisciplinary Knowledge and World Music Pedagogy

These additional examples offer opportunities for understanding music through selected interdisciplinary themes, namely gender equity (language/poetry), climate change (geography), autocracy and world peace (social science), and human migration (history). These themes illustrate ways in which the WMP dimension of Integrating World Music can be inserted at various times throughout the pedagogical sequence, so that students are learning aspects of the music's cultural content and meaning even as they are deeply listening and actively involved in producing the musical sound across the other pedagogical dimensions.

Interdisciplinary Theme 1: Islam, Women, and Music

Gender equity is a major issue of concern internationally, and the notion of *intersectionality* calls for reflection on how facets such as nationality and religion deeply impact attitudes and practices related to gender roles. In nations that are predominantly Muslim and commonly perceived as male-dominated, women may appear to be relegated in many social arenas. However, Episode 6.4 offers an exploration of Uzbekistan's most world-renowned singer of traditional music, Munojat Yulchieva, through a selection that reveals much about the actual diversity and expression of Islamic practices in Central Asia. While this episode demonstrates interdisciplinary understandings via Integrating World Music, this music can be experienced and studied through all five WMP dimensions (as can every selection presented within this volume).

€pisode 6.4: "Nihon €ttim" Uzbek classical *Ghazal* (Sung Poetry) (Uzbekistan)

Materials:

"Nihon Ettim" (I Concealed Myself), Munojat Yulchieva & Uzbek *maqam* ensemble, UNESCO Collection from Smithsonian Folkways Recordings

Procedure:

1. Explain that it is widely believed that Muslim-majority nations offer few opportunities for women artists, and stereotypes abound regarding women across the Middle East and in Muslim-majority countries that end with the suffix "-stan." However, as Central Asia is actually remarkably diverse, many women, including musicians, find creative ways to attain power.

2. Uzbekistan is an ancient Central Asian nation that shares borders with Afghanistan, Kazakhstan, Tajikistan, Turkmenistan, and Kyrgyzstan. It is one of the world's few doubly land-locked nations, meaning that neither Uzbekistan nor any of the nations surrounding it has access to the ocean.

3. Since becoming an independent nation in 1991, Uzbekistan has, by law, guaranteed equality of rights to women. Still, significant inequalities persist. When considered in the context of other Islamic majority nations today, there are many indications that Uzbekistan offers women more opportunities than do some peer nations. Although the vast majority of Uzbekistan's citizens are Muslim, it is a nation of great ethnic diversity, with many different minority groups.

4. On festival days in the city of Samarkand, many women dance—often without heads covered—and may even discretely sip alcohol. By day, women also drive cars in Uzbekistan and hold jobs as professors and attorneys, for instance, so the situation of Muslim women in Uzbekistan is different from that of Muslim women in, for example, Egypt or Saudi Arabia.

5. As to the featured performer, Munojat Yulchieva (b. 1960) is the most world-renowned singer of classical Uzbek traditional music, including *shash maqam*. Yulchieva is a frequent performer on Uzbek television as the most high-profile proponent of the tradition through several international tours and recordings.

6. Nihon Ettim ("I Concealed Myself") is a traditional piece of classical *ghazal*, or sung poetry, that describes extreme sorrow.

7. Discuss the meanings of the song lyrics for "Nihon Ettim (I Concealed Myself)":

Nihon Ettim

Falak subhin shom etdy
Hurshidin nihon etdi
Shafaq youngligh nihon kim
Bu hazian ku'nglumni gon etdi

I Concealed Myself (English Translation)

The sun turned its dawn into the sunset

And hid its glow

Like the hidden sunset

It turned my sad heart to blood

8. In the 50-second introduction to this music (before Yulchieva's voice enters), the ensemble establishes a slow rhythmic pulse that extends for the entire piece. The ensemble's slow groove is built on percussion and plucked strings (presumably the *doira* hand drum with a lute, either *oud* or *tar*), which is supplemented with sustained drone pitches, as well as bowed string parts featuring melismatic unison lines to support the sung melody (on *ghijak* bowed lute and *chang* dulcimer).

9. Upon entering (0:50), Yulchieva's contralto voice displays remarkable control, powerful phrasing, and timbral variations of what she calls her "Sufi tone." Yulchieva emphasizes singing the great classical works of Uzbek art music, many of which have profound lyrics based on Islamic mystic poetry.

10. For further information, students are encouraged to search online for videos containing "Munojat Yulchieva, "Sharq Taronalari," and "Shash Maqam," and also to consult the exemplary writings of ethnomusicologist Razia Sultanova on Uzbek women musicians.

Interdisciplinary Theme 2: Indigenous Peoples and the Environment

Across recent centuries, industrialization and modernization occurred in ways that were often destructive to the traditional lifestyles of Indigenous peoples worldwide. Population estimates for the number of Native Americans that inhabited North America prior to European colonization continue to vary widely (typically from 5 to 20 million), but today's populations amount to less than 1.5% of the population of the United States (including Alaska natives) and 4.9% of Canada's population. According to the UN Permanent Forum on Indigenous Issues, there are more than 370 million Indigenous people spread across 70 countries worldwide. As they explore their music, students enrolled in a world music course may wish to consult two notable international organizations for Indigenous peoples: NativeWeb (www.nativeweb.org) and First Peoples Worldwide (www.firstpeoples.org).

The following two episodes feature captivating songs that show a strong connection between Indigenous peoples and their geographic location in the natural world.

Figure 6.2   Sámi musician Mari Boine[1]

Episode 6.5 features an original song by leading Sámi (Indigenous Norway) musician Mari Boine (Figure 6.2), and Episode 6.6 presents a traditional Māori (Indigenous Aotearoa/New Zealand) song. Again, the description of elemental ideas for Integrating World Music are meant to be combined across the four sequential dimensions of World Music Pedagogy.

Episode 6.5: "Gula Gula" by Mari Boine Persen (Sámi, Lapland Norway)

Materials:

- "Gula Gula," Mari Boine Persen, Real World Records

  There are multiple versions and remixes of this song, which is sometimes subtitled "Listen to the Voices of the Foremothers." Music videos are retrievable from YouTube.

Procedure:

1. Explain that there are approximately 80,000 Sámi, the Indigenous peoples of Northern Europe, about half of whom live in Norway, and others who

live in Sweden, Finland, and Russia. Traditionally, they were nomadic people who lived in the Arctic region as reindeer herders and whose livelihoods also included fishing and fur trapping.

2. Mari Boine is widely regarded as among the most successful and influential contemporary Sámi musicians. She comes from the far north of Norway and is known for her sung expressions of experience as a member of a marginalized community that has known continuous prejudice.

3. Listen to the song (and/or watch the music video) and study the lyrics, which lament the conditions of environmental destruction worldwide, particularly as this impacts Indigenous peoples.

4. Students can copy the song lyrics and consider the meaning of images from the video.

5. Discuss with students the meanings of the song lyrics for "Gula Gula" (next).

Gula gula

Nieida, gánda

Gula máttut dál du èurvot

Manin attát eatnama duolvat

mirkkoduvvot

guoriduvvot

Gula jiena

Nieida, gánda

Gula máttaráhkuid jiena

Eana lea min buohkaid eadni

dan jos goddit ieza jápmit

Leatgo diktán ieèèat báinnot

Leatgo iešge mielde gilvvus

Gula máttut dál dus jerret

Itgo don muitte gos don vulget

Dus leat oappát

Dus leat vieljat

Lulli—ameriihka arvevuvddiin

Ruonaeatnama geadgerittuin

Itgo don muitte gos don vulget

English Translation:

Hear, hear, girl, boy!

Hear the cry of your forefathers ask:

Why you let the earth become polluted
Poisoned, exhausted?
Hear the voices, girl, boy
Hear the voices of our foremothers
The Earth is our mother
If we take her life, we die with her
Have you let yourself become stained?
Are you part of the game for yourself too?
Listen when the forefathers will ask you:
Don't you remember where you came from?
You have sisters, you have brothers,
in the jungles of South America,
in the stony shores of Greenland.
Don't you remember where you came from?

(*first stanza repeats*)

Episode 6.6: "Me He Manu Rere" ("If Only I Were a Bird") (Māori song, New Zealand)

Materials:

"Me He Manu Rere" sung by Mana Epiha on www.folksong.org.nz. "Me He Manu Rere" is retrievable on YouTube and from Folksong New Zealand website: www.folksong.org.nz/manurere/index.html

Procedure:

1. Explain that this New Zealand Māori song is often performed like a lullaby—vocally and without instrumental accompaniment. Birds are important symbols in Māori culture, which arose in a land of a wide variety of beautiful birds (but few other native animals). Pakeha (White New Zealanders) who reside in the land that the Māori call Aotearoa ("land of the long white cloud") refer to themselves as "kiwis," the name for the national (flightless) bird; the Māori generally do not use this term.

2. Students can learn pronunciation of the lyrics from the video:

   Me he manu rere ahau e,

   Kua rere ki tō moenga,

   Ki te awhi tō tinana,

Aue, aue!

E te tau, tahuri mai.

Kei te moe te tinana,

Kei te oho te wairua,

Kei te hotu te manawa,

Aue, aue!

E te tau, tahuri mai

English translation:

If only I were a bird,

I would fly to your bed

To embrace your body.

Oh, oh!

My darling, turn to me.

Although my body sleeps,

My spirit hovers near you,

And my heart beats with desire.

Oh, oh!

My darling, turn to me

3. This song is regarded as one of the most romantic in the Māori tradition, for the singer deeply longs to become a bird and fly to the beloved's bed. It has proven especially useful in teaching Māori language. See more of the use of this song on www.Maorilanguage.net.

4. Discuss the song's symbolism: What do birds and humans share in common? (Singing, nesting, a desire to fly.) What do you think birds might symbolize? (Sense of freedom, rapid movement, adventure.)

5. Note that birds have thrived for centuries in New Zealand partly because they face very few natural predators on the island nation. It follows that birds feature prominently in Māori mythology in which they are connected to spirituality. Have students search for videos of New Zealand's "tui bird" on YouTube, which sings with astounding virtuosity, alternating between hundreds of different sounds, almost like an orchestra.

6. Although the song can be sung *a cappella*, it is also often traditionally accompanied by a steel-string guitar. The simple chord sequence is repeated once for each verse:

    ‖: I I I I V^7 I I :‖

    This progression can be played in the key of G major (G/G/D7/D) or D major (D/D/A7/D).

7. Encourage students to sing as with improvised vocal harmonies, as Māori singers would do.

Interdisciplinary Theme 3: Autocracy and World Peace

Autocracy, a system of government by one person with absolutist power, has its incidence in empires and kingdoms since ancient times, and may to some extent be attributable to human nature. Autocratic leadership has arguably been the cause of many wars throughout history and has also been credited with ensuring civilization through social stability and rule of law. Autocratic power may be attributed to production of major artistic and cultural expressions, such as the pyramids of ancient Egypt and the Great Wall of China. The ancient court music of Japan, known as *gagaku*, arose at a time of Japan's strict hierarchical system of traditional governance. The music of *gagaku* is intended to evoke an atmosphere of absolute reverence toward magnificent eternal power. Today, Japan has a democratic political system with a strong appreciation of human rights and the rule of law. Historically, however, Japan was an empire with an absolutist system of hierarchical leadership, and at the pinnacle of this system was the emperor, for whom *gagaku* (court music) and *bugaku* (dance music) were traditionally performed in formal ceremonies. This culture of the emperor was continued over the centuries, although today's honoring of the emperor, while with all due respect to his royal role and to the honoring rituals, is now balanced by the principles of democracy that operate within the government.

Gagaku, as the ancient court music of Japan, is very closely associated with the emperor. Never at any point of Japan's history has *gagaku* been the music of the common people. Consequently, performances of *gagaku* are somewhat rare in Japan, much like performances of Gregorian chant in Europe. Nevertheless, the genre remains relevant, and brief excerpts of this music are frequently used today within historical dramas, whenever an ancient and powerful atmosphere might be desired. Arguably, the most immediately identifiable sound associated with *gagaku* is the *sho* (mouth organ), which produces a unique timbre much like a massive harmonica with rich and complex overtones. The music and associated dance are extremely slow and stately, and performers attend to a smooth delivery of sound over well-supported breath rhythms. In a typical *gagaku* piece, the *sho* sustains its drone tones while percussion instruments (drums and gongs) very slowly establish a rhythmic pulse and other string instruments and wind instruments play slow unison melodies. A well-selected (albeit brief) excerpt of a *gagaku* recording can readily be experienced via the four WMP dimensions, even as contextualizations are integrated throughout the days and weeks of this *gagaku* unit.

Episode 6.7: "Kuniburi no Utamai" from *Gagaku* (court music from Japan)

Materials:

"Gagaku" video on YouTube (Mainichi Productions, 2000): https://youtu.be/5OA8HFUNflk

(starting from 4:47) *[Note that this video recording is available via license on the official UNESCO YouTube channel.]*

Procedure:

1. Explain that *gagaku* is the ancient court music tradition of Japan. It is formal ritualistic music performed exclusively by men as a service to the imperial court. The main woodwind instruments of *gagaku* are the *sho* (mouth organ), *ryuteki* (transverse flute) and *hichiriki* (double-reed oboe). The string instruments include *koto* (zither) and *biwa* (lute), while the percussion instruments include the *shoko* (bronze gong) as well as both the *kakko* (small drum) and *taiko* (larger drum). Some *gagaku* pieces are accompanied by slow, formal dance movements known as *bugaku*.

2. To many Japanese, *gagaku* may be understood as a symbol of ancient Japan, in which hierarchies were very strict (e.g., elder over younger, male over female, samurai over merchant/farmer); the emperor was viewed as having absolute power.

3. Discuss the products of absolute rule in Japan and elsewhere in the world, including the beautiful ceremonial expressions such as *gagaku* and the architectural wonders of the world such as the pyramids. Additionally, consider the downside of absolutism, particularly the absence of the people's voice and the decisions by rulers to pursue aggressive acquisitions of land and power that lead to international tensions. For example, in the 20th century, Japanese emperors initiated wars with both Russia (1904–1905) and the U.S. (1941–1945). Since World War II, Japan has played an especially prominent global role in advocating reduction of nuclear weapons and in seeking avenues to international cooperation and world peace.

4. Listen to the music, both with and without the video image, and lead into discussion with these questions:

   1. What features of this music suggest it fits well into a strict and formal ritual context?

      A: *Very slow, serious, sustained drones, ritualized movements.*

   2. To what extent, would you assume, are the performers free to develop creative innovations in this style?

      A: *Not at all, strict imitation is enforced.*

   3. Does *gagaku* music permit a personalized style, including improvisation?

      A: *Traditional Japanese music, including the* gagaku, *is fixed and not improvised.*

5. Ask students to correctly identify each of the *gagaku* instruments in the video, both with and without the image displayed (by sound alone, or with visual cues).

6. Encourage students to respectfully imitate each of the slow *bugaku* dance movements in time with the dancers in the video.

7. While *gagaku* music is viewed as fixed and without permutation over a millennium of its existence, the melodic, rhythmic, and textural matter

of the music inspires and invites pedagogical possibilities for Creating World Music (see Chapter 5). Students can extend or vary small musical segments on available instruments. These phrases and techniques can be recombined, extended, and slightly varied so that the resulting music is performed in the *spirit* of *gagaku*, even as it is changed for pedagogical purposes. As always, of course, students should be directed to respect the original music and musicians as they are preserved on recordings.

8. Woodwind players can be invited to play the *ryuteki* melody on flute or *hichiriki* melody on oboe, while guitarists can pluck *biwa* parts with heavy picks, and percussionists can approximate the *gagaku* sounds on various Western orchestral percussion instruments. The *sho* parts can be sustained on chromatic harmonica or an electronic keyboard with harmonica sound.

9. Further recommended recordings include Tokyo Gakuso's albums *Gagaku: Court Music of Japan* (JVC, 1994) and *Gagaku and Beyond* (Celestial Harmonies, 2000).

Interdisciplinary Theme 4: Human Migration in History

Migration has been a natural phenomenon among humans and other mammals since long before the first walls, fences, and borders were ever constructed. In many parts of the world, nomadic peoples strive to continue maintaining a traditional migratory lifestyle—either herding animals or hunting and gathering across vast expanses of land—even while governments seek to contain them within enforced borders. In Europe, "wandering minstrels" (migrant musicians) were common during medieval times, and a similar phenomenon is seen in Central Asia, where bards perform epic songs from ancient lands. In 2015, Europe saw the largest mass migration for many generations, with more than one million refugees arriving from the Middle East and Africa during the span of a single year.

Migration is a complicated topic, as views differ across time and place. In the U.S., some perceive the only "real Americans" to be the indigenous "Native Americans," such that all others are a result of historic waves of either immigration (free or forced) or slavery. There is ebb and flow in the immigration of groups to the U.S. in the last century, with quotas set for citizens of individual nations to control the burgeoning population across the 50 states. Special diplomatic agreements such as the bracero program of 1942 allowed for temporary stays for Mexican farm laborers but with the understanding that such movement was time-limited. Short-term laborers from Mexico would work the farms and fields of California and Texas and never become rooted (or even known by name, by their employers), and permanent migration was never expected by anyone of either side. Recent restrictive immigration laws are aimed at the return of illegal immigrants to the country of their birth, thus affecting Mexicans without documentation but with extended lives in the American workforce to return to their homelands. Woody Guthrie's song pays tribute to the short-term laborers even as it brings attention to the journeys of other immigrants—legal and illegal—to the United States. "Deportees" can be learned vis-à-vis the WMP approach, with special attention given to the historical meaning behind the song as well as the issue of immigration at-large.

Episode 6.8: "Deportees" from *Pete Seeger Sings Woody Guthrie*
(American folk ballad, Guthrie & Hoffman, mid-20th century)

Materials:

- "Deportee (feat. Lyle Lovett)," Los Texmaniacs. Video available on Smithsonian Folkways Recordings (https://folkways.si.edu/video/deportee-feat-lyle-lovett-by-los-texmaniacs)
- "Deportees: Plane Wreck at Los Gatos," Pete Seeger, Smithsonian Folkways Recordings

Procedure:

1. Explain that the song lyrics were penned by the late American folk music legend Woody Guthrie (Figure 6.3). Another folk legend, Pete Seeger, became the first artist to release a commercial recording of the song. Recordings by others followed, including Bob Dylan, Joan Baez, The Byrds, Johnny Cash, Judy Collins, Bruce Springsteen, Dolly Parton, Ani DiFranco, Willie Nelson, Nanci Griffith, Concrete Blonde, Tom Morello, and Lyle Lovett. "Deportees" has become part of the canon of notable American songs.

Figure 6.3 Woody Guthrie, ca. 1968[2]

2. Explain that the lyrics of the song describe an incident from 1948 regarded as the worst airplane accident in the history of California. In all, 32 passengers died in the crash, including 28 migrant farm workers from Mexico. In most national news reports, only the names of the four U.S. citizen-passengers were mentioned, while the Mexican laborers went nameless and were described only as "Deportees." This situation troubled Woody Guthrie, provoking him to write the song.

3. Discuss the song lyrics for "Deportees (Plane Wreck at Los Gatos)":

    The crops are all in and the peaches are rotting,

    The oranges piled in their creosote dumps;

    They're flying 'em back to the Mexican border

    To pay all their money to wade back again

    Goodbye to my Juan, goodbye, Rosalita,

    Adios mis amigos, Jesus y Maria;

    Chorus: You won't have your names when you ride the big airplane,

    All they will call you will be "deportees"

    My father's own father, he waded that river,

    They took all the money he made in his life;

    My brothers and sisters they working the old church,

    They rode the big truck still laydown and died

    (Chorus)

    The sky plane caught fire over Los Gatos Canyon,

    A fireball of lightning, and shook all our hills,

    Who are all these friends, all scattered like dry leaves?

    The radio says, "They are just deportees"

    (Chorus)

4. Discuss migration in the social history of the United States, including the U.S.-Mexico agreement as to the bracero program of Mexican farm laborers to California and the Southwest. Discuss policies, the role of migrant workers over time in the U.S., and international laws concerning refugees and asylum seekers.

5. The chordal accompaniment to "Deportees" can be performed by strumming two chords on acoustic guitar: D major–G major–D major, a chord progression suitable for beginning guitarists. Depending upon the recording and class resources, other instruments can be added, such as the banjo fingerpicking on Pete Seeger's version.

6. For additional background information, lecturers are encouraged to consult a book by Tim Z. Hernandez entitled *All They Will Call You* (University of Arizona Press, 2017).

Faculty Feature:
Deborah Wong on Teaching World Music in Higher Education

Photo 6.1   Deborah Wong in Thai ritual to honor music teachers. The leader, dressed in white, is Asdavuth Sagarik, great nephew of renowned musician Luang Pradit Phairoh. Left to right: Consul Gunpirom Vichathorn, Prof. Christopher Adler, Prof. Helen Rees, Prof. Deborah Wong, and Prof. Supeena Insee Adler. Photo by Nattapol Wisuttipat.

> *"Ethnomusicologists use multiple methods to provide rich context for how and why music is meaningful. We show how music can create new contexts and shift the very terms for social connection. How can you teach world music without that?"*

Deborah Wong is Professor of Ethnomusicology at University of California, Riverside, a widely published author specializing in both Asian American and Thai musical practices, including *Sounding the Center: History and Aesthetics in Thai Buddhist Ritual*, *Speak It Louder: Asian Americans Making Music*, and *Louder and Faster: Pain, Joy, and the Body Politic in Asian American Taiko*.

Q: Can you tell us about your job, your institution, and its programs in world music?

A: I'm proud to teach ethnomusicology at the University of California, Riverside, which is a public research university with about 20,000 undergraduates and

3,000 graduate students. Our undergraduate student body is incredibly diverse. In Fall 2018, 41.5% of our students were Latinx, 33.8% were Asian Pacific American, and 55% were first-generation college students. These demographics inspire me and drive my teaching. In the Department of Music, we have a Music and Culture major (in addition to the usual Music major) and a PhD in Music with an ethnomusicology track. I regard all music as world music.

Q: What kinds of world music courses and ensembles do you have at your institution?
A: We offer numerous world music courses at all levels, with strengths in Latin American musics, Asian musics, and U.S. popular musics. Our world ensembles, Javanese *gamelan*, Philippine *rondalla*, Japanese American *taiko*, Latin American/Andean ensemble, Highland pipes, and Hindustani *tabla*, are taught by either faculty ethnomusicologists or community-based culture bearers who are part-time lecturers.

Q: What most motivates you personally in teaching world music cultures courses?
A: I love pushing through students' preconceptions about the world and defamiliarizing what they already know about their home communities.

Q: Can you describe how technologies are used in your world music courses, and how this has changed across time?
A: I've taught full time since 1991 so I've experienced many technological changes in higher education, for instance, the non-negotiable use of online learning management systems (e.g., Blackboard). Every year I teach a large lecture course for three hundred students with the help of four graduate teaching assistants, and a lot of our time goes into looking after the online and digital resources for the course, such as creating PowerPoint files for lectures that students can revisit afterward, helping students with the textbook's rich media online content, and creating and managing online quizzes and exams. I don't think that's the best or only way for students to learn, so we assign one review essay—usually on a biopic about U.S. popular music—which is submitted through our online learning management system and digitally checked for plagiarism by SafeAssign. My teaching is not only reliant on but also profoundly shaped by online digital resources that are now expected by my institution and indeed by my students.

For ethnomusicologists, the most sweeping technological change has been our pedagogical use of YouTube. What riches YouTube makes available! Everything from commercial audio recordings, to music videos from different corners of the world, to raw footage of amazing live events. I'm certain we've tapped only a small corner of the pedagogical possibility of YouTube. We often treat a YouTube clip as if it were a self-evident 'example' of something, and of course it never is. Any YouTube clip is the result of layers and layers of mediation, negotiation, and curation. We should build all that into our pedagogical use of it, though I'm often guilty of using it in the most literal way—you know, "Here's what 'La Bamba' sounds like!"

Q: Can you describe how research findings from ethnomusicology enrich the teaching of world music?
A: Actually, I can't imagine teaching world music *without* the knowledge that comes from ethnomusicological research. Ethnomusicologists use multiple methods to provide rich context for how and why music is meaningful. We show how music can create new contexts and shift the very terms for social connection. How can you teach world music without that?

Q: At your university, in what ways are you able to bring interdisciplinary knowledge—for instance, from social sciences, area studies, and other arts and humanities fields—into the teaching of world music?
A: My campus has a stunningly innovative PhD program in critical dance studies, so my contact with their faculty members and grad students has reshaped my own work. Dance scholars often begin with the body and deploy a range of theoretical approaches to parse how knowledge is embodied. I assign dance scholarship in my courses and I always teach music and dance as inseparable. Critical Ethnic Studies also has a powerful presence on my campus and it informs my thinking and thus my teaching. I approach music as a series of structural encounters between racial ideologies: transpacific currents and the Black Atlantic are basic to how I teach world music. More recently, Indigenous Studies has really taken off on my campus thanks to a series of brilliant new hires, so I'm learning about resurgence and sovereignty and am attending more carefully to immigrants as a different kind of settler. Finally, UCR has an amazing graduate program in public history, and I've learned a lot from those colleagues, for example, by creating undergraduate assignments that are directed toward creating public-facing work that addresses world music in our front yards here in Southern California.

Q: Can you briefly describe the highlights of your tenure as president of the Society for Ethnomusicology, and any important lessons you learned from it?
A: Any scholarly organization makes visible how personal/collegial relationships are the heart of disciplinary change and development. Listening, talking, exchanging, debating, playing, socializing, and sometimes taking stands together is what happens at conferences and on the pages of scholarly journals. Most of my work with/for the Society for Ethnomusicology has been at ground level, e.g., serving on committees and creating opportunities for good scholarship to flourish. Sometimes this has meant creating a new space: my long-time friend and colleague Elizabeth Tolbert and I created the SEM Section on the Status of Women in 1996, for instance. I served in a leadership role during the long decade when SEM was expanding how we addressed advocacy and diversity. No initiatives were mine alone but were rather the result of long discussions over many years involving many members. Two

highlights of my term as president were holding our annual conference in Mexico City (with many local partners, of course) and hiring SEM's first full-time executive director.

Q: Can you explain how guest lectures and performers benefit students in your world music cultures courses, and how you obtain funding for it?
A: One can and should learn about world music from lots of different kinds of knowledge-bearers. Learning from scholars and researchers is one way, but nothing lights up a classroom—and student engagement—like a culture bearer. As I said earlier, embodied knowledge is powerful and undeniable. When students meet a culture bearer who is grounded in a community of practice, and hear and see them in action, and then get to ask questions, they learn how music is most profoundly about lifeways. They learn how to respect that work and that knowledge in ways that commodity capitalism often discourages by valorizing an ownable artifact of that music, like an mp3 file. Funding visits or residencies by culture bearers means being resourceful. Ethnomusicologists constantly activate interdepartmental and collegial relationships on campus and jump on short-term opportunities. Also, any ethnomusicologist will tell you that hosting a culture bearer for a residency longer than a few days is a real commitment that involves extra effort and lots of person-to-person attention, but the payoffs in learning and lifelong friendship are so worth it.

Q: Do you have any predictions about the future status of world music in U.S. higher education?
A: I work at a public institution so I no longer try to predict what may happen next! But I think world music is urgently important to higher education. A world music curriculum prepares music professionals for a world where the lines between popular/classical and here/there seem porous but are often policed. As borders harden and hate rises, the need to learn about other people, other ways, and other worldviews couldn't be more important.

Integration for Robust Understandings

Based on the interdisciplinary field of ethnomusicology, the effective teaching of world music naturally requires a holistic approach that is informed by an array of academic fields across the arts, humanities, and social and physical sciences. Music faculty have many opportunities for connecting with other fields in exciting ways, leading to a co-taught course, a co-sponsored performance or lecture, or co-listed courses that feature as required courses in two or more departments. Faculty members can also, each to their own, embrace the backstories behind the music that are meaningful to the makers as well as to students on their way in to knowing music for its cultural contexts. As an inherently interdisciplinary subject, music of the world's cultures offers an excellent platform from which to examine various global challenges.

Glossary

Cultural Prism Model: Campbell's model (2004) for conceptualizing world music cultures in terms of musical beginnings, continuities, and meanings.

Functions of Music: As per Merriam's classic theoretical model (1964), a view of music from the perspective of its sociocultural meanings and uses.

Indigenous peoples: Original inhabitants of a region that was later colonized (e.g., Native Americans, First Nations, New Zealand Māori, and Sámi of Norway, Sweden, Finland, and Russia).

Integrating World Music: The study of music as it connects to culture and as it illuminates a prism-like grasp of integrated topics and interdisciplinary subjects in order to articulate music's cultural contexts and meanings. This WMP dimension assumes the integration of topical themes throughout the course of the learning process and is woven throughout the five dimensions.

Interdisciplinarity: An approach to the study of music that encompasses understanding across multiple disciplines, fields, and topics.

Notes

1. Public domain (Creative Commons). "Riddu Riđđu 18 Frokost med Mari Boine-7524" by Riddu Riđđu is licensed under CC BY-SA 2.0).
2. This work is from the New York World-Telegram and Sun collection at the Library of Congress. According to the Library, there are no known copyright restrictions on the use of this work.

References

Campbell, P. S. (2004). *Teaching music globally: Experiencing music, expressing culture.* Oxford University Press.

Clayton, M. (2016). The social and personal functions of music in cross-cultural perspective. In S. Hallam, I. Cross, & M. Thaut (Eds.), *Oxford handbook of music psychology.* Oxford University Press.

Merriam, A. P. (1964). *The anthropology of music.* Northwestern University Press.

Nettl, B. (2010). Music education and ethnomusicology: A (usually) harmonious relationship. *Min-Ad: Israel Studies in Musicology Online, 8*(1), 1–9.

Listening Links

"E Maru Rahi," Royal Tahitian Dance Company, Smithsonian Folkways Recordings. A Tahitian song about three brothers, one of whom died while diving for mother-of-pearl in the Lagoon of Takaroa in the Tuamotu Islands. https://folkways.si.edu/royal-tahitian-dance-company/e-maru-rahi/world/music/track/smithsonian

"Deportee (feat. Lyle Lovett)" by Los Texmaniacs, video made available on Smithsonian Folkways Recordings website. https://folkways.si.edu/video/deportee-feat-lyle-lovett-by-los-texmaniacs

"Deportees: Plane Wreck at Los Gatos," from *Pete Seeger Sings Woody Guthrie*, by Pete Seeger (1967, Folkways Recordings, FTS 31002). https://folkways.si.edu/pete-seeger-sings-woody-guthrie/american-folk-struggle-protest/music/album/smithsonian

"Dulce Sueño Mío," Ecos de Borinquen, Smithsonian Folkways Recordings. A Puerto Rican *jíbaro* (folk music) featuring a *trovador*, two *cuatros*, guitar, *guiro*, and bongos and using a *decimilla* (10 lines, 6 syllables) poetic song structure. https://folkways.si.edu/ecos-de-borinquen/dulce-sueno-mio-sweet-dream-of-mine/latin-world/music/track/smithsonian

"Gagaku," video licensed to official UNESCO YouTube channel (filmed by Mainichi Productions, 2000) ["Koniburi no Utamai," part 2, from 04:47]. https://youtu.be/5OA8HFUNfIk

"Gula Gula" by Mari Boine Persen, *Voices of the Real World* (Compilation album, Real World Records, 2000). Music video. www.youtube.com/watch?v=S3LPCITvYWc

"Me He Manu Rere," on *Folksong New Zealand* organization website. www.folksong.org.nz/manurere/index.html

"Me He Manu Rere" (sung by Mana Epiha), *Māori Language Net* organization website. www.maorilanguage.net/. Video performance also available at www.youtube.com/watch?v=7hsnGfYNY3k

"Nihon Ettim" (I Concealed Myself), *Uzbekistan: Echoes of Vanished Courts* (Smithsonian Folkways Recordings, 2014). https://folkways.si.edu/uzbekistan-echoes-of-vanished-courts/world/music/album/smithsonian

"Time to Have Fun," Rahim AlHaj, Smithsonian Folkways Recordings. An upbeat *khaliji* dance-style piece featuring *oud* (Iraqi lute), *santūr* (Iranian dulcimer), and percussion. https://folkways.si.edu/rahim-alhaj/time-to-have-fun

7

Surmountable Challenges and Worthy Outcomes

*"So perhaps we can claim that ethnomusicology has finally 'arrived' [to educa-
tion], as a source of musical materials, ideas about music, and ways of looking
at the world's music."*

—Bruno Nettl, 2010, p. 1

---

*Two floors down and a hallway away, the sound of a drum set outlines a clean swing
pattern: a jazz drummer is marking time resolutely by himself. The sharpness of his
ride cymbal has little trouble traveling past the hallway of practice rooms, where it
mixes with a lone clarinetist playing the* Rose Etude No. 21—*a conservatory favorite.
It is nearing the end of the day now, and upstairs, Dr. Carter is just concluding a late
afternoon of research, studying the metric evolution of Steve Reich's compositions for
an upcoming conference presentation. The mixed sounds of practicing students faintly
make their way through his closed office door in the Musicology wing, but he resolves
to continue working for a bit longer despite the distractions. Suddenly, from the other
end of the hallway comes the piercing timbre of two high-pitched drums. The combined
sonorities of these drums with the ride cymbal and clarinet build in discord, and a
frustrated Dr. Carter closes his laptop and packs up his belongings; no more work will
be getting done today. Leaving his office, he turns left instead of right, choosing to take
the long way to his car to find the source of this new sound—the culprit that ultimately
interrupted his workflow. He stumbles into the Ethnomusicology office area, a space he
concedes to have rarely visited. Ornate tapestries from far-off lands cover the bulletin
boards here, and nearby, Dr. Carter locates the source of the music.*

*On the floor carpet of a small office sits a man of North Indian descent, his knees
folded outward with the heels of his hands resting on the pair of* tablas *(Hindustani
drums) situated in front of him. A university student sits across from his teacher,
chanting rhythmic patterns as he plays with a flattened timbre. The teacher reaches
over wordlessly, reshapes the student's hands, and smiles at the immediately improved*

tone. They begin to play together, chanting the rhythm with a series of dhas, din*s, and* tin*s. Dr. Carter stands outside the room for a while, listening to the chants and strokes on the drums while the sounds from other studios converge. As he walks away, he is thinking of the incredible complexity of the* tabla *players' synchrony. For weeks now, Dr. Carter had been obsessing over the rhythmic evolution of Reich's music from the 1980s and 1990s, impassioned by the innovations of this 20th-century mastermind. But he had to smile to himself as thoughts of these rhythms mixed with the venerable Indian rhythms, likely centuries old now. Exiting through the side door of the music building, the drum set, clarinet, and* tabla *fade into the distance. With remnants of Reich still ruminating in his head, Dr. Carter suddenly feels a newfound, shared connection to every corner of his university school of music, where music of the West and of the rest of the world share space and time.*

Developing Musical-Cultural Understanding

The happy ending of a world music cultures course is the deeper understanding of music by way of its sonic features and cultural meanings and a recognition of music as a pan-human phenomenon that offers abundant cultural variation. On the first day of a world music course, students may hear a piece of music that initially seems incomprehensible. Perhaps this music contains a rhythmic structure that feels unsettled, a melody that appears unsingable, a harmony that just does not "fit" comfortably in their ears, or a timbre that seems aesthetically unnatural to them. To these students, culturally unfamiliar music may quite readily be felt as "Other," even "exotic," and beyond the realm of deeper comprehension. As students move through courses that feature meaningful experiences of teacher-facilitated listening, however, the music becomes increasingly familiar over time. What was once disquieting at first becomes welcomed through World Music Pedagogy's call for opportunities to listen, participate musically, enact the music in performance, creatively expand upon the music, and understand the music's meaning to people, cultures, and communities. From students' initial experiences come newfound anticipation, understanding, and even fondness for the music and the people whose music it is.

Soon, the music transforms for students from feeling "far away" and unobtainable to growing ever more accessible. A desire to make this music for oneself grows accordingly. Through Attentive Listening, students are invited to focus on particular musical components, to identify them, analyze them, and question the sonic structures of the music. Through Engaged Listening, or participatory musicking, students become directly involved in singing, playing, dancing, and moving to the music. Students then grow into opportunities to perform the music for themselves and for others, via Enactive Listening, and to actively engage with the music expressively. They can further indulge themselves through Creating World Music by providing extemporizations and inventions within the musical medium, delving ever more deeply through opportunities to create new possibilities within the style and structures of learned musical works. Throughout the process, students are learning more about the musical culture within which it is situated, through Integrating World Music—and knowing the social, geographical, political, and economic contexts of the music. In all its five dimensions, this is the World Music Pedagogy framework working as it is wholly intended, and it is a course of action for developing the musical-cultural understanding of students of music—be they music majors, minors, or students in a single course in study on the world's musical cultures.

Challenges and Solutions to Teaching World Music

World Music Pedagogy is intended as a useful instructional approach for preparing faculty in tertiary-level institutions to teach world music, many of whom are "sold" on the importance of cultural diversity in music but simply do not know what approach to take or where to begin. They are likely most familiar with Western-styled ways of teaching, based upon their experiences in teaching and learning Western European Art Music (WEAM). Many will have learned through one-on-one WEAM-based studio lessons deriving from time-honored teacher-student apprenticeship models. Most, if not all, faculty of higher education music programs are notationally literate and fully capable of reading and writing Western staff notation. They are probably well acquainted with the top-down lecture style of their academic courses, whether as students or seasoned members of music faculties. As the authors likewise share this inheritance of WEAM-based teaching and learning practices, we uphold a continuing reverence for WEAM's long-standing conventions. At the same time, however, we have experienced first-hand how WMP invigorates student learning by honoring sonic and social meanings, maintaining transmission processes of the world's oral traditions, and embracing the performative, creative, and cultural meanings of the world's music.

Still, there are valid and far-reaching challenges to teaching world music in higher education. These challenges might range from a faculty member's questioning of the validity of a course in world music cultures to questioning their capacity to teach music from outside their expertise. There are natural concerns, many that are shared by teaching faculty across institutional settings, as to "where to begin" and "where to draw the line" in determining course content from a seemingly infinite set of musical cultures. There are worries over which music cultures to teach (and by extension, which *not* to teach), which genres to select within a given culture, which musicians to highlight, and which musical works to feature. There is trepidation as to which resources to tap and whether there are course ancillaries and media technologies to provide to students. There are doubts about the amount of time it takes to enrich, entrain, and enlighten students as to the beauty and logic of a musical work and culture. There is the angst of authenticity and cultural appropriation and the anxieties of wondering whether expectations of students for learning music far afield from their experience are reasonable ones. There is the standard professional concern of how to assess and evaluate what students learn in the way of world music cultures, both musically and culturally. These challenges are briefly addressed in the following sections.

Preliminaries and Set-Ups

Early on in the journey toward teaching world music might come questions of "why world music?" and "who should teach world music?" First and foremost, situating world music at the very center of a tertiary music program's curriculum enables music programs to respond to timely initiatives and mandates to diversify and intercultural-ize course offerings through musical experiences that centralize and celebrate the diversity of human life. Many universities are seeking to increase global competence across the entire student body, thus prioritizing courses that examine local, global, and intercultural issues. Indeed, world music belongs in higher education for *all* students, and students of music do well to recognize the myriad of musical expressions across cultures—to savor the sounds, to puzzle through the different logical modes and means of these expressions, and to probe the uses and meanings of music within diverse communities. University faculty lines in ethnomusicology are the best bet for shaping course offerings in world music, in music of geographic regions, and in topical areas such as music and race, music and ritual, and music and social justice. An ideal music faculty composite in higher education encompasses those with expertise in performance, pedagogy, and academic areas, and one or more ethnomusicologists can readily design and deliver courses that serve diversity needs across the board. Still, the responsibility of teaching diversity, social justice, and equity is the responsibility of *all* within schools of music, regardless of subject area or expertise.

Course Content

Once a commitment is made to teaching a world music course, the immediate challenge is to then determine which content instructors should prioritize. The WMP dimensions can be applied compellingly to any of the world's art, folk, traditional, and popular music cultures and does not necessarily limit its usefulness to "Other" world cultures. Indeed, the WMP framework might be used in a listening-intensive study of Bach, Beethoven, Mozart, and Mahler to a similar degree of success, because the framework is rooted in the notion that *listening is core* to musical learning; that the unfamiliar becomes familiar (and embodied) given sufficient open-minded listening.

Nonetheless, a handful of questions appear to be consistent across faculty as to which musical cultures to prioritize; how to include art music, folk music, and popular music styles; balancing "big" cultures with "little" cultures (or better termed, "macro" and "micro" cultures); featuring both women's music and men's music; and pairing both vocal and instrumental music. In the planning stage, questions should begin to flow. For example, how should various regions be represented—especially considering that most are socially and politically constructed, such as the delineations of North, Central, and South America? Similar questions arise with respect to all continents and regions around the world. Furthermore, how does one achieve a balance of featured genres found throughout these regions? Among Andean *huayno*, Brazilian *samba*, Cuban *son*, Japanese *gagaku*, Korean *pansori*, Javanese *gamelan*, Indian *raga*, and a selection featuring Iranian *sehtar* and Chinese *pipa*, where does popular music "fit"? There are difficult choices to be made in planning these courses, and the music piles up, as do the concerns about whether there is sufficient time to feature enough of them.

To be clear, there is no single ideal way of achieving a perfect balance of musical selections across so many reasonable variables. Course content may simply reflect the world music textbook that has been selected for the course. Indeed, there are standard world music cultures that appear regularly in textbooks, including music from Asia (e.g., India, Indonesia, Japan); Africa (typically one or more cultures in West Africa or elsewhere among the many sub-Saharan cultures); the Middle East (e.g., Egypt or Iran); and Latin American countries (e.g., Brazil and Cuba) or regions (e.g., the Andes or the Hispanic Caribbean).

With regard to Asia, "high art" court music is prominently featured in these textbooks, so that Javanese and/or Balinese *gamelan* are a "must" in world music courses, as is the music of Hindustani North India (especially music for *sitar* and *tabla*). Textbook inclusions from North America may give focus to genres attributed to African Americans (blues or gospel), Native Americans (powwow), and Latin Americans (*mariachi*, salsa). Frequently missing from the standard mix of cultures are musical practices across Europe, the Pacific Islands, the many regions of the massive African continent, and of greater Asia (e.g., China, Korea, Central Asia, mainland Southeast Asia).

Furthermore, selecting music for a world music course sometimes comes as a result of the expertise and interest of the faculty member who is designing and delivering the course. Certainly, music may also be selected based on student interest and experience, and that mix may be not be known until course enrollment is clearer. Certain cultures come to light as a result of tapping the knowledge of faculty colleagues, too, such as the jazz studies professor who may be experienced in salsa, merengue, and cumbia; or the Korean American flute professor who happens to have studied Korean traditional flutes during a sabbatical; or the music education professor who spent a year abroad studying Japanese *koto* and *shamisen*. Community resources can color the course content as well, so that invited guests may include a Vietnamese *dàn tranh* (zither) player, a Spanish flamenco guitarist and dancer duo, a bluegrass banjo player, a player of Chinese *pipa* (lute), and a lead drummer of a Guinean drum and dance troupe.

Further still, there are faculty who prefer to go their own way, foregoing textbooks altogether and instead selecting cultures that best fit the circumstances of their students, their program, their institution, and the community that surrounds them. These faculty may develop their own set of listening and video selections, a coursepack of readings, and perhaps a set of digital materials for easy access. They may go independently and without textbooks for a number of reasons: Because they view no textbook as quite filling the needs of their course, because they view many valuable materials as scattered in various forms beyond the contents of a single textbook, or because they wish to respond to students' financial situations by providing free access to online materials. As they develop their own world music course, they would do well to consider the proposed set of recommended world music cultures (Table 7.1). Despite the personalized construction of the content of any world music course, the

TABLE 7.1 Recommended world cultures for a world music course

Africa	Asia	Europe	North America	South America	Oceania: The Pacific Islands
Egypt, West Africa (e.g., Ghana, Mali, Nigeria), South Africa	China, Japan, Indonesia (Java, Bali), India, Iran, the Arab World	Spain, Ireland, Bulgaria, Russia	Native American, African American, Latin American	Brazil, Mexico, the Hispanic Caribbean, the Andes (e.g., Peru, Bolivia, Ecuador)	Polynesia, Indigenous Australia, Māori

cultures offered in this list will represent the standard choices across settings and circumstances. (Note that the 16 selections featured within this volume span various world regions and cultures, including parts of Africa and Asia, the Americas, Europe, and the Pacific Islands.)

Sources and Resources

The sources and resources that make for an informed experience in the study of world music cultures are many and varied. There is a wide array of recordings, video recordings, online materials, books, book chapters, and articles from which to choose in the development of the course. Textbooks may become the principal resource for courses that choose to utilize them; see a sampling of such recommended textbooks among the resources in Appendix 2. Current textbooks for world music courses are typically comprehensive packages that include companion websites with ancillary items such as links to recordings and video clips, chapter reviews, and ideas for student projects and assessments. These textbooks are often available in hard copy and e-book formats, too, and may work in online as well as in standard in-person versions of the course. They may appear complete and comprehensive for teaching world music as a required or elective course to music majors, minors, and students from across many fields.

For those who prefer not to use a textbook or who recognize the need to supplement a textbook to further highlight specific cultures and genres, there are easily accessible resources from which to choose. A number of online resources, particularly within the realm of the online archival collections listed later, are a boon to teaching faculty and their students.

SMITHSONIAN FOLKWAYS RECORDINGS

As both a nonprofit record label and an archive associated with the national museum of the United States, Smithsonian Folkways Recordings (www.folkways.si.edu) is a collection of more than 4,000 albums and 60,000 tracks along with videos, podcasts, lesson plans for teachers, and the online Smithsonian Folkways Magazine replete with fieldwork recordings. The collection encompasses a sizable set of Americana recordings dating from the late 1940s from African American and Anglo-American communities, including Appalachian and Ozark fiddle and banjo tunes, spirituals and gospel songs, and children's singing games, and considerable documentation in music as well as spoken word (speeches and poetry) of the Civil Rights Era and the Labor Movement. Music from giants such as Woody Guthrie, Pete Seeger, and Lead Belly are well represented, as are more recent artists such as Rhiannon Giddings, Mariachi Los Camperos, Wu Fei and Abigail Washburn, and Laurie Anderson with Tibetan musician Tenzin Choegyal. More recent releases of recordings of Hispanic and Latinx musicians have diversified the collection further, and the 127 albums of music from the classic UNESCO Collection of Traditional Music are a valuable addition to the collection.

ASSOCIATION FOR CULTURAL EQUITY

Inspired by the work of folklorist-musicologist Alan Lomax, recordings and videos of music, dance, and spoken word are available via the Association for Cultural Equity (ACE) (www.culturalequity.org). There is considerable representation of song and instrumental music in African American and Anglo-American communities from as early as the 1930s, especially those located in the American South, from Georgia and the Carolinas to Alabama, Mississippi, Louisiana, and Texas. Additionally, music, dance, and oral traditions from Caribbean cultures and communities in Spain, Italy, Scotland, and England offer further evidence of musical diversity as recorded by Alan Lomax and his associates. Related to ACE is the Global Jukebox, a site which contains fieldwork recordings from the world's diverse cultures, including peoples in Africa, the Americas, Asia, Europe, and the Pacific Islands, in addition to many Indigenous American and Australian communities. A world map categorized by region, culture, and function makes this treasury of 6,000 digitized songs from over 1,000 cultures more easily accessible.

ETHNOMUSICOLOGY: GLOBAL FIELD RECORDINGS

As a project of the UCLA World Music Center with Adam Matthew Digital, an academic publisher based in the United Kingdom, this collection features 15,000 audio field recordings and interviews, plus film footage and more than 8,000 images from across the world. They are derived from the fieldwork of ethnomusicologists during the period 1950–1980, such as Mantle Hood, Jacqueline Cogdell DjeDje, Harold Courlander, Robert Garfias, Lorraine Sakata, Charlotte Heth, Cheryl Keyes, Jose Maceda, David Morton, and many others, mostly associated with UCLA and the University of Washington. The various materials offer musical, social, and cultural views in African, Asia, the Caribbean, Central and South America, Europe/Caucasus, the Middle East, North America, and the Pacific Islands, and altogether comprise opportunities for students to study original field recordings and their associated documentation. Of interest to students may be interviews by scholars with musicians, field notebooks, and contemporary finding aids.

HUMAN RESOURCES AND CULTURE BEARERS

For all the value that print resources can afford instructors, there may be no adequate substitution for "human resources." Artists, scholars, and community members can be invited to a world music course whether in person or digitally (through Skype or Zoom). Not only can such "culture bearers" provide tangibility and creative energy, but they will additionally serve as human verification and extension of the music cultures under study. Through these special visitations, students can both experience the music as it is performed live by artists and absorb the compelling stories that they may have to share. Culture-bearing community musicians may have much to stay about the music they share just as scholars from other programs (e.g., African Studies or East Asian Studies) also provide insights into the contexts that formed the musical culture over time. In addition to human resources who appear in person as visitors to a course, there are those specialists who can be consulted by faculty for advice and good counsel for materials to help frame the music to be studied. These specialists may also be useful, as their time allows, to individual students whose course assignments and research projects may require further guidance. Importantly, it should be mentioned that human resources should not be treated as *free* resources under most circumstances, particularly when experts from marginalized communities are asked to share their musical culture with others. Whenever their expertise is called upon, they should be compensated for their time and preparation just as any consultant would. Of course, most human resources would be enthusiastic to share their music with others even when institutional budgets might be tight, but they ought to be compensated fairly for their time and work.

Pedagogical Essentials

When university faculty break free from the traditional lecture model in order to open into ways of internalizing the music and honoring the cultural origins and developments of the music, students often come to develop a genuine love and passion for the music in question. Contemporary pedagogical essentials in higher education require a balance of tried-and-true traditions with innovative teaching strategies. Of primary importance is the age-old wisdom of selecting musical works that entice and invite the curiosity and involvement of learners. Chapter 2 outlines characteristics to be considered in choosing culturally unfamiliar music and recommends attention to music that features structural repetitiveness through repeated melodic and rhythmic motifs, phrases, and patterns. Naturally, these considerations became the primary criteria for choosing the 16 recordings for this volume's Learning Pathways and teaching episodes.

Meanwhile, several well-established principles of effective music teaching continue to serve instructors favorably within the WMP framework. These may include both newfound technological approaches as well as tried-and-true educational strategies, including the following:

- Recognizing "the artist within" students, faculty, and guests and prioritizing plentiful opportunities for active musicking so that music can be sounded live in the classroom whenever and however possible;
- Inviting students into the decision-making processes to centralize their ideas for engaging in participatory activities with chosen WMP selections;
- Further promoting a student-centered environment by having small groups choose and teach a musical culture from resources such as Smithsonian Folkways Recordings or the Association for Cultural Equity;
- Drawing students into unfamiliar musical selections through video representations of the music as well as through thoughtful comparisons to familiar examples;
- Mixing up the students' experiences within the course, even in single class sessions, by providing opportunities to listen, discuss in small and large groups, and to sing, move, and play music; and
- Inspiring students to seek further understanding of world music cultures beyond the scope of the course expectations.

Given that most university students are expectedly literate with technology, it is also pedagogically essential that technology play a role in world music courses. The incorporation of digital resources like GarageBand, Logic, and Pro Tools brings students further into the realm of Creating World Music, aiding in composing and producing music in particular cultural styles (whether in class or on their own). Students may likewise benefit from exploring free online world music tools like Virtual Tanpura (www.anubodh.com/

tanpura.php), Tanpura: The Indian Drone Convertor, or similar websites for virtual *tabla* and other digital instruments (also see Chapter 5). Other useful online tools for world music teaching and class performance projects include Sufi Plug Ins (www.beyond-digital.org/sufiplugins/) and the "Free Ethnic Drum Loops and Samples" tools on the Looperman website (www.looperman.com/loops?gid=15&cid=1).

Developing a World Music Syllabus

With these ideas and principles in mind, addressing how a semester-long world music curriculum might be designed remains a timely concern for instructors. Offered here is a sample syllabus for a lecture- or seminar-style world music cultures course that is designed for undergraduate students (but could be easily adapted into a graduate context as well). Included within the sample syllabus are a possible course description, course objectives, required resources, suggested grading criteria, assignment descriptions, and a recommended 15-week course outline. The rundown of weekly sessions also includes recommendations for the specific selections used throughout this volume.

SAMPLE SYLLABUS
Undergraduate-Level World Music Class
[Lecture- or Seminar-Style]

Course Description

Introduction to world music cultures, including both sonic and sociocultural dimensions of music in culture. Topics include instruments, pitch, rhythm, form, composition and improvisation, music and race, gender, politics, economy, and religion and ritual, with case studies of traditional and contemporary practices in selected world regions.

Course Objectives

Upon completion of the course, students will be able to:

1. Articulate the various ways in which culture is celebrated through music within the following geographic locations: West Africa, Asia (China, Japan, Korea, India), the Pacific Islands (Tahiti, New Zealand), the Middle East (Iran, Iraq, Uzbekistan), Europe (Western, Eastern, Nordic), the Caribbean (Puerto Rico), South America (Bolivia), and North America (United States, Native American)

2. Sonically identify musical concepts and techniques as they are both shared and exclusive among various musical cultures [WMP Attentive Listening]

3. Participate in and perform music from various world music cultures through singing, playing, and movement [WMP Engaged and Enactive Listening]

4. Develop unique expressions of cultural practices through extension, improvisation, composition, and other creative expressions [WMP Creating World Music]

5. Articulate the ways in which world music cultures both influence and are influenced by sociocultural factors, current events, and social life through interdisciplinary discussions and activities [WMP Integrating World Music]

Required Resources

Textbook selection, audio/visual resources, and additional readings to be selected by the course instructor, with recommended use of corresponding Learning Pathways and Episodes found within this book.

Grading Criteria (Suggested)

Participation	20%
On-Campus Student Performance	*5%*
World Music Creativity Performance (small groups)	*5%*
General Class Participation	*10%*
Assignments	**30%**
World Music Concert Mini-Ethnography	*15%*
Music & Social Justice / Current Events Project	*15%*
Quizzes & Exams	**50%**
Quizzes (3)	*15%*
Midterm Exam	*15%*
Final Exam	*20%*
	Total: 100%

Assignment Descriptions

- **On-Campus Student Performance**
  As a class, enrolled students will briefly perform altogether for the university student body during the "Friday Free Hour," either (a) in the student union or (b) on the quad (weather permitting). We will choose 2–3 favorite musical cultures featured throughout this course and perform

selections of our choice through singing, playing, movement, and/or dancing. This performance will act as an "informance," or an informal presentation in which the primary goal is not to perform a "polished" work but to offer an experienced with a musical style or practice.

- **World Music Creativity Performance**

  In small groups, students will develop a unique musical experience with a chosen musical culture that features some sort of extension, improvisation, composition, arranging, or other creative musical development. These brief and informal creations will be performed in class for peers.

- **World Music Concert Mini-Ethnography**

  This project is intended to replicate, on the small scale, the work of an ethnomusicologist studying a particular culture. Attending any "world music" performance of your choice during the semester, write a 7–10 page mini-ethnography of the performance. The following steps should be taken to complete the project:

  (a) **Attend a world music performance.** Take detailed "fieldnotes" at the performance. Include notes about the music, space, context, performers, audience members, event sequence, performers' behaviors, audience's behaviors, etc. Write a complete and detailed account of what you experienced as soon as possible afterwards.

  (b) **Make a recording of the performance.** If this is not possible, you may use a commercial recording. Refer back to your recording throughout step d.

  (c) **Interview a musician, dancer, knowledgeable audience member, or culture bearer.** If possible, arrange for an audio-recorded interview with a musician, dancer, audience member, or culture bearer present at the performance. Questions on repertoire, performer histories, community values (e.g., cultural orientation, musical function), and history and values will help to explain the musical culture. Transcribe the interview into written form. If an interview cannot be arranged, please document steps taken to attempt to secure an interview with someone (e.g., emails, social media messages).

  (d) **Develop your mini-ethnography.** Plan to submit your 7–10-page (double-spaced) mini-ethnography that interweaves (a) your fieldnotes and personal narrative, (b) interviews, and (c) your recording of the performance. The ethnography should be primarily about the particular performance you attended, but with attention to the interviews and your personal research to contextualize the performance within a broader musical culture.

Tip: Recall our discussion from the first day of classes regarding what constitutes "world music." You might choose to attend a performance of a musical culture not well represented within the U.S., or you might choose to take an "ethnomusicological" view of a well-regarded musical practice such as popular, hip-hop, or jazz. The focus should be on examining the music through a *cultural* lens, which is the ethnomusicologist's primary interest in studying music.

- **Music & Social Justice/Current Events Project**

  This final project might take the form of a (a) written paper [5–7 pages]; (b) podcast [15–20 min.]; (c) PowerPoint presentation [15–20 min.], or (d) other method of dissemination (to be approved by the instructor). The purpose of this project is to explicitly connect music with a timely matter of social justice and/or current events.

Some possible examples:

- Protest songs and the Civil Rights Era
- Work songs and incarceration
- Music of immigrant communities in the U.S.
- Music of Indigenous people around the world
- Music and environmental sustainability
- The music of Islam in a time of Islamophobia
- Marginalized musicians and composers around the world (e.g., women, people of color, LGBTQ+)
- Music and environmental sustainability

Sample Course Outline
(15-Week Semester)

Week	Topic	Assignments/ Presentations	Suggested Learning Pathways/Episodes
Week 1	**Fundamentals of Music of the World's Cultures**		
Week 2	**Asia: East**		• Episode 2.1 • Episode 5.6 • Episode 6.7
Week 3	**Asia: South and Southeast**	*Quiz #1 (weeks 1–3)*	
Week 4	**Asia: The Middle East**	*Midterm Exam*	• Learning Pathway #1 • Episode 6.4

Week 5	Africa: Sub-Saharan (West)	*Prepare Creativity Performance*	• Episode 2.6 • Episode 3.6 • Episode 5.4
Week 6	Africa: Sub-Saharan (East)		
Week 7	Africa: Central and South		
Week 8	The Americas: South and Central	*Quiz #2 (weeks 6–8)*	• Episode 3.5 • Episode 5.5
Week 9	The Americas: The Caribbean	*Social Justice/ Current Events Project Due*	• Learning Pathway #3
Week 10	The Pacific Islands		• Learning Pathway #2
Week 11	Concept: Music and Immigration		• Episode 6.8
Week 12	Concept: Improvisation & Creativity	*Quiz #3 (weeks 10–12)*	• Revisit Learning Pathways #1–3: Creating WM
Week 13	Concept: Diasporas of Music Cultures	*On-campus performance rehearsal*	
Week 14	Concept: Musical Hybridity	*On-campus performance rehearsal*	• Episode 3.4 • Revisit Learning Pathway #1: Integrating WM
Week 15	Review and Performance	*On-Campus Student Performance*	
Finals Week	Final Exam and Project	*Final Exam (cumulative) Mini-Ethnography Due*	

Designing Short- and Long-Term Assignments

Assignments spanning the duration of a world music course may be short-term or long-range, and will frequently include both so that there are daily or weekly assignments as well as midterm and final projects of various sorts. Short-term tasks may run the gamut from required reading and listening selections, to written responses and reflections on these readings and listenings, to online explorations of further music or dance of particular genres or cultures, and so forth. Students may be tasked, for example, with viewing a video of an Irish *seisún* (session) and identifying the instruments, figuring out the form, and perhaps even learning the melody of the opening eight bars by ear. They may be asked to search independently on Spotify for live recordings of Turkish *saz* players and compare renditions of older and more recent productions of the music. They may be expected to attend one of several upcoming performance experiences on campus or in the vicinity—such as a concert by a Latin jazz band, a Near Eastern ensemble, an evening of blues, or a powwow event—and to write a report of the music, the commentary by the musicians, and the audience behaviors and reactions to the music. And there may be an expectation for students to "journal" their musical experiences over several days, or several weeks, and to describe these diverse musical expressions both musically and in terms of where and when they experienced it.

Weekly quizzes, midterms, and finals frequently play a hefty part in assessing knowledge acquired in the course. Multiple choice, true-false, matching, short answer, and essays are among the typical techniques found in such exams. These sorts of assessments generally check student knowledge in a convergent fashion by asking students to recite information about musical cultures—including sonic properties, historical and social contexts, instruments, the music's function, and so on. Occasionally, never-before-heard selections might be used to test students' ability to transfer their understandings to new (but stylistically similar) works.

Importantly, the limited use of summative assessments (i.e., quizzes, tests) should allow for greater freedom in designing more open-ended, creative, and constructivist assignments and projects that arguably test students' thinking in deeper ways. For example, consider the Mini-Ethnography assignment outlined in the sample syllabus. Conducting an ethnographic account of a given musical culture provides students with a deep sense of the holistic nuances of a musical practice—including behaviors, performance venue, clothing, movement, and musician-audience participation. They may target a campus hip-hop club, a student *mariachi*, a residence hall multicultural music revue, or a chapel choir's Baltic (and/or Balkan) program. In the process, they may find themselves facing matters of social behavior and identity that are inseparable from the music—race, gender, ritual and religion, oral tradition, stylistic fusion, and sustainability, for example. The end product of an ethnographic project may even turn into a scholarly paper, with citations to relevant publications, recordings, videos, and interviews that they can share to the course site.

Ethnomusicological Principles for Pedagogical Application

Because World Music Pedagogy evolved at the cusp of ethnomusicology and music education, there are principles honed by ethnomusicologists that are especially relevant to the work of those who are teaching world music in higher education. Some concepts that may have originated from ethnomusicology have long ago migrated to educational practice, especially by those educators whose work has been aimed at issues of diversity, equity, and inclusion. The use of culture bearers, for example, has become standard practice in classrooms, following on the ethnomusicological valuing of the voices of cultural insiders. Other concepts such as "identity" and "social justice" have found their ways from ethnomusicology into a myriad of specialized music studies, with reinforcement by insights from anthropology, sociology, and general education. These concepts are realized in distinctive musical ways within the content of world music courses. Several relevant issues of this nature are briefly defined and described for their relevance to World Music Pedagogy, with attention to their ethnomusicological origins and how they are meaningful to teaching world music.

Emic-Etic Views

Ethnomusicology shares with anthropology and folklore studies the necessity of understanding how people from within social and cultural groups understand their world. The *emic* perspective gives weight to the local people, their behaviors, meanings, and values, and pays tribute to the knowledge of those within a culture. The *etic* approach shifts from the perspective of local people to the observations and interpretations of research-oriented outsiders, so that fieldworkers and scholars follow a scientific path in interpreting cultures through generalizations about human behaviors. They seek cross-cultural facets and features of a culture, often in the non-Western world or in marginalized communities, and offer comparisons of the studied culture with their own (typically Western) culture. Best practices in fieldwork research is found in the combination of emic and etic views, when collaborations of visiting ethnographers with local community members can bring about the richest understandings of a culture. This complementarity of views can get to the heart of the local knowledge within a framework of understandings but with serious intent to remain culturally neutral—that is, for cultural outsiders to remain wary of their own ethnocentric biases.

It is this balancing of emic and etic views that has so inspired ethnomusicologists in their own teaching, by seeking to incorporate visiting artists and culture-bearing community musicians into their classes, course assignments, and projects. As discussed throughout this book, culture bearers offer powerful means for knowing culturally unfamiliar music. Because they grew up in the culture, they know the context of the music more deeply than an outsider could ever hope to provide, and they can share the tales of the songs they sing and the instruments they play.

Orality-Aurality

Across the world, face-to-face transmission has been the gold standard for genres classified as folk, traditional, and popular music. Furthermore, the teaching and learning of art music beyond the West—such as Persian classical music, Hindustani and Karnatic music of India, and music of Asian courts such as at Bangkok, Phnom Penh, and Yogyakarta—continues to transpire through an oral process of teaching without notation and learning by listening, watching, and imitating the master musician-teacher. While *orality* had long existed in places where literacy was unfamiliar, as in rural and remote villages of the distant past, it unsurprisingly remains a steadfast process of musical transmission still today. Even in practices where notation is used, such as in piano studios, jazz ensembles, and Japanese *koto* and *shamisen* practices, a kind of partial orality is still in play as students listen and learn the nuances of repertoire as well as technical matter by watching and listening to master musicians who model what can never be sufficiently captured in print. Ethnomusicology's tales of the field provide evidence of the primacy of the oral tradition—from blues to bluegrass, reggae to rap, *gamelan* to *ngoma*, and on fiddles, fifes, and fretless lutes in many of the world's regions.

As celebrated through WMP, listening is central to learning all the world's music, and it is the time-honored tradition of orality that can flavor the manner in which world music courses are conducted. Alongside lectures and discussions, as well as brief moments of passive listening to recorded excerpts, the opportunities for students to tune their aural skills toward the sonic features of a given selection are clearly rewarding. In the process, students experience orality as they also exercise their personal *aurality* that leads to a deeper knowledge of music. Students can gain an understanding of the oral tradition as a pan-human process through class-based experiences in guided listening, followed by direct invitations to observe and imitate the recorded (or live) musical model. In the case of culturally unfamiliar music, the passage through listening to the making of a public performance (or "informance") of a piece is an exercise in the power of the oral-aural process. Ethnomusicologists who study music as sound, behavior, and values are well aware that learning by ear is an important—and prized—element to grasp.

Interdisciplinarity

Given that ethnomusicology is the holistic study of *music in and as culture*, it would follow that it is best studied through multiple academic lenses including language and linguistics, economics, politics, history and geography, and the related arts (dance, drama, visual arts, poetry, and literature). Interdisciplinarity, or interdisciplinary study, is the combining of insights from two or more disciplines and fields in order to shine light on a given idea or issue. Just as global warming requires an understanding of several different scientific disciplines together in order to frame and interpret its complexities, so can musical cultures be better known by crossing boundaries of sound to social meaning. Through the interdisciplinary study of music, it is possible to recognize the economic advantages of playing brass band music for weddings in India and to understand why a Bulgarian community will choose certain repertoire for the cultural shows they put on for tourists, for instance. It is useful to know music as it sounds now and sounded then, and to recognize how the location of people—geographically at sea level or in the high desert, for example—can determine how instruments are developed and played. An understanding of music's cultural contexts and an embrace of the backstories behind the songs are a result of interdisciplinary, integrated approaches to teaching and learning.

Just as ethnomusicologists examine music through interdisciplinary realms, innovative educators are facilitating student learning through the integration of multiple perspectives. In many teaching-learning contexts, educators who seek to improve student achievement in one discipline or field are doing so through rigorous and relevant curricula that draws in other disciplines and fields. Aspects of Western music history may be underscored by slides of paintings, sculpture, and architecture of the same historical period, even as knowledge of migratory groups—the Jewish diaspora from the Eastern Mediterranean to Spain, and the seafaring traders from southern Indian to Cambodia and Vietnam, for example—awaken an awareness of reasons for music that is a result of cultural mixes and mergers. The interdisciplinary integration of subject matter is as critical to teaching, and the many-splendored meanings of music are known for their culturally specific religious, ritualistic, social, political, and environmental circumstances. Following in the footsteps of ethnomusicologists, the teaching of world music cultures benefits from delving beyond the sound to the surrounding conditions and features.

Othering, Tokenizing, and Essentializing

Emanating from contemporary postmodern and feminist theories, ethnomusicologists with sensitivity toward marginalized voices in mind have cautioned music instructors (and students) of the potential dangers of participating in actions or dialogues that are *othering, tokenizing,* or *essentializing.* World music courses without attention to these facets are liable to offend or confound students, or to lead them down the road toward misconceptions and false notions of music and the people the music is meant to represent.

Othering occurs when someone brings negative attention to the ways in which a culture is dissimilar from a privileged or dominant culture (such as Western European and European-American groups). One example of Othering in higher education is the instance of a professor lamenting the lack of melodic material in hip-hop music, and then comparing it pejoratively to the *bel canto* vocal quality of the Puccini aria. Dominant-culture music genres, from orchestral to opera forms, typically comprise the standard to which other styles must measure up, which is ubiquitously observed when four-year music major programs center dominant musical forms and marginalize others (i.e., world, folk, and popular music) in single "one-off" courses. Misguided but well-intentioned comparisons are also offered in the act of Othering, where someone marvels at unfamiliar music because it sounds "exotic." In short, the practice of Othering is observed whenever the norms of one culture are viewed—whether implicitly or explicitly—as naturally superior to other "strange" or "exotic" cultures.

Tokenism regards the surface-level inclusion of marginalized groups in a feeble attempt to establish the appearance of diversity. In a world music course, tokenism can be seen when a professor offers students only a passing moment of collective focus or discussion on Balinese *gamelan*, for example, never to be repeated or provided explanation of the meaning and value of this music to the Balinese culture. Beyond music, prominent examples of tokenism in university settings are found when people of color are appointed to committees in order to offer the appearance of diversity. The result is that underrepresented faculty are disproportionately asked to load up on service responsibilities in order to fulfill these institutional expectations.

Essentialism is the attribution of stereotypical and blanketed characteristics toward members of a particular cultural group and their music. Consider, for instance, a professor who characterizes "African" music (notably referencing an entire continent rather than a specific country such as Nigeria or specific culture such as Yoruba) as "especially rhythmic" and percussion-oriented—with no mention of the pervasiveness of the plucked lutes, zithers, and harps that pervade many musical cultures across the continent. Likewise, Chinese music might be broadly described as "pentatonic" with no mention of the elaborate improvisations that reach far beyond these five tones, just as the music of Mexico is sometimes personified exclusively through *mariachi* despite its richly diverse expressions. Such essentialist descriptions oversimplify and promote rough generalizations about an entire culture group.

Cultural Appropriation vs. Cultural Appreciation

Cultural appropriation and cultural appreciation are two sides of one coin, both of which usually arise from an effort to understand a heritage that is different from one's own. The impetus may be cultural curiosity or even an intent to celebrate distinctive features of a community, but the difference between appropriation and appreciation is ultimately a question of cultural sensitivity. Specifically, cultural appropriation is the inappropriate and unacknowledged adoption of practices from one social or ethnic community by members of another (typically dominant) community. It is often seen as a byproduct of colonization, oppression, and assimilation, with a deep history of the dominant social group becoming defensive or reputative of the possibility that their actions might indeed be appropriating another's culture. Musically, it is the borrowing of music without concern for its owners, origin, history, or contextual meaning. Well-known examples include the song "Hound Dog," which was made famous by Elvis Presley in 1956 but originally recorded by Big Mama Thornton in 1952;[1] the Zulu "Mbube" melody being adapted for folk recordings of "Wimoweh" and the pop hit "The Lion Sleeps Tonight" despite very little compensation being attributed to the original composer (Solomon Linda); the American choir Roomful of Teeth being accused by First Nations artists of appropriating the practice of Inuit *katajjaq* (throat singing);[2] and the recent use of the Japanese penname Keiko Yamada by American composer Larry Clark.[3]

The flip side of the "coin" of recognizing difference is cultural appreciation, the result of conscious and culturally sensitive efforts to learn about valued traditions and to understand their significance to people. Understanding the music of the Burmese *nat pwe* festival, or the powwow ceremony of the Northern Plains Indians, or the Japanese theater form of *kabuki* requires an honest effort to unravel layers of meaning as they are understood by those who know these forms. Such unraveling may require the permission and guidance of cultural insiders and a desire to understand the expressions that have been collectively shaped and embraced by a community over the ages. Cultural appreciation is a recognition of and respect for the qualities of a collective group, including their aesthetic, cultural, social, and structural features and values. As a result of dedicated time to follow through the five dimensions of World Music Pedagogy, for example, students learn to understand and appreciate the music for its aesthetic, cultural, social, and structural composite. Cultural *appreciation* is thus an honest recognition of the qualities of a community, even approval and admiration of the culture, which arises through understanding (see Howard, 2020).

Authenticity

The concept of *authenticity* refers to the necessity of music to be maintained precisely as it was conceived by those from within the culture. Some hold a conservative view of authenticity, arguing that any performance should pursue an exact re-creation of a traditional performance. In contrast, others hold a more liberal view, reasoning that all music becomes recontextualized once it is performed (Campbell, 2018). Given even a more liberal conceptualization of authenticity, however, performances of world music should nevertheless attempt to remain true to its original sound and context whenever possible. Although the music will always become recontextualized in the process, performers should conduct personal research to promote a musical presentation that sounds similarly in its new context as it would sound in its original context. However, as many ethnomusicologists and music educators have attested, authenticity is an elusive target that may never be objectively achieved (Schippers, 2010). Instead, by approaching musical experiences with the utmost of *integrity*, instructors can maintain the contextual parameters of the music while allowing the musical performance to be reasonably recontextualized as students breathe new life into it.

Toward a More Mindful Pedagogy of World Music Cultures

Active musical participation enables students to viscerally experience a remarkable diversity of unique traditions through embodied performance, resulting in a profound and enduring impact beyond mere academic learning. As they immerse themselves within various musical cultures through listening, singing, playing, and dancing, students are simultaneously gaining deeper insights into the cultural contexts associated with the music. In the process, they come to understand not just the sonic properties of the music but the distinctive histories, stories, and values of the people they represent. Thus, a student's decision to participate in a world music course during their college years can initiate an eternal affinity for cultivating artistic citizenship and learning beyond oneself. These opportunities should not be squandered through talk and lecture but seized through participation and action.

Teaching world music in higher education institutions is both a challenging and fulfilling endeavor. But above all, it is *necessary* in today's times. Despite political interests that swing back and forth like a pendulum, isolationism will remain a transitory sickness because no amount of policy and no degree of xenophobic nationalism can halt how the world seeks to transform. And institutions of music within higher education are not independent of these social realities. With migrations that are quickly changing the landscape of the world's cities and nations, our neighbors, our colleagues, and our students look less like the musical "giants" of bygone eras and more like those whose music is centralized through a globalized music curriculum. The time is ripe for us to make reparations in music programs, to encourage students to decentralize dominant narratives and supplement opportunities to more deeply embrace and celebrate those whose songs have been silenced within higher education. Just as migrants cross our borders and reach our shores out of a desire to *join us* rather than *replace us*—despite troubling messages to the contrary—a culturally diverse music curriculum likewise seeks to unite Diabaté and Debussy, AlHaj and Holst, and de Borinquen and Beethoven on a mutual, artistic level.

Glossary

Aurality: The quality of learning by ear, aurally, which forms the basis of World Music Pedagogy's embrace of listening as a critical avenue of learning culturally unfamiliar music.

Authenticity: The necessity for music to be maintained precisely as it was conceived by those from within the culture; a conservative view of authenticity argues for performance as an exact re-creation of a traditional performance, while others recognize the reality of music as likely to be at least slightly personalized or recontextualized by the performer (or performing group).

Cultural appropriation: The inappropriate and unacknowledged adoption of practices from one social or ethnic community by members of another (typically dominant) community.

Emic: An approach that gives focus to local people and their behaviors, meanings, and values, attributing value to the knowledge of those within a culture.

Essentialism: Attribution of stereotypical characteristics toward members of a particular cultural group or their cultural forms, leading to oversimplified and misleading generalizations.

Etic: An approach that shifts from the perspective of local people to the observations and interpretations of research-oriented outsiders, in which scholars follow a scientific path in interpreting cultures through generalizations about human behaviors.

Hybridity: The condition of combining musical traditions.

Interdisciplinarity: The combination of insights from two or more disciplines and fields in order to shine light on a given idea or issue.

Orality: The quality of transmitting or teaching music by singing, chanting, or playing an instrument, as opposed to teaching via notation.

Othering: The act of bringing negative attention to the ways in which another culture is dissimilar from a dominant or privileged culture, often highlighting characteristics that seem "strange" or "exotic."

Tokenism: Surface-level inclusion of marginalized groups in a feeble attempt to establish the appearance of diversity or comprehensive coverage.

Notes

1. However, even this example of cultural appropriation is not quite black and white. The claim of appropriation in this case comes from the fact that Elvis made the song famous, selling over 10 million copies, while Big Mama Thornton, who recorded a version four years before Presley, earned comparatively little. However, the song was actually written by Jerry Leiber and Mike Stoller, who were both Jewish American songwriters. However, regardless of the song's origins, the disproportionate earnings between Presley and Thornton illustrate the immense racial discrimination that has been pervasive in the music industry.
2. George, J. (2019, October). Acclaimed American choir slammed for use of Inuit throat singing. *Nunatsiaq News.* https://nunatsiaq.com/stories/article/acclaimed-american-choir-slammed-for-use-of-inuit-throat-singing/?fbclid=IwAR3xRteuqPU8IO4ra8Jflde OSkTaspSD0hznVn9mDhWiNePaHds_PRh9jFs
3. Jolley, J. (2019, November). The curious case of Keiko Yamada. *New Music USA.* https://nmbx.newmusicusa.org/the-curious-case-of-keiko-yamada/

References

Campbell, P. S. (2018). *Music, education, and society: Bridging cultures and communities.* Teachers College Press.

Howard, K. (2020). Equity in music education: Cultural appropriation versus cultural appreciation—Understanding the difference. *Music Educators Journal, 106*(3), 68–70. https://www.doi.org/10.1177/0027432119892926

Nettl, B. (2010). Music education and ethnomusicology: A (usually) harmonious relationship. *Min-Ad: Israel Studies in Musicology Online, 8*(1), 1–9.

Schippers, H. (2010). *Facing the music: Shaping music education from a global perspective.* Oxford University Press.

Appendix 1
Learning Pathways

The following three Learning Pathways represent a beginning-to-end manifestation of the five dimensions of the World Music Pedagogy approach. Together, they constitute the pedagogical episodes on three musical works that were featured across the chapters; they are conveniently located as follows so that the flow between dimensions can be recognized, and one continuing pathway of learning the music and its cultural purposes can be clearly delineated. These progressive WMP episodes may be parceled out over many class sessions, repeated in part, or varied and extended in order that students can orient themselves to the nuances of new musical expressions. Alternatively, they can be economically pressed into a single session, as necessary. The intent of the Learning Pathways is to map how teaching and learning proceeds over the course of the World Music Pedagogy, where listening, participatory musicking, performance, creating, and integrating experiences open students to the many splendors of a musical culture.

Learning Pathway #1
"Time to Have Fun" (Iraq/Iran)

Materials:

- "Time to Have Fun," Rahim AlHaj Trio, Smithsonian Folkways Recordings. https://folkways.si.edu/rahim-alhaj/time-to-have-fun
- Students' and instructor's instruments of choice

Attentive Listening

Procedure:

1. Ask, "how many instruments do you hear?"
2. Play track [0:00–0:38] and field responses.

    A: Three instruments.
3. "Pick one of the instruments that you hear in this selection and try to describe it in your own words. Does it sound like a wind instrument, string instrument, percussion instrument?"
4. Play track [0:00–0:38] and field responses.

    A: Two string instruments [one plucked, one hammered]; percussion.
5. Display an image of the *oud* and *santūr* (Figure 2.3). Briefly discuss that both instruments can be found across the Persian Gulf in many forms and musical styles. Both instruments represent a long and diverse history of the lute family (*oud*) and dulcimer family (*santūr*) around the world.
6. "What function do you think this music might serve? What do you think the music attempts to communicate?"
7. Play track [0:00–0:38] and field open answers.

    A: The piece is related to dance and celebration.
8. "Throughout this section of the recording, does the melody appear to repeat or change each time it's presented?"
9. Play track [0:00–0:38] and field answers.

    A: It repeats.
10. "Close your eyes and raise your hand when you think you finally hear the melody change." *By directing students to close their eyes, they are encouraged to focus on their own assessment of the recording rather than raising their hands only by seeking agreement with peers.*
11. Play extended track [0:00–1:07].

    A: Students should raise their hands around 0:38.

Figure 2.3   Painting of a *santūr* and *oud* player by Ibrahim Jabbar-Beik

Engaged Listening

1. "Can you trace the *oud* and *santūr* melody with your finger? After you do so, describe how the A-section melody moves."

2. Play track [0:00–0:38] and field responses.

    A: It ascends and then descends several times within the A section.

3. "While you continue tracing your finger along with the melody, sing it on a neutral syllable (e.g., 'doo')."

4. Play track [0:00–0:38].

Figure 3.1 Melody to "Time to Have Fun (transcribed by W. J. Coppola)"

5. Show students the notated melody on the board or projector (Figure 3.1).

   Note: For upper-level seminar courses, it might be preferable to have students transcribe the melody on their own or place it on their instruments by ear.

6. "Please sing along once again, using the following notation to help make corrections as you go."

   Note: It is important that students are able to demonstrate their internalization of the melody before being shown the notation, which reflects a "sound-before-sight" method. Because this music was likely composed/learned aurally between Rahim AlHaj and Sourena Sefati, it is recommended that students learn the melody in a similar fashion.

7. Play track [0:00–0:38].

8. Ask students to individually line up the pitches of the melody in order from lowest to highest (they should also omit the A-natural, as it represents a passing tone to the melody).

9. Discuss: "Just as most music in Western traditions are based upon a series of pitches, which we call *scales*, much of the music throughout the Middle East use what are called *maqams*. *Maqams* are similar to scales, but they tend to have different arrangements than our Western scales, and they don't always use the same types of pitches (for example, sometimes they might include microtones). Check with your neighbor to see what type of *maqam* you've discovered in this song. We'll give it a name later."

10. Show the scale on the board or projector (Figure 3.2).

11. "The *maqam* used in this particular example is called the *maqam kurd*. In this case, it is a *maqam kurd* starting on G."

12. Guide students toward an understanding that the scale's pitches indicate that the key signature would be Eb major, with three flats (Bb, Eb, and Ab).

Figure 3.2 *Maqam kurd*

"However, we can't quite say that the song is in E♭ major, because the song doesn't seem to rest on E♭ as its 'home.' What pitch *does* appear to be the song's 'home' or resting place?"

> **A:** G.

13. "We place 'G' as the first and last note because it is the 'home,' or 'tonic,' of the song. In Western music, this is a special type of scale called a *mode*. If we are thinking about E♭ major, but starting on the note G, which number mode would this be?"

> **A:** The third mode in E♭ (Note: This might require assistance from visual cues of the E♭ major scale for students to recognize this relationship).

14. Depending on the students' prerequisite knowledge, ask students to relate the scale to the mode used in Western notation (if not, skip to step 15). Ask, "does this *maqam* resemble a mode used in Western music?"

> **A:** Yes, the Phrygian mode.

15. Discuss: "In Western music, there's a special name for modes that start on the 3rd degree of the major scale. We call it the *Phrygian mode*. So, the Phrygian mode and the *maqam kurd* are actually the same scale. However, since we are studying this piece within the context of Middle Eastern music, we will refer to it only as the *maqam kurd*."

Enactive Listening

1. "Now, let's focus our attention on the percussion. Can you tap the beat along with the recording?"

2. Play track [0:12–0:38].

3. "Can you hear the basic pattern of low and high pitches in the percussion? Place the low pitches on your lap (or stomp feet) and place the high pitches in your hands (clap) or on the desktop."

4. Play track [0:12–0:38]. The pattern should be *low-low-high*.

5. "How many times does this *khaliji* pattern of *low-low-high* repeat during each phrase? What happens after?"

6. Play track [0:12–0:38].

> **A:** Seven times. After the seventh pattern, the percussion plays the eighth note figure along with the *oud* and *santūr* (see measure 8 of Figure 3.1).

7. Split the class into two halves. Have one half of the class sing the melody on a neutral syllable while the other half of the class performs the basic *khaliji* rhythm.

8. Play track [0:00–0:38]. Repeat as needed, and be sure to allow the class to switch roles.

9. "As an added challenge, try to tap/clap the *khaliji* rhythm while singing the melody. If you're not ready for that step, continue to perform only your role."

10. Play track [0:00–0:38].

11. Repeat without the recording. Immediately after, play the track again [0:00–0:38] and have students compare their performance with the recording. Repeat this step until the students feel comfortable performing it on their own.

12. Repeat this process for the rest of the recording, paying special attention to when and how the music shifts and continually comparing their performances to the recorded model.

Creating World Music

1. After students are able to perform the selection confidently through various Engaged and Enactive Listening activities, divide the class into small groups of 4–8. Try to include at least one student who can read and write using Western notation, if possible. This student will act as the group's scribe.

2. "Let's sing the main melody once through and assign letters to each 4-beat measure to figure out the micro-form of the melody."

3. Play track [0:00–0:38]. Hold up fingers for each measure to guide students who may not be familiar with concepts like a "measure."

   A: The micro-form is ABAB'ABA'C.

4. "In small groups, we are going to compose brand-new melodies using the *maqam kurd* and the existing form of the song." Display the pitches of the *maqam kurd* (Figure 3.2) on the board.

5. "There are two different levels of participation for this activity, which you may self-select as a group. For Option 1, you will compose a completely new melody. For Option 2, you may keep the 'A' motive and just compose new 'B' and 'C' motives."

6. To help facilitate the activity, have students write out their three independent motives separately before putting them in the order of the song's form. Provide the following parameters:

   • The A motive should lead melodically into the B motive;

   • The C motive should be 2 measures long (to make the full phrase 9 measures) and should end on the root of the *maqam kurd* (G);

   • Students may choose to honor or ignore the need to write slightly different motives for the A' and B' sections.

Note: As presented, these steps are highly structured to give students the necessary parameters to feel comfortable with a potentially unfamiliar task. However, to be responsive to the students' level of comfort, the instructor should readily remove parameters as needed to allow students more creative freedom, as appropriate.

7. Have small groups perform their new compositions for the class.

8. Reincorporate the percussion part (learned during Enactive Listening) into these compositions.

9. If desired, have the class choose a handful of their favorite melodies and perform them as a class, creating an arrangement from these several motivic ideas.

Integrating World Music

Geography

There are approximately two million Arab Americans, with over 215,000 immigrants from Iraq and nearly 400,000 from Iran. Students can explore for information on Iran and Iraq using the search functions on such websites as CIA World Factbook and National Geographic.

Sample discussion questions:

1. How and when were the current borders developed in the region in which Iran and Iraq are situated?

   A: 1639 Zuhab Treaty with Ottoman Turks.

2. What is the strategic importance of such countries as Djibouti, Qatar, and Kuwait in relation to the larger Gulf States?

   A: All have access to sea and oil.

History

Students can seek out information on some of the world's very earliest known musicians, many of whom lived in present-day Iraq and Syria, from the period 2300–970 BCE: Enheduanna (ca. 2300), Dada (ca. 2040 BCE), and Risiya (fl. ca. 1790 BCE). They can explore examples from the Golden Age of Islam (600–850 BCE), including Barbad (ca. 600 CE), Jamila (715 CE), Ibrahim al-Mawsili (742–804 CE), Ishaq al-Mawsili (767–850 CE), and Ziryab (ca. 790–850 CE). Ziryab was an accomplished African musician who had a profound on European music in medieval times. Students can also explore important 20th-century musicians such as Wadi al Safi, Fairuz, and Um Khulthumm.

Sample discussion questions:

1. Where do you think our knowledge of these earliest known musicians come from?

   A: Archaeology, ancient writings.

2. What was the Golden Age of Islam, how was it important for music, and how did it ultimately impact scientific development in Europe?

   A: This is the historical period spanning the 8th–13th centuries, a time of the development of robust music theory by Al Farabi, and scientific methods by such figures as Avicenna and Averroes.

3. How did music of Iraq and Iran change in the 20th century?

> **A:** Relevant processes include westernization, standardization, and application of technologies.

Social Sciences

Students can learn about the "Translation Movement," along with Avicenna (one of the earliest known proponents of music therapy), Averroes (who reintroduced Aristotle to Europeans), and Al Farabi (one of the world's first prolific theorists of music, who had a major impact on both Middle Eastern and European thinkers of later generations).

Sample discussion question:

1. How did Avicenna, Averroes, and Al Farabi impact European science?

> **A:** They deeply influenced the most well-known European scholars to come later, such as Francis Bacon and Thomas Aquinas

Laboratory Sciences and Mathematics

Some of the greatest mathematicians of all time were associated with Iraq and Iran. Students can explore this important legacy from the age of Al-Khwarizmi (ca. 780–ca. 850), to the Golden Age when Avicenna (ca. 980–ca. 1037) lived in Baghdad, to Jamshid al-Kashi (ca. 1380–1429), and eventually Maryam Mirzakhani (1977–2017), winner of the 2014 Fields Medal for achievement in mathematics.

Sample discussion question:

1. How have Iraqi and Iranian scholars contributed to the global advancement of mathematics at various points in history?

> **A:** House of Wisdom in Baghdad, invention of algebra by al-Khwarizmi.

World Languages:

Iran is home to many influential poets, particularly Mevlana (Mevlevi), known to Europeans as Rumi (1207–1273). His poems continue to be popular all across the Middle East, in Arabic, Turkish, Farsi, and other languages. The typical graduate of Iranian schools can recite hundreds of poems that were memorized as an essential part of the educational system. Select some of Rumi's poetry to explain to the class. Locate recordings, including by video, of these poems recited in the original languages (Farsi and Arabic).

Sample discussion question:

1. Can you identify and interpret some poems by Rumi, referring to both the original language and English translation?

> **A:** See "This Marriage," "Gone to the Unseen," and selections from Masnavi Book I.

Learning Pathway #2

"E Maru Rahi" (Tahiti)

Materials:

- "E Maru Rahi," Royal Tahitian Dance Company, Smithsonian Folkways Recordings. https://folkways.si.edu/royal-tahitian-dance-company/e-maru-rahi/world/music/track/smithsonian
- Ukuleles (or substitutes), shakers

Attentive Listening

Procedure:

1. "What instruments in this recording are providing the underlying groove or rhythm?"
2. Play track [0:00–0:54] and field responses.

   A: Ukulele, shaker.
3. "Is the groove in duple or triple meter?"
4. Play track [0:00–0:54] and field responses.

   A: Triple meter.
5. "What adjectives would you use to describe the mood of this song? Is it energetic or calming? Celebratory or mourning? Reflective or showy?"
6. Play track [0:00–0:54] and field open responses.
7. "How many musicians do you think are performing in this selection? Specifically, see if you can keep track of how many instrumental and vocal parts there are."
8. Play track [0:00–0:54] and field responses.

   A: There are at least 4 instrumental parts (1 ukulele, 1 bass, 1 shaker, 1 rhythm instrument) and about 3–4 vocal parts.
9. Play track again to check responses.
10. "Can you 'pretend-play' along with the strumming pattern of the ukulele?"
11. Play track [0:00–0:54] and repeat as necessary.
12. "Given what you've heard so far, where in the Pacific Islands might you place this song? (Hint: If you listen closely, the singers will make reference to the island in the song.)"
13. Play track [0:00–0:54].

    A: Tahiti. (Note: The singers mention Tahiti at 0:49 in the song.)

Engaged Listening

Procedure, Melody:

1. "Can you sing along with the melody on a neutral syllable?"
2. Play track [0:00–0:54].
3. Post the lyrics on the board or projector. "Now, can you sing along with the melody with the lyrics? We will sing it several times through so you can hear how the lyrics fit the melody."

   E maru rahi e aue

   ua moe to tino

   e ita to mata

   e ite faaho e

   e ita to mata

   e ite faaho e

   to'u aia here

   o Tahiti rahi e
4. Play track [0:00–0:54] and repeat as necessary.

Procedure, Harmony:

1. "Now, let's focus on the harmony played by the ukulele. Can you 'air play' the ukulele part to try to figure out the strumming pattern?"
2. Play track [0:00–0:54].
3. While the strumming pattern is sometimes performed somewhat differently in an improvised manner, guide students toward the following strumming solution:

   Note: This pattern is more difficult to read through notation than it is to learn aurally. Instructors should consider using Figure 3.3 as a personal reference rather than providing it to the students.

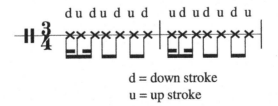

d = down stroke
u = up stroke

Figure 3.3 Strumming pattern to "E Maru Rahi"

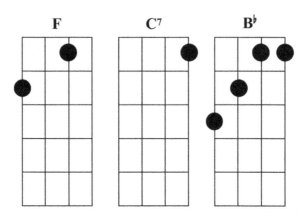

Figure 3.4   F, C7, and B♭ chords in "E Maru Rahi."

4. When ready, provide ukuleles (or guitars) to a handful of students. (Depending on how many are available, rotate the instruments so all students have an opportunity to attempt the activity. Refer to the activity in the opening vignette for one possibility.)

5. Guide students toward the two main chords of the song, F and C7 (see Figure 3.4). These chords are considered to be straightforward enough for unexperienced students to attain quickly. For more advanced students, also provide the third chord, B♭, and allow students to self-select their desire to attempt this more challenging chord. At this time, it is not important for students to be able to switch fluently between these chords, which is usually the most challenging aspect of playing the ukulele.

6. Split the ukulele-playing students into three groups: those playing only the F chord, those playing only the C7 chord, and those playing only the B♭ chord. For students with prior experience playing the ukulele, allow them to switch between all three chords on their own.

7. Displaying the below chord progression on the board, have students play along with the recording [0:00–0:54] on their instruments by playing only their respective chords (or self-selecting if they would prefer to play all chords):

Intro:	F	C⁷	F	C⁷
Verse:	‖: F	F	F	F
	F	C⁷	C⁷	C⁷
	C⁷	C⁷	C⁷	C⁷
	F	F	F	F
	B♭	B♭	B♭	B♭

F	F	F	F
C⁷	C⁷	C⁷	C⁷
F	C⁷	:‖	

8. "Now, let's continue playing the ukulele harmony along with the recording, but let's add the singing back in as well. Try to sing the lyrics while playing, or sing on a neutral syllable again if necessary."

9. Play track [0:00–0:54] and repeat as necessary (until students become more comfortable with singing and playing).

Enactive Listening

1. "Now that we are becoming more comfortable with the singing and playing, let's focus once again on *how* the singers are singing the lyrics. How would you describe their singing style? Are they singing with an open sound? A forward sound? Let's see if you can match their timbre."

2. Play track [0:00–0:54]. The sound should be resonant and somewhat dark with a slightly forward tone.

3. Add the shaker rhythm back into the song. Provide shakers to several students and have them play along with the recording while singing (no ukuleles). Remind them that the rhythm is a fixed ostinato, or repeating pattern, so they should repeat the same rhythm once they've figured it out.

4. Play track [0:00–0:54].

5. Now, with all of our musical elements—the sung melody, ukulele harmony, and shaker rhythm—let's try to put it all together along with the recording.

    Note: Once again, the instructor may ask the ukulele-playing students to self-select their difficulty level with two considerations: (a) whether they should divide the chords (each group only playing one chord) or play all of the chords (switching between them), and (b) whether they should sing and play or just play (allowing the non-ukulele students to sing on their own).

6. Play track [0:00–0:54].

7. "Finally, let's try to play this whole section on our own, without the recording."

8. Perform as a group without the recording. Immediately after, play the track again [0:00–0:54] and have students compare their performance with the recording. Repeat this step until the students feel comfortable performing it on their own.

9. Ask, "what else can we do to further bring our performance closer to the recording?"

    A: Add the sung harmony, add Polynesian dance, etc.

Creating World Music

1. This activity involves students writing new lyrics to accompany the "E Maru Rahi" melody. As the instructor, decide whether students should be asked to use the existing topic of the song (the loss of the singers' brother) or an entirely different topic (to be decided by the class).

2. In small groups (or individually), have students compose poetic verses regarding their topic, in English. If using the existing topic of the song, students might tell the story of how the brother died, how the family mourned his loss, or about the spirit of the brother, for example.

3. Optional: Have students first count the number of syllables in each phrase and compose their poetic verse with the same number of syllables. (If this step is not desired, students can conduct the same activity but will slightly change the rhythm to fit the new lyrics.)

    E maru rahi e aue (**8**)

    ua moe to tino (**6**)

    e ita to mata (**6**)

    e ite faaho e (**6**)

    e ita to mata (**6**)

    e ite faaho e (**6**)

    to'u aia here (**6**)

    o Tahiti rahi e (**7**)

4. Have a small group of students play ukuleles and shakers as each group's newly-composed verse is displayed on a projector.

5. While the instrumentalists are playing the harmonic accompaniment (Episode 3.2), have the rest of the class sing the new lyrics using the original melody.

Integrating World Music

Geography:
Students can explore for information on French Polynesia and Tahiti using the search functions on such websites as CIA World Factbook and National Geographic. Around 200,000 people live in the Society Islands, an archipelago of French Polynesia in which Tahiti is the major island.
Sample discussion question:

1. How do geography and landscape impact the materials available for construction of musical instruments, and how is this reflected in Tahiti?

    A: Tahiti's traditional instruments include *ihara* (struck bamboo percussion), the *vivo* (nose flute), and the *pu* (conch trumpet)

History
Reliable resources can aid in telling of Tahiti's "discovery" and colonization by Europeans. Tahiti has been long associated with dance, and Tahitians know that there is great beauty in how these ensembles attain unified gestures with harmonious singing and instrumental accompaniment.
Sample discussion question:

1. What factors have contributed to the evolution of an eroticized image since the earliest colonial contacts?

    A: See Captain William Bligh's Mutiny on HMS Bounty and Paul Gauguin's paintings of Tahiti.

Social Sciences
Notable industries and products associated with the island economy of Tahiti are pearls, coconut products, vanilla, and tourism. Students can locate and watch videos about pearl diving in Tahiti, then read about the hazards of pearl diving profession. Students can search online for articles about the perils of pearl divers. They can explore, too, the place of music and dance in Tahiti's cultural tourism.
Sample discussion questions:

1. What the notable risks are faced by pearl divers?

    A: Drowning, oxygen deprivation, sharks, stingrays, and health problems
2. How can cultural tourism have both positive and negative impacts on traditional island communities?

    A: Increased income streams, commodification of both nature and culture

Laboratory Sciences and Mathematics
Some low-lying regions of Tahiti are not above sea level anymore. Governments of the Marshall Islands (and the Maldives) have even begun seeking to negotiate options for evacuation of the human population within a few generations. For reference, students may consult the Majuro Declaration from the 44th Pacific Islands Forum summit (2013) and further developments since that time.
Sample discussion questions:

1. Is it possible to calculate how much longer each of these islands is likely to last before evacuation of the human population may become necessary under current rates of climate change?

    A: Debatable; many calculations exist, but the exercise of exploring this timely issue is the primary point rather than arriving at an absolute answer

2. Is climate change represented in any musical examples from Tahiti or the vicinity?

   A: Yes, it is a common theme in popular music

World Languages

Many words in Tahitian are similar to Māori and other Polynesian languages. The dissection of a song text can offer culture-specific insights or universal principles that are understood by people of many cultures. See the translation of "E Maru Rahi" for a launch to discussion.

E maru rahi e aue (Great tenderness and how)

ua moe to tino (lost is your body)

e ita to mata (and your eyes)

e ite faaho e (and see how that)

e ita to mata (and your eyes)

e ite faaho e (and see how that)

to'u aia here (my beloved)

o Tahiti rahi e (is tucked nearby)

Learning Pathway #3
"Dulce Sueño Mío" (Puerto Rico)

Materials:

- "Dulce Sueño Mío (Sweet Dream of Mine)," Ecos de Borinquen, Smithsonian Folkways Recordings. https://folkways.si.edu/ecos-de-borinquen/dulce-sueno-mio-sweet-dream-of-mine/latin-world/music/track/smithsonian
- Instruments of students' and instructor's choice

Attentive Listening

Procedure:

1. "Which instruments can you identify during the opening of this selection? Don't worry about identifying the exact name of it, but try to at least identify the timbre or the instrument family."

2. Play track [0:00–0:42] and field responses.

   A: 2 guitar-like instruments (cuatros); 1 rasp- or shaker-like instrument (guiro); 1 bass-sounding instrument (guitar); 1 percussion instrument (bongos) singer (trovador).

3. "What musical role is each instrument playing in this selection?"

4. Play track [0:00–0:42] and field responses.

   A: Cuatros provide melody and harmony, guitar provides bass line, guiro and bongos provide rhythm.

5. "Pay attention to the singer/*trovador*'s singing. What language does he seem to be singing in?"

6. Play track [0:00–0:42] and field responses.

   A: Spanish

7. "Listen to the *trovador*'s words after he sings his introductory "le-le-la"s. Does it sound like he is repeating any lyrics?

8. Play new segment of the track [0:21–1:07] and field responses.

   A: He repeats his first line as well as his last

9. Post the lyrics of the first verse on the board or projector. "Listen to the lyrics again, and see if you can determine a pattern from what is being sung."

   Sueño de mi vida

   Porqué me despiertas

   Cerrando una puerta

   Y abriendo una herida

   Hoy en mí se anida

   Un mundo de hastío.

   Y ya en mi plantío

   Marchita una flor.

   No me seas traidor

   Dulce sueño mío.

10. Play track [0:21–1:07]; repeat as necessary.

11. Guide students to identify that there is a rhyming pattern at the end of each line.

12. "Can you write down the rhyming scheme that you see/hear in the first verse of the song? Use letters A, B, C, and so on."

13. Play track [0:21–1:07]; repeat as necessary.

14. Guide students toward uncovering the correct rhyme scheme: *ABBAACCDDC*.

Engaged Listening

Procedure, *Cuatro* Melody:

Before this class session, request that students bring any instrument they may play outside of class (e.g., guitar, ukulele, melodica, wind instrument). For those without instruments, students can use a mobile piano app such as GarageBand. Remember, many students enrolled in these courses may be active musicians outside of class, or may even be music majors. Alternatively, the instructor might provide pitched instruments such as xylophones or metallophones (which might be available for loan from the music education department).

1. "Trace the *cuatro* melody with your finger, outlining separate arches for each 8-beat phrase."

2. Play track [0:00–0:21].

3. "Can you determine which of your arches were the same, and which were different? Let's listen again, and try to think of the melody's pattern in terms of As and Bs. What's the form?"

4. Play track [0:00–0:21]

    A: AABB' (Students might respond with AABB, but direct their ears toward the slightly different ending of the second B section).

5. "Since the introduction is just made up of two simple 8-beat sections, let's try to figure out how to play this melody. First, let's sing the melody on a neutral syllable."

6. Play track [0:00–0:21].

7. "Now, let's try to place these pitches on instruments. We'll start with the A melody together." In small/medium groups, allow students to use their own instruments to locate the melody. Use Figure 3.5 as a personal guide, but avoid showing it to students; encourage them to transcribe the melody fully by ear.

    Note: Although this may feel like an advanced activity, remind students that this is how folk musicians often learn to play what they hear in their heads, and they should use their instruments as tools to help them decipher and translate the music they hear. To facilitate this activity further,

Figure 3.5 "Dulce Sueño Mío" *cuatro* melody (transcribed by W. J. Coppola).

it is recommended that the instructor maintains an inventory of students' musical expertise and carefully divides groups so that experienced and inexperienced musicians are grouped together for more efficient facilitation of the activity. Most importantly, it is important to remain patient of each student's individual progress with this task.

8. Play track on a loop [0:00–0:10] and facilitate progress by working with individual groups throughout (as well as TAs that might be assigned to the class). Continue until most students are able to place the full A melody on their instruments.

   This step might also require students to return to step 5 (singing the melody) as needed. In fact, students should be encouraged to continually sing-then-play the melody to match what they sing to their instruments.

9. Repeat steps 7 and 8 for the B melody [0:10–0:21].

Procedure, Sung Melody:

1. "Can you sing along with the melody on a neutral syllable?"

2. Play track [0:21–1:08].

3. Post the lyrics on the board or projector. "Now, can you sing along with the melody with the lyrics? We will sing it several times through so you can hear how the lyrics fit the melody."

   Sueño de mi vida

   Porqué me despiertas

   Cerrando una puerta

   Y abriendo una herida

   Hoy en mí se anida

   Un mundo de hastío.

   Y ya en mi plantío

   Marchita una flor.

   No me seas traidor

   Dulce sueño mío.

4. Play track [0: 21–1:08] and repeat as necessary.

Enactive Listening

1. Divide the class into three groups: vocal, instrumental, and rhythm: *Vocal* students will sing the *decimilla* [0:21–1:08]; *Instrumental* students will perform the *cuatro* melody [0:00–0:21] on instruments of their choice (see step 2 for more information); *Rhythm* students will perform the *guiro* melody with *guiros* and/or shakers [0:00–1:08].

Note: while students should emulate the basic guiro rhythm, they do not need to be concerned with performing it exactly as heard in the recordings, given the improvised nature of the guiro.

2. With students, engage in a discussion about which instruments should be responsible for playing the *cuatro* part (see the "Embrace Approximations" suggestion under "The DIY of WMP" section at the end of the chapter). Allow students to decide between using pitched percussion instruments (metallophones/xylophones) and other available instruments.

3. Along with the recording, have students perform their respective *cuatro* (instrumental), vocal, and rhythm parts. Repeat as necessary.

4. When the instructor deems the class to be ready, fade out the music and have students perform without the recording.

5. Perform all three parts (separately and/or together) without the recording and compare their performance with the recording. Ask, "in what ways can we make our performance more similar to the recording?"

6. Keep performing the recorded segment without the recording and continually compare to the recorded model.

7. A new interlude is played at 2:05. Allow students to either continue playing the original AABB' melody for this section, or learn this new melody by ear by once again following the Engaged Listening steps provided earlier.

Creating World Music

1. "Describe the content of the *trovador*'s improvisation. What is he singing about? How does he communicate his ideas? Through imagery? Metaphor? Literal depiction?" Review the Spanish/English lyrics of "Dulce Sueño Mío" for the sake of understanding the content about which the *trovador* sings.

2. Play track [0:21–1:08] and field responses.

   A: He sings about unrequited love. He communicates it through poetic metaphor and similes.

3. As a class, collectively decide upon a single topic for use in a new *décima*. Topics are often philosophical (e.g., love, freedom, nationalism), but can also be about a current events topic or other context-specific topic.

4. In small groups, have students compose 10-line *décimas* (in English or Spanish) following the proper rhyme scheme of *ABBAA CCDDC* and 8 syllables per line.

   Note: While décimas *would traditionally be improvised spontaneously, allow students time to compose their* décimas *and appreciate the difficulty of the trovador's task.*

5. Once each group has written their full *décima*, have them speak it aloud with a clear, even rhythm (no pitches yet). Students should repeat this until a clear rhythm develops from their chanting of the words.

6. Have students create a harmonic backing with *cuatros* (or instrumental facsimiles) and percussion instruments. Use a non-complex harmonic progression (such as oscillating I–V⁷ chords) to allow students to focus on successfully improvising melodies that fit the harmonic progression.

   Note: The focus here is not on re-creating the harmonic background of the original recording, but to create something new using the tradition of décima improvisation. Thus, using a simple I–V⁷ allows students to maintain focus on the lyric-writing aspect of the activity rather than harmonic or melodic concepts.

7. Cue students to continue chanting their non-pitched lyrics as a separate small group performs the harmonic progression in a loop. Encourage students to begin taking note of where their lyrics might be taking them melodically. Repeat as necessary.

8. Display each group's newly composed *décima* verse on a projector or white board.

9. While the instrumentalists are playing their invented harmonic accompaniment, have each small group perform their *décima* using either (a) an improvised melody or (b) the melody from the original recording.

Integrating World Music

Geography:

Students can explore for information on Puerto Rico using the search functions on such websites as PuertoRicoReport.com (https://welcome.topuertorico.org) and National Geographic. They may try to solve some free online quizzes (locatable via common internet search engines) such as "Do You Really Know Puerto Rico?" and "Puerto Rico History Test."

Traditionally, Puerto Rico has been famous for sugar cane and rum production. Note that today pharmaceuticals manufacturing is by far the largest specialized industry in Puerto Rico, followed by biotechnology and medical device manufacture.

Sample discussion question:

1. How is the Puerto Rican product rum made?

   A: Through a complex distillation process that is explained on the websites of famous rum makers.

History:

Students can explore the island's past as a Spanish colony (1493–1898), and its transition to its current designation as an unincorporated U.S. territory (1898–present). The earlier Arawak and Taino indigenous populations were overtaken by the Spanish during a long colonial period (1493–1898) and the arrival of enslaved Africans, the late 19th century saw the struggle of Puerto Ricans for autonomy, and the Spanish-American War, which led to the country's establishment as an American territory and commonwealth.

Sample discussion question:

1. What were some of social and economic changes in Puerto Rico as an American territory?

   A: The island agrarian culture was rapidly developed into a modern economic society, with the sugar, tobacco, and coffee industries leading the way. Schools, hospitals, roads, and communications reflected the American influence.

Music History:

Leonard Bernstein's *West Side Story* depicted the Nuyorican (Puerto Rican diaspora in U.S. mainland) community as part of its plotline, which also served as the conceptual basis for some of that well-known musical's complex rhythms. Some Puerto Rican and Nuyorican (New York-based) musicians became well-known for establishing salsa and Latin jazz styles, including Tito Puente, Willie Colon, and Tito Rodriguez (who also interacted with great Cuban and Cuban American musicians such as Celia Cruz, Perez Prado, Machito, and Xavier Cugat), and later came such popular stars as Ricky Martin, Daddy Yankee, and Luis Fonsi. However, *jíbaro* is the traditional *folk* music of Puerto Rico's rural Hispanic population (rather than the popular style of salsa), and famous *cuatro* virtuosos include Edwin Colon Zayas and Yomo Toro.

Sample discussion question:

1. What are some of the musical subgenres and styles attributed to Puerto Rican (and Cuban) musicians since the early 20th century?

   A: Examples include salsa, cha-cha-cha, son, rhumba, and merengue.

Social Sciences:

There is a difference between a U.S. state and a U.S. territory, the latter of which is Puerto Rico's current status. Referendums have indicated that the vast majority of Puerto Ricans would like the territory to become a U.S. state.

Sample discussion question:

1. What are the potential gains and challenges for Puerto Rico, were it to become a U.S. state?

   A: Greater political power is given to residents of states rather than to territorial residents. The shifting of language could prove challenging, since Spanish rather than English is the preferred language of the territory.

Laboratory Sciences and Mathematics:

Puerto Rico's economy has gradually shifted from an emphasis on agricultural products to pharmaceutical production and biotechnologies. However, the region still struggles with high unemployment.

Sample discussion question:

1. How do major economic indicators—such as Gross Domestic Product (GDP) and Purchasing Power Parity (PPP)—of Puerto Rico compare with the wealthiest and poorest U.S. states?

   A: Puerto Rico is one of the poorest parts of the U.S., where wages are low and jobs are not available for all citizens.

World Languages:
Spanish is among the most widely-spoken languages in the world. Unlike English, spelling and grammar in Spanish is relatively consistent with few exceptions to basic rules.

Sample discussion questions:
Are there alternative ways of translating the lyrics to "Dulce Sueño Mío"? Spanish-fluent students can be called on for deciphering various interpretations and metaphors used. Note the approximate translation of the Spanish lyrics to "Dulce Sueño Mío" that can be displayed by projector (see Chapter 2).

Dream of my life

Why wake me up

Closing a door

And opening a wound

Today in me it nests

A world of weariness.

And already in my plantation

Withered a flower.

Don't be a traitor

Sweet dream of mine.

Appendix 2
Additional Resources

This list provides important resources and references relevant to teaching and learning world music cultures in higher education. Included are readings regarding the need for global approaches to music education, strategies to culturally relevant and responsive music teaching, and discussions of matters of social justice. Additionally, this list supplies notable internet resources for locating recordings, films, and discussions that support the application of World Music Pedagogy in tertiary music education.

Ethnomusicology

Blacking, J. (1973). *How musical is man?* University of Washington Press.

Bohlman, P. V. (2002). *World music: A very short introduction.* Oxford University Press.

Hebert, D. G., & Rykowski, M. (2018). *Music glocalization: Heritage and music in a digital age.* Cambridge Scholars Press.

Merriam, A. P. (1964). *The anthropology of music.* Northwestern University Press.

Nettl, B. (1974). Thoughts on improvisation: A comparative approach. *The Musical Quarterly, 60*(1), 1–19. https://www.jstor.org/stable/741663

Nettl, B. (1983). *The study of ethnomusicology: Twenty-nine issues and concepts.* University of Illinois Press.

Nettl, B. (1992). Recent Directions in Ethnomusicology. In H. Myers (Ed.), *Ethnomusicology: an Introduction* (pp. 375–399). W. W. Norton.

Nettl, B. (1996). Ideas about music and musical thought: Ethnomusicological perspectives. *Journal of Aesthetic Education, 30*(2), 173–187. https://doi.org/10.2307/3333198

Nettl, B. (2005). *The study of ethnomusicology: Thirty-one issues and concepts.* University of Illinois Press.

Nettl, B. (2010a). Music education and ethnomusicology: A (usually) harmonious relationship. *Min-Ad: Israel Studies in Musicology Online*, 8(1), 1–9.

Nettl, B. (2010b). *Nettl's elephant: On the history of ethnomusicology*. University of Illinois Press.

Nettl, B. (2015). *The study of ethnomusicology: Thirty-three issues and concepts*. University of Illinois Press.

Nettl, B., & Bohlman, P. V. (Eds.). (1991). *Comparative musicology and anthropology of music: Essays on the history of ethnomusicology*. University of Chicago Press.

Rice, T. (2013). *Ethnomusicology: A very short introduction*. Oxford University Press.

Small, C. (1998). *Musicking: The meanings of performing and listening*. Wesleyan University Press.

Smith, M. P. (2003). Buffalo Bill and the Mardi Gras Indians. In M. Gaudet & J. C. McDonald (Eds.), *Mardi Gras, Gumbo, and Zydeco: Readings in Louisiana culture*. University Press of Mississippi.

Solís, T. (Ed.). (2004). *Performing ethnomusicology: Teaching and representation in world music ensembles*. University of California Press.

Taylor, T. D. (1997). *Global pop: World music, world markets*. Routledge.

Thompson, D. (Ed.). (2002). *Music in Puerto Rico: A reader's anthology*. Scarecrow.

Pedagogical Issues

Allsup, R. E. (2016). *Remixing the classroom: Toward an open philosophy of music education*. Indiana University Press.

Banks, J. A., & Banks, C. A. (Eds.). (2004). *Handbook of research on multicultural education* (2nd ed.). Jossey-Bass.

Banks, J. A., & Banks, C. A. (Eds.). (2019). *Multicultural education: Issues and perspectives* (10th ed.). Wiley.

Brookfield, S. D. (2017). *Becoming a critically reflective teacher* (2nd ed.). Jossey-Bass.

Campbell, P. S. (2004). *Teaching music globally: Experiencing music, expressing culture*. Oxford University Press.

Campbell, P. S. (2018). *Music, education, and diversity: Bridging cultures and communities*. Teachers College Press.

Church, I. M., & Samuelson, P. L. (2016). *Intellectual humility: An introduction to the philosophy and science*. Bloomsbury.

Fung, C. V. (2018). *A way of music education: Classic Chinese wisdoms*. Oxford University Press.

Gay, G. (2010). *Culturally responsive teaching: Theory, research, and practice*. Teachers College Press.

Howard, K. (2020). Equity in music education: Cultural appropriation versus cultural appreciation—Understanding the difference. *Music Educators Journal*, *106*(3), 68–70. https://www.doi.org/10.1177/0027432119892926

Lind, V. R., & McKoy, C. (2016). *Culturally responsive teaching in music education: From understanding to application.* Routledge.

Sarath, E. W., Myers, D. E., & Campbell, P. S. (2017). *Redefining music studies in an age of change: Creativity, diversity, and integration.* Routledge.

Schippers, H. (2010). *Facing the music: Shaping music education from a global perspective.* New York, NY: Oxford University Press.

World Music (Textbooks)

Bakan, M. B. (2011). *World music: Traditions and transformations* (2nd ed.). McGraw-Hill Education.

Miller, T. E., & Shahriari, A. (2016). *World music: A global journey* (4th ed.). Routledge.

Nettl, B., & Rommen, T. (2016). *Excursions in world music* (7th ed.). Routledge.

Shelemay, K. K. (2015). *Soundscapes: Exploring music in a changing world* (3rd ed.). W. W. Norton & Co.

Titon, J. T., Cooley, T. J., Locke, D., McAllester, D. P., Rasmussen, A. K., Reck, D. B., . . . Sutton, R. A. (2009). *Worlds of music: An introduction to the music of the world's peoples* (3rd ed.). Cengage Learning.

Wade, B. C. (2012). *Thinking musically: Experiencing music, expressing culture* (2nd ed.). Oxford University Press.

Wade, B. C., & Campbell, P. S. (2021). *Global music cultures.* Oxford University Press.

See also Oxford University Press's Global Music Series, edited by Bonnie Wade and Patricia Shehan Campbell (2004–2008) with 28 books and recordings in all.

Archives and Media

The Association for Cultural Equity (ACE). www.associationforculturalequity.com

Ethnomusicology: Global Field Recordings (Adam Matthew Digital). www.ethnomusicology.amdigital.co.uk

Smithsonian Folkways Recordings. www.folkways.si.edu

University-Curated Archives

Archives of Traditional Music, Indiana University. https://libraries.indiana.edu/archives-traditional-music

UCLA Ethnomusicology Archive. https://schoolofmusic.ucla.edu/resources/ethnomusicology-archive/

University of Washington Archives. https://music.washington.edu/archives

Index

Made in the USA
Columbia, SC
14 June 2022

61732098R00134